Crime

Key Concepts Series

Barbara Adam, *Time*
Alan Aldridge, *Consumption*
Alan Aldridge, *The Market*
Jakob Arnoldi, *Risk*
Will Atkinson, *Class*
Colin Barnes and Geof Mercer, *Disability*
Darin Barney, *The Network Society*
Mildred Blaxter, *Health 2nd edition*
Harriet Bradley, *Gender 2nd edition*
Harry Brighouse, *Justice*
Mónica Brito Vieira and David Runciman, *Representation*
Steve Bruce, *Fundamentalism 2nd edition*
Joan Busfield, *Mental Illness*
Margaret Canovan, *The People*
Andrew Jason Cohen, *Toleration*
Alejandro Colás, *Empire*
Patricia Hill Collins and Sirma Bilge, *Intersectionality*
Mary Daly, *Welfare*
Anthony Elliott, *Concepts of the Self 3rd edition*
Steve Fenton, *Ethnicity 2nd edition*
Katrin Flikschuh, *Freedom*
Michael Freeman, *Human Rights 2nd edition*
Russell Hardin, *Trust*
Geoffrey Ingham, *Capitalism*
Fred Inglis, *Culture*
Robert H. Jackson, *Sovereignty*
Jennifer Jackson Preece, *Minority Rights*
Gill Jones, *Youth*
Paul Kelly, *Liberalism*
Anne Mette Kjær, *Governance*
Ruth Lister, *Poverty*
Jon Mandle, *Global Justice*
Cillian McBride, *Recognition*
Anthony Payne and Nicola Phillips, *Development*
Judith Phillips, *Care*
Chris Phillipson, *Ageing*
Robert Reiner, *Crime*
Michael Saward, *Democracy*
John Scott, *Power*
Timothy J. Sinclair, *Global Governance*
Anthony D. Smith, *Nationalism 2nd edition*
Deborah Stevenson, *The City*
Leslie Paul Thiele, *Sustainability 2nd edition*
Steven Peter Vallas, *Work*
Stuart White, *Equality*
Michael Wyness, *Childhood*

CRIME

The Mystery of the Common-Sense Concept

Robert Reiner

polity

First published in 2016 by Polity Press

Polity Press
65 Bridge Street
Cambridge CB2 1UR, UK

Polity Press
350 Main Street
Malden, MA 02148, USA

ISBN-13: 978-0-7456-6030-1
ISBN-13: 978-0-7456-6031-8(pb)

Library of Congress Cataloging-in-Publication Data

Names: Reiner, Robert, 1946-
Title: Crime : the mystery of the common-sense concept / Robert Reiner.
Description: Malden, MA : Polity Press, 2016. | Includes bibliographical references and index.
Identifiers: LCCN 2015043505 | ISBN 9780745660301 (hardback : alk. paper) | ISBN 9780745660318 (pbk. : alk. paper)
Subjects: LCSH: Crime. | Criminal justice, Administration of.
Classification: LCC HV6025 .R516 2016 | DDC 364–dc23 LC record available at http://lccn.loc.gov/2015043505

A catalogue record for this book is available from the British Library.

Typeset in 10.5 on 12 pt Sabon
by Toppan Best-set Premedia Limited
Printed and bound in the UK by Clays Ltd, St Ives PLC

For further information on Polity, visit our website:
politybooks.com

To the carriers of the future:
Jacob, Ben, Charlotte and David, Toby and Meg

Contents

Introduction: Crime: Conundrums of a Common-Sense Concept

> 'This is criminality, pure and simple, and it has to be confronted and defeated.'
>
> (David Cameron, quoted in Sparrow 2011)

Contrary to these shoot-from-the-hip remarks by the British prime minister, reacting to the 2011 London riots, crime 'is rarely pure and never simple' (to borrow Oscar Wilde's characterization of the truth). Crime hardly seems an example of purity, and it is far from simple, either as a concept or as a problem to be 'confronted and defeated', as this book will show.

Spectacularly gory crimes are prime water-cooler moments, uniting all healthy consciences in abhorrence and condemnation, just as Durkheim (1973 [1893]: 80) argued more than a century ago. Yet behind the apparent consensus that crime must be fought, there is considerable conflict about what should or should not be treated as criminal. Even the most shocking crimes divide as much as they unite. The massacre in July 2015 of nine black worshippers in a Charleston church caused revulsion around the world. The South Carolina legislature voted against displaying the Confederate flag, and many major retailers stopped stocking it. Yet sales of the Confederate flag are reported to have soared (Guzman 2015). The suspect, Dylann Roof, was treated to a Burger King by the cops driving him to jail (McCormack 2015). There are clearly conflicting perspectives on even the most horrifying slaughters, especially when divisive loyalties – such as those of race, nationality, class or religious belief – come into play.

Crime has long been a central theme in popular culture and prominent in measures of public anxiety (as registered by opinion polls – although it has been slipping down the hierarchy of concern in the last decade). But what crime *is* has largely been taken for granted (even though how to explain and tackle it generates fierce controversy). Crime can be seen perhaps as an essentially *uncontested* concept (to turn on its head the influential notion of 'essentially contested concepts' introduced by Gallie in 1957) but one that ought to be highly contested. The discipline of criminology is evidently defined around the idea of crime, even though some of its most celebrated theories have sought to deconstruct it. But despite all the problems in defining crime that will be elaborated on in this volume, discussions of this underpinning concept have generally been confined to opening chapters (frequently perfunctory) in criminology textbooks. These usually skip rapidly through some controversies and conundrums, before proceeding with the more substantive matters of measurement, explanation and policy.

The general playing down of the issue is indicated by the absence of a text that focuses on the concept of crime, although there is a valuable volume of articles that collects important classic and contemporary contributions (Henry and Lanier 2001). This book will systematically review the problems posed by the concept of crime, and how these have affected criminological theories as well as public and policy debates. It will confront the paradox that the term 'crime' features prominently in public debate and popular culture as if it was straightforward and uncontested, but it is deployed in multiple, frequently contradictory, ways.

The book will also discuss the historical emergence of the concept of crime, and what its broad conditions of existence are. Chapters 1 and 2 trace how crime as a distinct element of law, conceived of as a technical realm of universal and objective rules, emerged out of much more amorphous notions of sin and morality, hand in hand with the development of modern capitalism. The broad political and cultural preconditions of the concept of crime include: strong centralized states; a culture of individualism, with associated notions of personal responsibility; and a degree of social stabilization and pacification.

Crime connotes an *intermediate* level of threat to norms shared within a fundamentally settled order. 'Trivial' nuisances are problematically conceived of as crime, as are massive occurrences of violence and destruction in war at the other end of the scale. Contemporary debates about antisocial behaviour and terrorism indicate these limits, as does the breakdown of order in many parts of the world that are deemed to be failed or threatened states.

Crime: concept and conceptions

Crime is an example of what has been called an 'essentially contested concept', 'concepts the proper use of which inevitably involves endless disputes about their proper uses on the part of their users' (Gallie 1957: 169). 'The key to Gallie's idea of essential contestability is a combination of normativity and complexity': normative concepts with a certain internal complexity are essentially contested (Waldron 2002: 150).

Crime is an essentially contested concept because it is complex but, more fundamentally, because at heart it raises normative rather than technical or factual issues. It is common for people to argue about whether something ought to be a crime or not, whether it really is criminal, how it should be treated, and so on. These exchanges are usually interminable because they invoke differences in moral or political beliefs or involve the conflicting interests, values, experiences and practices of different cultures or social groups. Yet, in the first place, people assume they mean the same thing when talking about crime, and indeed that it is an important matter about which all right-thinking people agree. In short, crime is an essentially contested, conflict-ridden concept that is treated as if it were essentially uncontested and consensual.

This can be illuminated by a distinction, drawn by many philosophers, between an underlying concept and specific conceptions of it (e.g. Rawls 1971, which distinguishes between an underlying concept of justice and contested particular conceptions of what it entails). I suggest that there is a fundamental deep-level agreement on what is meant by crime, the basic *concept*, but that there are different, essentially contested, *conceptions* of what this means in terms of specific acts, practices, contexts and meanings.

The deep agreement about the concept of crime is not, in my view, the one generally proposed. The idea of crime as an infraction of criminal law is the definition found in most dictionaries and, in my experience at least, the one most people would offer if asked. Moreover, it is anchored by certain processes – labelled as criminal procedure – which, if followed, result in people accused of breaking criminal laws being punished, i.e. having 'pain' inflicted on them. However, there is nothing contradictory about arguing that actions proscribed by criminal law ought not to be, and vice versa. Criminal law has a complex and problematic relationship with different views of morality, as chapter 2 will explore. It is also the case that criminal laws have a tortuous relationship to social practice, and laws are in fact violated by most people, including the apparently respectable, as chapter 3 will show. The criminal law that is applied in action constitutes a tiny proportion of the laws in the books, and it is systematically biased against the poor and powerless, as chapter 5 demonstrates. At the same time, law breaking and serious harms and wrongs committed by the powerful usually escape with impunity, as elaborated in chapter 4.

The picture of crime that most people have is not rooted in their own experience but in highly slanted images derived from the mass media, and it is these that (mis)inform popular and political debate, as chapter 6 illustrates. Finally, chapter 7 explores the ideas of crime, causation and control developed by criminology over the years, and will show that each is problematic as a general theory. Nonetheless, they can be the basis of an eclectic model, synthesizing the core perspectives, which can illuminate trends and patterns over time (although the explanation of the recent fall in crime in western countries presents formidable difficulties). Thus the legal notion of crime is only one of several competing conceptions, even though it is anchored in the power of the state, which confers upon it the threat of official punishment for breaches.

The basic concept of crime that people agree upon (although they differ about what it means in terms of specific practices) is elusive because it is not a cognitive concept, referring to a particular reality outside itself. Rather, it is an expressive concept, embodying an attitude of revulsion, fear, pain or disapproval. In the everyday meaning of the term, it is a censure,[1] an expression of 'strong criticism or disapproval' (*Cambridge English Dictionary* online).

To call something a crime is to register disapproval, fear, disgust or condemnation in the strongest possible terms and to demand urgent remedies – but not necessarily the pain of criminal penalties. A neat way of putting this is the characterization by Egon Bittner of why people call the police. Someone calls the cops, he argued, when she experiences 'something that ought not to be happening and about which something ought to be done' (1974: 30). This neatly fits the basic concept of crime, an expression of condemnation and concern, which may be provoked by various specific conceptions of what exactly the problem is. It may be that a criminal law has been broken, and the demand is for the invocation of the criminal process. But more often it will be an expression of moral condemnation, disgust, or a cry for help against some threatening harm that may or may not be subject to criminal law. As the chapters of this book will elaborate, conceptions of crime can be legally based, or they could derive from other moral perspectives. Either way, they can differ substantially from conceptions of crime as deviance, i.e. departures from normal social practice, and from media, political or criminological conceptions of crime.

Constructivism vs realism

Two broadly contrasting perspectives on how to define crime can be found in criminology: 'constructivist' and 'realist'. These are not mutually exclusive, and indeed I would argue that both have a degree of validity. Nonetheless, they have often been presented imperialistically, denying any truth to the opposing viewpoint. The contrast between these approaches runs through most of the debates considered in this book.

The constructivist position claims that 'crime' is purely a product of perception and political process, not any intrinsic characteristic of the behaviour so labelled. It is quintessentially encapsulated in an influential assertion by Louk Hulsman, a leading Dutch penal abolitionist: 'Crime has no ontological reality' (Hulsman 1986: 71). By this he meant that 'Crime is not the *object* but the *product* of criminal policy' (ibid.). In Hulsman's analysis, criminalization occurs when a person or organization 'deems a certain "occurrence" or "situation" as undesirable...attributes that undesirable occurrence to an individual', and wants this individual punished through law and criminal justice, rather than other styles of conflict resolution, sanctioning or peace keeping. His conclusion is that the concept's lack of 'ontological reality...makes it necessary to abandon as a tool in the conceptual framework of criminology the notion of "crime"' (1986: 71).

At one level, Hulsman is correct by definition. Without the labelling of particular behaviours as criminal, they would not be crimes. Crime could be abolished at a stroke by wholesale decriminalization. But, as the realists argue, many activities that are treated as crime by criminal law are widely regarded as harmful, especially to the most vulnerable people in society, and these should not continue unchecked. Whether the standard modes of criminalization and punishment are justifiable, effective or counterproductive is an urgent debate, but the harm and suffering that are inflicted by crime would not be abolished by removing the label. Indeed, critical criminologists have argued that there are very serious harms, committed with relatively impunity by the powerful and privileged, that should be regarded as at least as serious as mainstream volume crime.

The constructionist position is often presented in abstraction from analysis of the wider structures of power and advantage in contemporary capitalist societies. Conflicts over whether to label activities or people as criminal are not carried out on a level playing field. The wealthy and powerful have disproportionate power to shape law making, and to evade its enforcement. The idea of a 'criminal justice system' is at best an unrealized dream, and at worst an ideological cloak disguising injustice, as chapters 4 and 5 will show. The title of a classic critical criminology text sums it up well: *The Rich*

Get Richer and the Poor Get Prison (Reiman and Leighton 2012). What complicates matters is that it is also the poor who get disproportionately victimized by crime. All of this has been accentuated by the political triumph of neo-liberalism since the 1970s throughout the western world (Streeck 2014), vastly exacerbating the injustices of criminal justice (Reiner 2007; Bell 2011, 2015; Turner 2014).

The realist position straddles a wide spectrum of political and theoretical ones, united only by their acceptance that crime represents real problems, which exist whether or not they are labelled as crime. Most criminological research, past and present, has operated with what can be regarded as naive realism. It has simply taken for granted the categories of criminal law as the objects of analysis. Criminology in practice has focused on the small part of criminal law that gets to be formally measured and processed, and the even smaller group of criminal justice lottery losers, those who are caught and convicted (sometimes incorrectly).

Self-declared realist approaches originated in the 1970s as a conscious reaction to the critical criminology that proliferated in the 1960s and early 1970s. The key aspects of critical criminology that realists of all stripes targeted were its tendencies to extreme constructivism and to crime control scepticism.

Right-wing realism was spearheaded by James Q. Wilson's seminal 1975 book *Thinking about Crime*. Wilson sidestepped any issues about defining or measuring crime, focusing on 'predatory street crime', not only because it was what most frightened the public but because he saw it as a truly menacing and immoral threat to civilized existence. Wilson dismissed liberal-Left criminology's pursuit of 'root causes' of crime as a pointless and misguided distraction from seeking innovative, workable solutions to crime. His goal was the identification of promising policies that could economically and effectively reduce crime in the here and now, without waiting for social 'root causes' (which he was dubious about anyway) to be tackled by social reform and redistributive welfare (which, as a conservative, he opposed).

Wilson's book was symptomatic of the rapid ousting of the post-war Keynesian welfarist consensus by neo-liberalism. Wilson himself stressed smart, evidence-based initiatives, rather than tougher, 'zero tolerance' policing and punishment. However, his realist blueprint provided an intellectual boost not only to what has come to be known as administrative criminology, developing more effective security and opportunity-reducing situational prevention, but also to a prison boom in many countries. Such strategies have been celebrated as the source of the crime drop since the 1990s by can-do criminal justice policy makers and governments. These claims will be considered critically in chapter 7.

In parallel with the growth of Right realism and administrative criminology, there also developed a vigorous Left realist perspective, a reaction against what some critical criminologists had come to disown as their own earlier 'Left idealism' (Young 1975; Lea and Young 1984). Crime, they argued, was not just an ideological construction aiming to demonize the poor. It was a real scourge precisely in the poorest communities, as most crime was intra-class. A major source of Left realism was also the growing influence of feminism, and a sensitization to the reality of the pervasive victimization of women (and children), in working-class and other communities, by violence and abuse.

Although Left realists did accept that there were deeper, fundamental causes of crime, they argued that the Left must develop effective and practicable interventions to tackle crime now, and not just talk of reducing the long-run sources. The answer was not tougher but more legitimate, evidence-led policy. For example, the police would be more effective if they could regain legitimacy in poor and/or black and minority ethnic (BAME) areas, which had become alienated by militaristic tactics, through more consensual, community-oriented styles which facilitated the flow of information.

Both constructivism and realism make important points that can and should be reconciled (as recognized for example by a new 'ultra-realism', cf. Hall and Winlow 2015). Criminal law making and enforcement are largely shaped by the massively unequal structures of power and wealth in capitalist societies, which are growing ever wider under neoliberalism. The constructivists are thus right to problematize processes of criminalization.

However, much criminal law does have popular support, even though the law in action focuses almost exclusively on the street crimes committed by poor, marginalized young men. Popular support for criminalization of such predatory offences is only in small part a matter of media-fomented false consciousness, though no doubt the media do purvey a distorted representation of crime (see chapter 6). At its core, the popular legitimacy of much policing and penal policy is grounded in the reality of serious harm perpetrated by poor young men against others, and also against women, children and older people, in their neighbourhoods.

Critical criminology has rightly emphasized the massively greater harms against property and people perpetrated by the crimes of the powerful (Hillyard et al. 2004; Green and Ward 2004, 2012; Tombs and Whyte 2015). Many of these most dangerous actions are not unequivocally criminalized because of the power of elites to erect barriers of impunity around their depredations (as chapter 4 demonstrates). However, there are various reasons why it is harder to generate popular concern about the suffering inflicted by state and corporate wrongdoing, apart from low visibility fabricated by the operation of power itself. One is the longer, more complex, chain of causation, running from decisions made at the top of organizational hierarchies to the pain of the mass of people suffering from these policies.

Even more fundamentally, there is a gulf between the immediate fear and injury engendered by face-to-face confrontation, and the possibly more serious, even life-trashing, but less visceral anguish caused, say, by financial skulduggery or by austerity policies that can kill people. Recently, my teenage son and I had to get our car from a dark, deserted underground car park in the small hours. We both acknowledged relief as I drove out. I may have lectured for many years about the small risk of being attacked by a robber compared, say, to my crashing the car on the way home. I know that I am actually suffering greater financial loss from being mis-sold payment protection insurance (PPI)[2] and other products, and from such crimes as organized rigging of key lending and exchange rates, than I would even from several thefts of my money and mobile. None of these truths comforted me in those few frightening minutes.

The realists of the political Right and Left correctly stress the seriousness of the core of ordinary criminal law offences.

However, the constructionists also underline validly that the formation and the enforcement of criminal law are shaped by unequal and unjust structures of power and advantage.

Social injustice and criminal justice

Criminal law in the books and in action has a Janus-faced character. On the one hand, it contributes to a degree of order that is necessary for coordination and peaceful coexistence in a minimally civilized society. On the other hand, all known complex societies have been built on unjust, unequal hierarchies of power and privilege. As pithily formulated by policing scholar Otwin Marenin, criminal justice deals with both 'parking tickets' and 'class repression' (Marenin 1982). So even if criminal law contributes to maintaining order in a fair way, without acerbating inequality, the order that is reproduced is structurally unjust. But for reasons similar to those that vitiated Stalin's doctrine of 'socialism in one country', social justice is unachievable in one institution that is encircled by an unequal society. In reality, all criminal justice institutions acerbate the social inequalities in the societies they are embedded in.

The concept and conceptions of crime are intricately interconnected with the development and operations of modern capitalism. We will see this in subsequent chapters, when the development and ramifications of conceptions of crime are explored. The project of developing a supposedly objective, technically administered, neutral code of right and wrong that applies to everyone and is accepted by everyone may be an impossible dream in a society structured by deep inequalities of class, ethnicity, gender and other lines of cleavage. At the same time, the essentially contested ideal of the rule of law, as the optimal way of settling disputes and enforcing norms, may be of universal value, as the Marxist historian E. P. Thompson argued powerfully against a majority of his fellow radicals (Thompson 1975: Part 3, iv). Nonetheless, as Thompson's own historical research demonstrated, the formulation and practice of criminal law are a far cry from the ideals of legality and are grotesquely distorted by inequalities of class and power.

The subsequent chapters of this book will consider the multiple specific conceptions of crime, contesting the amorphous basic concept of crime – an assertion that something seriously problematic and wrong is happening and that something needs to be done. We will look at: the anchored conception of crime as criminal law violation; the problematic relationship of this to morality and social practice; the unequal application of it to the powerful and the disadvantaged; how media and political discourse misrepresent crime; and how crime patterns and trends (especially the recent crime drop) might be explained. Running through all these conceptions will be the key structuring relationship between crime and capitalism and how this has mutated over time and between places.

1
Legal Conceptions of Crime

Crime and criminal law: anchored pluralism

A while ago, a friend asked me what I was working on. I told him it was a book about the concept of crime. He replied 'it must be the shortest book ever written. A crime is something that's against the criminal law. What else is there to say?'

The concept of crime is complex and multifaceted, however, condensing a number of partly conflicting, partly overlapping meanings. A plurality of meanings of 'crime' are at play in popular culture, policy debate and academic discourse. Nonetheless, the idea of crime as infraction of criminal law anchors this diversity. The profusion of definitions can be seen as an example of 'anchored pluralism', borrowing a term originally used in the analysis of security (Loader and Walker 2007: 192–4).

The notion of crime as those actions that breach criminal law anchors the diversity and ambiguity of different conceptions in a number of ways. It would probably be the primary definition offered by most people, even if they have only a sketchy idea of what is entailed by criminal law. Certainly, most dictionaries define crime primarily as violation of criminal laws.

More substantially, the identification of crime and criminal law is anchored in social practice. It is only formal criminal law that is explicitly promulgated by government processes. And only infractions of it are subject to *state punishment*, as distinct from informal sanctions or legally imposed restitution.

The main definition of crime offered by dictionaries is in terms of criminal law. The online *Oxford Dictionary*, for example, gives as its primary definition of crime: 'An action or omission which constitutes an offence and is punishable by law.' This primary definition is followed by a second: 'An action or activity considered to be evil, shameful, or wrong.'

A crucial and problematic issue is to what extent do these definitions overlap? Actions or activities may often be condemned as 'evil, shameful, or wrong', but nonetheless not be offences criminalized and punishable by law. Contemporary examples of behaviour that outrage many people, whilst perhaps staying just the right side of criminal law breaking, include: egregious tax avoidance schemes exploiting 'loopholes' in the law to avoid their being illegal tax evasion; MPs' expenses claims that seem excessive but are within the rules; and the 2003 US/UK invasion of Iraq.

Conversely, some criminal law breaking may not be seen as evil, or morally wrong, by many people. Judging by frequent arguments with friends and family, and by everyday observation, such activities as speeding, using mobile phones whilst driving or paying for services in cash when it is clear earnings are not being declared are widely regarded as not 'real' crime. The spheres of criminal law and morality may overlap to some extent, but they are certainly not identical, and social practice may differ from both. A key feature of late or post-modern culture is the erosion of consensus about acceptable behaviour and a greater tolerance of a diversity of social practices.

The formal doctrinal content of law 'in the books', however, is not only much less coherent and straightforward than either popular or dictionary definitions assume. It is also hugely different from the 'law in action' – how the criminal justice system operates in practice. Indeed, as chapters 4 and 5 will demonstrate, the phrase 'criminal justice system' is itself a euphemistic misnomer. The law in action scarcely tackles most crimes, is far from just in its operation, and is systematic only in its remorseless focus on the crimes of the poor and powerless, whilst the rich and apparently respectable enjoy virtual immunity for their wrongdoing.

The mass media, furthermore, greatly distort the picture of crime and criminal justice, typically promoting a highly simplistic drama of straightforward good vs evil, as chapter 6 will show. Chapter 7 suggests that this is also true of the academic study of crime which, for much of its history and to an increasing extent, has bracketed out fundamental analysis of causes, focusing on immediately practicable projects and fine-tuning the functioning of criminal justice conceived in very narrow and technocratic ways.

A Mephistophelean maze: formal criminal law

In this chapter, the focus will be on analysing the concept of crime as violations of criminal law 'in the books', i.e. as promulgated in statute and case law. It will trace the emergence and development of a distinct criminal law and consider various attempts by legal, criminological and social theory to delineate its specific nature and functions.

The concept of 'crime', in any of the contemporary versions that will be explored in this book, is not a universal one, and this is particularly true of criminal law-based definitions. Criminal law has specific historical conditions of existence, and its emergence is related to the rise of capitalist political economies and certain associated features of modern culture, notably liberal individualism.

Although not accepting the perspective of legal positivism – the position that questions of identifying what law *is* should be sharply distinguished from moral or political evaluation of what law *ought* to be – this chapter will focus primarily on analytic and explanatory theories of criminal law, postponing the deeply intertwined normative issues of evaluation and prescription to chapter 2.

As a preliminary health warning, however, it is worth stressing the massive extent and apparent diversity of contemporary criminal law 'in the books', profoundly challenging simple explanation or evaluation. The number of separate offences created by legislation is hard to calculate and sensitive to complicated definitional issues of what counts as a separate crime. A much-cited assessment has claimed that, in its first nine years, Tony Blair's New Labour government in Britain sought to deliver on its celebrated promise to be 'tough on crime' by creating some 3,000 new criminal offences, more than one per day (Morris 2006). Whilst subsequent governments have distanced themselves from 'Blair's "frenzied law-making"' (ibid.), new crime statutes have continued to proliferate,[1] as governments have passed new criminal laws as a panacea for all kinds of social problems.

The UK list of 'Notifiable Offences' (which the police have a statutory obligation to record) includes more than 1,500 types of criminal offence (each type containing many separate offences), which have been criminalized over the centuries by common law and statute.[2] The broad miscellany of behaviours that have been criminalized calls into question any simple generalizations about characterizing crime.

Criminal law 'in the books': historical and cultural variation

Defining the scope of criminal law in substantive (rather than formal or procedural ways) is notoriously problematic because of the multitude of different kinds of function and character apparent in the vast, rapidly growing and shifting corpus of criminal law (Farmer 1996; Ashworth 2000; Lacey, Wells and Quick 2003: 1–15).

This is underlined by the huge cultural variation across space and time in what has been counted by the law as criminal. The business of the English courts a few centuries ago would be largely unrecognizable to their contemporary counterparts, as illustrated by a historical study of felony indictments in Essex between 1559 and 1603 (Cockburn 1977). In line with contemporary crime patterns, property offences predominated (110 highway robberies, 320 burglaries, 1,460 larcenies), with a smaller proportion of violent (129 homicides and 28 infanticides) and sex crimes (28 cases of rape, eight of buggery). But a striking difference between the Essex courts of the first Queen Elizabeth and those of the second was the 172 cases of witchcraft tried in the former!

The change in conceptions of crime is even more striking in the lower courts. A study of Essex quarter sessions between 1628 and 1632 found that, out of 3,514 offences prosecuted, 144 were thefts and 48 assaults. But these figures are dwarfed by the 480 prosecutions for allowing bridges or roads to fall into decay, 229 for keeping a disorderly alehouse, and – the most numerous offence category – 684 prosecutions for failing to attend church (Wrightson 1980). Prosecutions in ecclesiastical or manorial courts show a yet wider range of offences that are not recognized today (Sharpe 1984: 50–3), such as adultery, fornication, bridal pregnancy, scolding and disrupting the sabbath in a variety of ways such as working, drinking in an alehouse or wearing a felt hat. On the other hand, the English courts of the first Elizabethan England knew nothing of such matters as parking tickets, cybercrime or drug-related offences (alcohol apart).

It can plausibly be argued that there has to be a 'minimum content of natural law' if a society is to survive as more than a short-term suicide club (Hart 1961: 189–94), involving some protection of person and property. However, the variation in how this 'minimum' is achieved, and what activities are proscribed at different times and places, makes the content of law contingent on a host of social, political, economic and cultural circumstances that underpin the processes of criminalization (Duff et al. 2014).

The emergence of crime as a concept

All societies, perhaps all relationships, are characterized by deviance. Some basic reasons for this were well set out a century ago by Emile Durkheim, one of sociology's founding fathers. Statistical deviance from the norms of any group, in the sense of behaviour departing from its central tendencies, is inevitable. 'It is impossible for all to be alike, if only because each one has his own organism and that these organisms occupy different areas in space' (Durkheim 1964 [1895]: 69). Thus, even in a 'cloister of saints', there will be deviance and punitive reactions sanctioning it, even though the precise nature of the 'sins' in such an environment might not cause any concern in our own more blasé, morally insensitive cultures (ibid.: 68–9).

But, whilst deviance and control may be perennial, there are distinctive features of modern concepts of crime and of the associated repertoire of formalized responses. As anthropologists have shown, it is only in relatively complex societies, with a developed division of labour, that specific 'legal' mechanisms for dispute resolution and order maintenance emerge. In simpler societies, these functions are achieved through other institutions, notably kinship and religion.

Anthropological studies have been conducted on many pre-literate societies that lacked any formalized system of social control or policing. In his famous ethnography of *Crime and Custom in Savage Society*, the pioneering social anthropologist Malinowski analysed processes of conflict resolution and order maintenance in a small-scale pre-literate society (Malinowski 1926). In the absence of 'codes, courts and constables', conflicts were resolved, and wrongs were punished, by mobilizing informal communal and kinship sentiments and structures. Subsequent anthropologists have explored the subtle, complex processes adopted in different stateless societies without specialist legal systems, based on kinship, religion and feuding patterns (Roberts 1979).

A classic cross-cultural study of the relationship between legal evolution and societal complexity found that 'elements of legal organization emerge in a sequence, such that each constitutes a necessary condition for the next' (Schwartz and Miller 1964: 160). The emergence of the core elements of a distinct legal system followed a definite order – counsel, mediation, police. This was related to the development of a more complex division of labour.

Specialized criminal law institutions emerge only in relatively complex societies, but they are not a straightforward reflex of a burgeoning division of labour. They develop hand in hand with social and economic inequality and hierarchies of power. They are means for the emergence and protection of more centralized and dominant class and state systems. A wide-ranging review of the anthropological literature concluded that the development of specialized law enforcement 'is linked to economic specialization and differential access to resources that occur in the transition from a kinship- to a class-dominated society' (Robinson and Scaglion 1987: 109). During this transition, communal policing forms are converted in incremental stages to state-dominated ones, which begin to function as agents of class control in addition to more general social control (Robinson, Scaglion and Olivero 1994).

This intimate interrelationship between inequality and the emergence of crime and criminal law was anticipated by Adam Smith, supposedly the prophet of free-market economics. In less developed societies, order can be maintained by informal community 'interposition' he argues, because: 'Property, the grand fund of all dispute, is not then known...But...when some have great wealth and others nothing, it is necessary that the arm of authority should be continually stretched forth...Laws and government may be considered in this and indeed every case as a combination of the rich to oppress the poor, and preserve to themselves the inequality of the goods which would otherwise be soon destroyed by the attacks of the poor' (Smith 1982 [1782–4]: 208).

Codes of law backed up by adjudication and enforcement personnel did emerge in some ancient societies. Well-known examples include the Babylonian Code of Hammurabi (approximately 1800 BC), the Hebrew Bible (dated by contemporary scholars as developing between about 1200 and 165 BC), and, most elaborate of all, the corpus of Roman Law that proliferated from the eighth century BC up to the sixth century AD. The Bible and Roman Law are crucially important sources of western law, and many aspects of present-day criminal and civil law clearly reflect these origins. Nonetheless, whilst all these codes penalize acts that are core offences in contemporary criminal law, such rules are not distinguished from what would now be seen as religious, civil, family or administrative law. All types of law were subject to similar procedures and punishments.

Criminal law: an ideal-type

The development of specifically 'criminal' law, as distinct from other forms of order maintenance, adjudication and enforcement of norms, is associated with the advent of modernity. To clarify this, it is helpful first to construct an ideal-type of 'criminal law', as it has come to be understood in modern industrial capitalist societies since the late eighteenth century. The distinctive features of 'criminal' law, contrasted with other areas of law and conflict regulation, include the following:

- close procedural association with the state,
- punishment not compensation as the outcome of cases,
- the notion of individual responsibility,
- a tacit background assumption of a reasonably stable and peaceful society.

These elements form an ideal-type, and many aspects of actually existing criminal law systems do not comply with them all. Moreover, there are distinct tendencies away from these features in recent years, in particular the growth of absolute offences not requiring individual responsibility, or *mens rea*, and a pre-emptive turn towards preventing future threats rather than punishing past infractions (Lacey 2001; Ramsay 2012; Ashworth and Zedner 2014; Horder 2014). Nonetheless, these elements do distil the quintessential paradigmatic aspects of the idea of criminal law, so that the legitimacy of such developments is highly contentious.

The centrality of the state in criminal law

Criminal laws are deemed to be offences against the public realm, as distinct from private interests, even if there is also harm to specific individuals. The legislative and judicial arms of the state have the authority to determine what is treated as criminal, i.e. subject to state-organized punishment rather than to private redress or revenge. This is symbolized clearly by the way criminal cases are named, as (in the United Kingdom) the Crown against the defendant, *R. v. X*, with the name of the victim (if any) not featuring. This was the culmination of a long set of processes by which state agencies (the police, and now also the Crown Prosecution Service) gradually became responsible for the investigation and prosecution of offences. Hitherto, these had been primarily private initiatives (Hay and Snyder 1989; Godfrey and Lawrence 2014: ch. 3).[3]

The nature of criminal proceedings has become one of establishing whether a defendant has committed an offence against a universalistically framed, state-defined rule of law. This is distinguishable from judging conduct as a sin against religious law, an affront to sovereignty, an interpersonal harm to other individuals, or a violation of local community notions of correct conduct, as courts had done from medieval to early modern British society (Jeffery 1957; Gatrell, Lenman and Parker 1980; Sharpe 2001; Lacey 2014).

Establishing the authority of an apparently impersonal, universalistic law involved protracted and often violent conflict, for example over redefining as theft what had been seen as customary perquisites of the poor (like gleaning crops or gathering fallen wood). Theft itself was a highly disputed category, constructed slowly over centuries (Hall 1952 [1935]; Lacey et al. 2003: ch. 4). It only became established as a general offence during the eighteenth century, as capitalist relations became dominant. Until then, in the absence of violence (making it robbery) or physical trespass, taking something claimed by another was widely seen as a civil issue to be settled between the parties as late as the publication of Blackstone's *Commentaries on the Laws of England* in the 1760s (Palmer 1977).

The proliferation of capital punishment for minor property offences during the eighteenth century paradoxically underlines the severity of the struggle over definition (Thompson 1975). It reflected the tighter conception of property rights in capitalist market relations, which displaced the 'moral economy' embedded in traditional networks of obligation and entitlement. Nonetheless, a never fully submerged sense of some crime as 'social' – defiance of the power of the privileged orders – survived in subterranean fashion (Thompson 1971, 2009; Hobsbawm 1972; Linebaugh 1976, 2006, 2014;

Lea 1999). Victims came to feature in criminal cases as witnesses rather than principals, although there has been some movement in recent decades to alleviate their marginality to proceedings (Rock 2004).[4]

State punishment and criminal process

A key feature of those laws designated as criminal is that the end result of successful prosecution is punishment, not restitution. Indeed, the threat of punishment, and the consequent need for special criminal procedure, are often said to be the defining characteristics of criminal law. In other 'civil' proceedings between private individuals, such as for breach of contract or tort, the aim is restitution, compensating the party deemed to be injured for the loss or harm suffered.

Because criminal cases pitch the power of the state against a defendant, and because the possible outcome is punishment, i.e. infliction of pain of some kind, the rules of criminal procedure are intended to offer defendants greater protection against incorrect outcomes (Ashworth and Redmayne 2010). For example, the rules of evidence are tighter and cases have to be proven 'beyond reasonable doubt', rather than the weaker standard of 'the balance of probabilities' that applies in civil cases. These rules are far from foolproof, and there is of course a sad history of miscarriages of justice (Nobles and Schiff 2000; Naughton 2012). The rules have also often been regularly criticized from the police and prosecution side as offering guilty people too much protection. The just balance in criminal procedure is a matter of frequent, almost constant, controversy.

Individual responsibility

Violators of criminal law are usually regarded as personally responsible, a crucial element in most justifications of state punishment (Lacey et al. 2003: ch. 1, Part II). In principle, conviction for a criminal offence is supposed to require not only proof that the defendant has carried out the prohibited act, the *actus reus*, but also a fault element, *mens rea*. However, many contemporary laws that are criminal (in that their alleged breach may incur prosecution and punishment) are strict liability offences, without a requirement of individual culpability. These are regarded as problematic by many theorists of criminal law, and indeed treated as different from criminal law 'proper' in many jurisdictions (Ashworth 2000), although the growth of such offences is arguably an inevitable concomitant of the need to regulate not only human actors but also organizations (Horder 2014).

Modern notions of crime as a specific type of problem and process are related to key characteristics of capitalist political economy and culture (Kennedy 1970; Lea 2002). The growth of strong centralized states is clearly a precondition of the first feature, the notion of crime as a public offence, with harm to individuals being neither a necessary nor a sufficient condition of criminalization.

The idea of individual moral responsibility is related to the liberal conception of people as autonomous subjects, capable (at least in principle) of rational choice (Norrie 2014; Roberts 2014). It is the criminological extrapolation of the rational economic actor model of classical political economy, developing in the eighteenth century with the rise of capitalist industrialism. The eminent Soviet legal theorist Evgeny Pashukanis pointed this out in his seminal 'commodity exchange' analysis of law (Pashukanis 1978 [1924]). This stressed the isomorphism of the individual owner (of labour power or of capital) in the capitalist marketplace, and the figure of the individual accused of crime. The latter is regarded by law only as an abstracted autonomous subject, stripped of all the concrete circumstances that are relevant to fully understanding and judging her or his actions. Liberal political and legal theory are constructed on the same model of 'possessive individualism' (Macpherson 1962).

The notion of individual responsibility is clearly an ideal-type, presenting people as equal wielders of a primeval and abstract will, excluding all factors that could explain why people act differently. As the novelist Anatole France put it pithily, 'The law, in its majestic impartiality, forbids the rich as well as the poor to sleep under the bridges of Paris, to beg in the streets, and to steal bread' (France 2002 [1894]: ch. 7).

Relatively stable order as a prerequisite of the concept of crime

A further condition of existence of the fully fledged modern idea of crime is the stabilization of modern capitalism during the nineteenth century (Lea 2002: chs 2–4). 'Crime' is essentially an intermediate level of wrongdoing or threat to social relations, attributable to individuals or at most to small groups ('gangs'). Criminalizing nuisances below a certain threshold of seriousness and specificity (as has been done in Britain from the late medieval vagrancy laws to the contemporary anti-social behaviour order [ASBO]) is always controversial and attributable to varying levels of insecurity, 'respectable fears' (Pearson 1983), about the threat posed by 'dangerous classes'. These insecurities have multiplied in recent times, as neo-liberalism generates ever larger numbers of people in marginal, precarious economic positions – the 'precariat' (Standing 2011) – generating fear amongst them and about them (Winlow and Hall 2013).

Conversely, levels of violence and disorder above a certain threshold are also frequently seen as somewhat distinct from 'ordinary' crime, even though they involve many very severe 'crimes': 'terrorism', civil war, genocide, war (as will be discussed in chapter 4). Part of the appeal of the popular British television series *Foyle's War* is the implicit irony of the eponymous detective painstakingly unravelling individual murders in Hastings during the Second World War against a backdrop of wholesale killing just a few miles away, above and across the English Channel.

When there is perceived to be a complete breakdown of order, as in 'failed' states, or wars between states, it is hard to distinguish between crime and politics, the evils of war and war crimes (Cohen 1997). The notion of 'crime' as an offence against a fundamentally consensual public interest, committed by individuals who are separately culpable and subject to adjudication, presupposes a degree of settled order. This was achieved during the nineteenth century and for most of the twentieth in the liberal democracies of Europe, North America,and the rest of the 'western' world, the heyday of modern criminal justice. However, the last quarter of the twentieth century saw profound changes in political economy and culture, namely the embedding of neo-liberal hegemony, that continue to threaten the conditions of existence of modern criminal justice.

The nature and functions of criminal law: antinomies of analysis

As argued above (p. 12), conceptions of crime display 'anchored pluralism'. Different conceptions are found in ethical discourses, social practices, the criminal justice process, the mass media, popular culture and criminological theories. Anchoring this pluralism, however, is the idea of crime as infraction of criminal law. This is the dominant conception, most often offered by dictionary and popular definitions and authoritatively promulgated and enforced by state institutions. Unlike less formal notions of sin and deviance, criminal law, as a specific mode of regulating and reproducing order, has crucial conditions of existence: social complexity, an advanced division of labour, social inequality and hierarchy. The core features of the ideal-typical criminal law paradigm sketched above emerge only in modern societies.

How can this emergent phenomenon of modern criminal law be analysed and assessed? The main disciplines that have grappled with understanding crime are criminology and criminal law, which have had at best curiously cursory relationships with each other, despite their overlapping subject matter (Zedner 2011; Lacey and Zedner 2012; Nelken 2012).

Nonetheless, the concept of crime has been a central question for both criminal law scholars and criminologists at different times, and the subject of controversy between different schools of thought within each discipline. The following are four key axes of argument that have divided analysts. I am presenting these as sharply contrasted antinomies for ease of exposition. Few if any writers could be identified with such simply dichotomized ideal-types. On all these polarities, I would declare my own position as not 'either/or' but 'both/and'.

Positivism vs normative perspectives

'Positivism' has been a crucial reference point for debates about crime, both in criminology and criminal law, albeit with somewhat different meanings. The term 'positivism' was originally popularized in the early nineteenth century by one of the founders of social science, Auguste Comte (who also coined the label 'sociology'). It has gone through many developments and sub-movements.

Positivism is primarily an attempt to analyse the nature of science and its claims to objective knowledge of the world. It postulates that claims to knowledge are valid if and only if they are based on empirical observations that are testable, or on logical deductions from such propositions. Everything else is 'meaningless'; extreme versions consign to the dustbin of cultural history all other philosophical enterprises such as metaphysics, ethics, aesthetics and religion.[5]

Applied to social science, positivism refers to the aspiration that knowledge of the human world can comply with the same epistemological strictures about valid knowledge as physical science, albeit with different specific techniques of verification (primarily statistical analysis of social data rather than laboratory experimentation). This position has been influential in the study of crime. Indeed, the term 'criminology' was coined to name the positivist 'science of the criminal' developed in the late nineteenth century by Lombroso and his disciples (cf. chapter 7).

Positivism as an analysis of physical science has been the subject of much critical debate. But this is as nothing compared to the arguments against it as an aspiration for social science, which studies human actors endowed with consciousness. And these problems apply a fortiori to the study of law and crime, which seeks to understand norms and deviance, and thus has values as the beating heart of its subject matter.

Positivism as a philosophy of social scientific knowledge has had a chequered career, criticized in its strongest forms even by some of its supposed adherents. Karl Popper, for example, is often regarded as a leading positivist philosopher, and indeed he introduced the criterion of 'falsifiability' (rather than verifiability) as the criterion of empirical testability

(Popper 1959 [1935]). Yet he is even better known for his work developing an approach to political and social philosophy that draws on social democracy, liberalism and indeed conservatism (Popper 1945).[6]

Ludwig Wittgenstein ended his *Tractatus Logico-Philosophicus* (originally drafted in the trenches during the First World War) with a famous aphorism: 'Whereof one cannot speak, thereof one must be silent' (Wittgenstein 2001 [1921]). The *Tractatus* offered an austere distinction between what can be known and said about the world scientifically and the *evaluation* of this. His formulations were highly influential on Bertrand Russell and subsequently on the logical positivists. However, those areas about which 'one must be silent' – consciousness, spirit, values and their philosophical discourses, metaphysics, ethics, aesthetics and so on – were neither 'meaningless' nor unimportant to Wittgenstein.

Positivism occupies a somewhat paradoxical position nowadays in both social science (including criminology) and in law. As Giddens has said, 'Positivism has today become more of a term of abuse than a technical term in philosophy' (Giddens 1977). It has come to be identified with the a-theoretical quantitative analysis that C. Wright Mills unforgettably castigated as 'abstracted empiricism' (Mills 1959: ch. 3).[7] However, this much-lampooned ritualistic numerology prevails not only in economics, still the dominant social science in academe despite its partial discrediting by the post-2007 credit crunch, but in teaching and publication in criminology and sociology, especially in the United States.

Both the critics and the practitioners of this cod-positivism have smothered the important issues raised by positivist philosophers over the last century. Rigorous testing of propositions is vital, but so is the interpretation of meaning and the attempt to develop defensible normative analysis of institutions and policies. As Max Weber, often (mis)characterized as a critic of positivism, argued, explanation and understanding had to be both 'causally adequate' and 'adequate at the level of meaning' (Weber 1964: 99–100).

Beyond this, claims Weber – supposedly the prophet of 'value-free' sociology – the social scientist, a human being studying other sentient, interpreting and evaluating actors, cannot but be influenced by values, certainly in the choice of topics and any policy inferences, but inevitably also in analysing material (Weber 1949). There is no licence to misuse the lecture hall for propaganda (Weber 2004 [1917–19]). But the guise of a value-free, apolitical and amoral eunuch is not the way to scientific objectivity. As with Popper, the key to an asymptotic approach to value-free knowledge lies in vigorous testing and debating of ideas. A necessary condition is the open declaration of value positions, not hiding them in thickets of algebra or jargon.[8]

The debate with positivism has also been pivotal in jurisprudence, in a different, albeit related, sense. Legal positivism is not the quest to model the analysis of law on the logic ascribed to the physical sciences. But what it shares with all positivism is the emphasis on the sharp differentiation between facts and values. Identifying what *is* the law is an absolutely distinct question from its normative evaluation. Law can be judged as morally bad without losing its status as valid law. This is expressed most bluntly in the nineteenth-century jurist John Austin's formulation that law is the command of a sovereign backed up by threats.

More sophisticated versions of a fundamentally legal positivist approach are sensitive to issues of ethics, politics and legitimacy, but nonetheless distinguish the questions of identifying law from its evaluation. The identification of a law as valid if it satisfied the 'rule of recognition' accepted by a society's officials (Hart 1961: chs 5–6) in no way precluded the more important consideration of whether it was morally right to obey it (Hart 1958: 75). As Hart made most explicit in his famous debate with Lon Fuller, most Nazi law might have been valid, but nonetheless thoroughly bad; the overwhelming moral duty was thus legal *dis*obedience (Fuller 1958; Hart 1958; see also Lacey 2008; Rundle 2013: 66–76).

Formalist vs substantive definitions

Most criminal law texts define crime in a positivist, formal and essentially circular way, following the arguments advanced fifty years ago in a celebrated lecture by Glanville Williams: 'crime is an act capable of being followed by criminal proceedings having a criminal outcome, and a proceeding or its outcome is criminal if it has certain characteristics which mark it as criminal' (Williams 1955: 107). Contemporary textbooks continue to define crime in formalistic ways, although usually they go on to consider broader normative issues of the reasons for criminalization, its limits and consequences. To give a recent example, 'A criminal offence is a legal wrong for which the offender is liable to be prosecuted on behalf of the State, and if found guilty liable to be punished' (Card, Cross and Jones 2014: 1).

This formalism has been matched in jurists' pronouncements over the years.[9] It is confirmed by recent jurisprudence, in the United Kingdom and continental Europe, which continues to demarcate criminal law in essentially procedural terms. The European Convention on Human Rights (ECHR), incorporated into UK law by the Human Rights Act 1998, has stimulated much case law and legal debate about what makes proceedings criminal. Article 6 of the ECHR seeks to protect the right to a fair trial. It sets out various specific rights for those facing 'any criminal charge', notably the presumption of innocence, and adequate legal assistance with the preparation of a defence. There are further due-process requirements specifically for criminal cases in Article 7 and several Protocols. This has resulted in extensive ECHR jurisprudence seeking to delineate the criminal/civil borderline (Emmerson and Ashworth 2012; Amatrudo and Blake 2014). The ECHR case law delineates the criminal/civil borderline in essentially formal and procedural terms and does not offer a substantive theory of the nature of crime.[10]

The issue of legal definitions of crime has become even more complex in the last decade with the rise of hybrid offences whereby criminal sanctions (often severe) attach to breach of orders that are initially determined by civil processes. The most significant of these in the United Kingdom is the ASBO under section 1 of the Crime and Disorder Act 1998, which may be made by a magistrates' court in civil proceedings (Squires 2008; Burney 2009; Ramsay 2012). Breach of this order without reasonable excuse can attract a penalty of up to five years' imprisonment on indictment.

The ECHR principles would seem to suggest that this potentially severe penalty should make the proceedings as a whole (including the initial imposition of the order) 'criminal', but against this the House of Lords has held that an ASBO is preventive not punitive in purpose.[11] The imposition of an ASBO thus represents 'a position midway between the civil and the criminal paradigms' (Ashworth 2004: 277), in that the Lords have held that it requires the criminal standard of proof because of the potential severity of penalties, but with the more relaxed civil rules of evidence, including hearsay. ASBOs have been controversial as an extension of criminal sanctions to vaguely defined behaviour, requiring judgements of value about what is 'reasonable' in specific contexts that are likely to vary according to the social position of the defendant, and subject to procedures less rigorous than the criminal.

Although the formalist definition of criminal law continues to be repeated in textbooks and in judicial pronouncements, there has been an increasing concern to identify normative or other principles for identifying criminal law, avoiding the circularity of formalism. Andrew Ashworth has suggested that we *can* 'identify a principled core of criminal law' (Ashworth 2000: 253–4), comprising 'four interlinked principles'. The last three of these are procedural: equal treatment and proportionality in enforcement; the human rights protections of Article 6 of the ECHR for suspects; and proportionality in sentencing. The first, however, proposes a fundamental principle to delineate the ambit of criminal law: 'the criminal law should be used, and only used, to censure persons for substantial wrongdoing.' This clearly raises the issue of whether there is or can be agreement on what constitutes culpable 'substantial wrongdoing', and indeed Ashworth's explicit purpose is 'to re-kindle debate about the functions and characteristics that the criminal law ought to have' (ibid.: 256). This and other normative perspectives will be the focus of chapter 2.

Consensus vs conflict

The tension between 'conflict' and 'consensus' perspectives has been one of the central threads in social theory (Dawe 1970; Giddens 1979; van Krieken 2002). As with other such dualisms, the two poles represent ideal-types never actually embodied in the work of any major thinker, even if textbook caricatures of the classical theorists have been constructed by selecting one-sided quotes. The contrast between consensus and conflict perspectives, although a huge oversimplification of actual authors, is a useful way of pointing up clear tendencies in the analysis of criminal law. The consensus view regards crime as a violation of the common values and interests of all people in a society, crystallized in modern democratic societies in criminal law.

This consensus view is expressed explicitly by Durkheim. Noting that 'There are many acts which have been and still are regarded as criminal without in themselves being harmful to society', he suggests that what is regarded as criminal cannot be explained by the intrinsic features of the acts themselves. 'The only common characteristic of all crimes is that they consist...in acts universally disapproved of by members of each society...Crime shocks sentiments which, for a given social system, are found in all healthy consciences' (Durkheim 1973 [1893]: 72–80).

So many diverse actions have been and are treated as criminal, however, that the only common feature uniting them is the social reaction of censure. Durkheim's definition is circular: crime shocks 'healthy' consciences. But how are these defined except as those which are shocked by 'crime'?

The problem is that, whilst there are probably some crimes in any society that do have the Durkheimian unifying effect, others are more or less clearly contested. Rare spectacular crimes may draw almost everyone together in horrified condemnation, such as those of the Yorkshire Ripper in the 1970s and 1980 (and his eponymous London forebear in the 1880s), or the killing of appealing children like the Liverpool toddler James Bulger or the Soham schoolgirls. But many other crimes are the focus of heated controversy and diametrically antagonistic responses: drug taking, tax evasion or avoidance. One side's just war is another's state crime. Who is the 'terrorist', who is the freedom fighter, or war hero?

Conflict perspectives emphasize precisely such examples of contentious crime. They also seek to expose how even apparently consensual crimes may conceal different interests behind a seemingly universalistic criminal law. All known societies are characterized by inequalities and hierarchies, primarily based on economic class, ethnicity and gender. These are a source of conflict, whether latent or manifest. As we have seen, criminal law and its enforcement machinery evolved in relation to the emergence of domination and inequality.

Criminal law purports to address all people equally, a crucial condition of the ideal of the rule of law. However, the formulation of criminal law could not claim democratic legitimacy until the gradual achievement during the nineteenth and early twentieth centuries of the universal franchise (Lacey 2014). As chapter 5 will show in detail, the criminal law in action follows the patterns of inequality and injustice in society, bearing down unequally on different classes and ethnic groups. Nonetheless, there is little evidence of systematic or widespread questioning of the legitimacy of criminal law in contemporary western liberal democracies, apart from such subterranean aphorisms as 'one law for the rich, one for the poor'.

This is partly achieved by the focus of the media, popular culture and political debate on the most serious and atypical crimes of homicide and sexual violence. These are most likely to achieve the Durkheimian consensus, rather than the much more commonly processed 'volume' offences like theft, which are more evidently related to inequality.[12] Public images of crime are dominated by rare serious violent offences, not the mass of poor property and drug offenders who actually populate the prison boom.

However, as more sophisticated analyses of the ideology of criminal justice show, this is not just a case of *Sun*-stroke, tabloid-driven false consciousness, but derives from the ambivalent experience and life situation of most people (Sumner 1979). The functioning of criminal law and criminal justice is Janus-faced. In his recollections of the hiatus between the collapse of Nazism at the end of the Second World War and the re-establishment of some semblance of order by the victorious allies, Ralf Dahrendorf vividly described the terror of a society in which there was no authority at all to provide any protection of life, limb or personal property (Dahrendorf 1985: 80). Of course, for the many victims of the Nazis, the previous 'order' held the systematic terror of state-sponsored annihilation for those deemed

Untermenschen. But Dahrendorf's brief anomic interval created fear and insecurity for everyone. A functioning system of criminal law and justice (at least outside despotism) provides a minimum bedrock of *general* order, social cooperation, civilization, that is in the universal interest of everyone. However, at the same time, criminal law and justice reproduce a *particular* order, riven by inequality, injustice, hierarchy and oppression. The functioning of criminal justice thus has an inevitable ambivalence, memorably described by Otwin Marenin as 'parking tickets and class repression' (Marenin 1982). It is characterized by both consensus *and* conflict.

Constructivism vs realism

'Crime has no ontological reality. Crime is not the object but the product of criminal policy' (Hulsman 1986: 71). This is a concise statement of the constructionist perspective on crime, which is implicit in the positivist and formalist interpretations of criminal law discussed above, as well as in much critical criminology, especially labelling theory. The behaviours that are criminalized by law are hugely diverse and changeable, so that the quality of criminality cannot be seen as present in the act itself but is purely the product of social perception and reaction.

This was not the view of crime held by earlier generations of radical thinkers, such as Marx or Bonger (Cowling 2008; Moxon 2014), or social democratic liberals like Merton or Mannheim. Whilst fully aware of the links between class power and the making and enforcing of law, they also recognized that at least some of what was labelled as criminal included practices that were harmful and wrong, not least because they victimized the vulnerable and disadvantaged. However, the dominant strains of radical criminology that flourished in the 1960s and 1970s emphasized the harms of labelling and social control, implicitly, and sometimes explicitly (e.g. Becker 1967), minimizing the evils often perpetrated by criminal victimization.

A realist reaction to constructivism developed in the 1970s, originating amongst conservative criminologists. The pioneer was James Q. Wilson, in his seminal *Thinking about Crime* (Wilson 2013 [1975]). He argued forcefully that the crime that mattered was 'predatory street crime', not all criminal law violations, because it was uniquely fear provoking, destructive of social relations and objectively evil.

Wilson's book also blazed the trail for a burgeoning field of 'administrative', policy-oriented research that disregarded issues of causation of crime and focused instead on 'what works?' Based on rational choice, routine activities and situational crime-prevention theory, it focused on practical initiatives and their evaluation (Clarke and Mayhew 1980; Cornish and Clarke 1986; Felson and Clarke 1998; Tilley 2005; Felson and Eckert 2015).

During the 1980s, a self-styled school of 'Left realist' criminology developed, shaped by similar concerns about the considerable growth of crime (chapter 5 will consider the trends in detail). The essence of the position was that the Left should take crime seriously. Using a combination of the government's newly launched crime surveys, and important local surveys of their own (Jones, MacLean and Young 1986; Crawford et al. 1990), the new Left realists emphasized how the main burdens of crime fell on the poorest and most vulnerable sections of society, precisely the groups the Left should primarily be concerned about. They argued that the Left had to develop concrete policies to alleviate crime and reform criminal justice in the short run, rather than relying on long-term reforms to tackle the root causes of crime.[13]

The at times highly polarized and polemical debate between constructionist and realist perspectives is unnecessary and unhelpful. On the one hand, it is tautologically true that, in the absence of labelling, crime as it is currently regarded and processed would not exist. On the other hand, the harms, pains, suffering and injustice associated with the core behaviours that are indeed censured and sanctioned in all viable societies *would* still occur, albeit perhaps with different forms of social reaction, some of which might be preferable. What, if any, normative justification there is for criminal law, and what should be its ambits and limits, will be discussed in the next chapter.

The core parameters of the legal idea of 'crime' have been discussed above, and it has been seen that there is considerable diversity of interpretation concerning what criminal law itself is. Cross-cutting or running alongside the formal criminal law's framing of crime, at least the following five further conceptions of crime can be distinguished in contemporary discourse, each itself signifying a complex web of perspectives, practices and values: morality; social practice; criminal justice system labelling and measurement; mass-media images; and the academic field of criminology. These will be examined in subsequent chapters.

2
Moral Conceptions of Crime

Arguments about what should or should not be part of criminal law are commonplace in public discourse, as well as in jurisprudential debate. 'There ought to be a law against [pet hate]' is a frequently expressed sentiment. At least as common are aggrieved complaints from Jeremy Clarkson wannabes about supposedly unjustified prosecutions for speeding and other traffic offences, whilst 'real' crime (such as assaulting junior colleagues?) is neglected.[1]

The boundaries of criminal law often seem to evade simple or clear moral justification. To take a currently controversial example, the rules demarcating criminally proscribed tax evasion from legally permissible avoidance often arouse indignation at their apparent injustice. This is especially so when the seemingly lax handling of tax evasion is contrasted with the draconian treatment of much more minor sums that may be involved in alleged welfare fraud (Cook 1989, 2006).

The Department of Work and Pensions' 'no ifs, no buts, benefit fraud is a crime' campaign offers an especially egregious example.

> However, if benefit fraud is 'theft', then so is tax evasion. The difference is that the former is committed by the weakest and most vulnerable of society, while the latter is committed by the richest and the most powerful, and costs the country tens

> of billions of pounds in illegally withheld revenue [...] an appalling 8% to 12% of the nation's GDP. (Taylor 2007)

This chapter will review various attempts within criminology and criminal law theory to offer criteria for determining what should or should not be criminalized. These issues are at the heart of several celebrated jurisprudential debates. Should criminal law enforce traditional moral beliefs, as conservatives from James Fitzjames Stephen to Patrick Devlin have argued (Devlin 1965 [1959])? Or should law's ambit be restricted to preventing 'harm to others', as postulated by liberals from John Stuart Mill to Hart (Hart 1968; Feinberg 1984–1990; Lee 1987)?

More radically, should the concept of crime, hard to justify on a coherent normative basis, be replaced by a clear principle denoting the basis of censure and sanctioning? Examples of such principles include the protection of human rights or the minimization of harm, as radical scholars and 'zemiologists' have suggested (Schwendinger and Schwendinger 1975; Hillyard et al. 2004; Davies, Francis and Jupp 2014; Pemberton 2015). This chapter will review these arguments about the vexed relationship between criminal law and different conceptions of morality and harm.

Positivist or formalist legal definitions of crime open themselves to normative critique, as shown in the previous chapter. From different moral perspectives, it can be claimed that criminal law proscribes and sanctions actions that ought not to be punished because they are acceptable or perhaps even desirable. There is a long and honourable historical lineage of harshly punished lawbreakers who have subsequently been hailed as moral heroes, from Socrates, Spartacus and Jesus to Nelson Mandela, Aung San Suu Kyi and Alan Turing. Even if behaviour is generally regarded as wrong, moreover, it can be argued that criminalization is – for a variety of possible reasons – not the most appropriate means of control. Conversely, the scope of criminal law can be criticized normatively for failing to include behaviours that should be proscribed and punished. Why are the banks not only too big to fail, but their directors too big to jail, despite the havoc of the financial crash of 2007–8, dubbed 'the crime of our time' by Danny Schechter (Schechter 2010; Garrett 2015)?

Normative criminal law theories

As seen in the previous chapter, modern criminal law emerged during the late eighteenth and early nineteenth centuries in line with the march of industrial capitalism. It slowly distinguished itself from civil law, although overlap remains as some offences can also give rise to civil actions (for example, assault is both a crime and a tort).[2] Modernity was also associated with a gradual distinction (but not separation) between law and morality.

Moralistic perspectives

Modern criminal law had its roots in older, and indeed ancient, moral and religious values and rules. Hart described what he called 'the classical thesis' on law and morality, dating back at least to Plato and Aristotle, stressing their absolutist view of an objective and timeless morality underpinning the law.

> According to this thesis not only may the law be used to punish men for doing what morally it is wrong for them to do, but it should be so used...This theory is strongly associated with a specific conception of morality as a uniquely true or correct set of principles – not man-made, but either awaiting man's discovery by the use of his reason or (in a theological setting) awaiting its disclosure by revelation. (Hart 1983: 248)

During the Middle Ages, classical and biblical influences combined as the basis of the 'natural law' position developed by the leading theologians of Christianity (and to some extent also Judaism and Islam). In the words of Aquinas, the great Catholic thinker, reflecting Augustine's dictum 'that which is not just seems to be no law at all': 'every human law has just so much of the nature of law as is derived from the law of nature. But if in any point it deflects from the law of nature, it is no longer a law but a perversion of law' (*Summa Theologica* 1265–74, I–II, Q. 95, A. II). In this view, the authority of law is derived from analysis of reason and nature, embodied in religious tradition.

The shadow of these moral and theological origins remains in the naming of the best-known offences (murder, rape, theft, etc.), and in how they are regarded and discussed, by popular culture. Echoes remain in legal culture, too. For example, the Latin terminology *mala in se* (offences evil in themselves) versus *mala prohibita* ('evils' merely prohibited by political authorities) is still found in some texts, as is the distinction between the *actus reus* (the guilty act) and the *mens rea* (the perpetrator's guilty state of mind).

The emergence of modern liberal criminal law theory: Beccaria to Blackstone

During the eighteenth and nineteenth centuries, there were many debates about the proper scope and ambit of criminal law. An emerging split was discernible between more conservative views that continued to see criminal law as underpinned by universal, absolute moral principles, and secular, more liberal interpretations inspired by the Enlightenment. The latter approaches saw law as having a human and contingent basis, at least in large part. Cesare Beccaria, an Italian nobleman and professor of political economy, wrote the 1764 treatise *On Crimes and Punishments*, which is generally regarded as the foundational text for the so-called 'classical' perspective in modern criminal law and criminology.

Beccaria's work was heavily influenced by earlier liberal political thought, lauded by Enlightenment thinkers such as Voltaire and Bentham, but castigated as heresy by the Church (Harcourt 2014). Beccaria typified liberal conceptions of crime and punishment in regarding the latter as an unfortunate necessity. It was only justified by the notion of a social contract entered into for fear of a Hobbesian state of nature. 'Every punishment which does not arise from absolute necessity, says the great Montesquieu, is tyrannical' (quoted from *Dei delitti e delle pene*). Crimes were acts that breached the social contract and threatened a return to the insecurity that had prompted people to cede a small measure of their autonomy to the sovereign. Punishment was justified to deter this but to the minimum extent necessary to outweigh the attractions of violation and only if regulated strictly by the rule of law.

Beccaria was hugely influential over Bentham and other reformers of criminal law in Britain and throughout Europe. However, he was also virulently opposed by those conservatives who continued to preserve the idea of law as based on traditional morality, and he saw violations as meriting punishment for retribution and not just utilitarian crime prevention. His impact on Blackstone's seminal *Commentaries on the Laws of England* (1765–9) exhibits this double-faceted influence (Stern 2014).

Blackstone's *Commentaries* are generally read as an attempt to rationalize and justify the common law of England, and this is largely true of the fourth part, which is on criminal law. However, Blackstone had been deeply influenced by Beccaria before he wrote his account, and he expressed some criticism of the legal system reflecting this. For example, he opposed the overuse of capital punishment for minor property offences, which had proliferated in the eighteenth century. The critique is formulated in the mildest terms, and the problems were largely portrayed as the lingering influence of less advanced stages of civilization, but the Beccarian influence is clear. The criminal law should be founded on universal and incontestable moral principles, and in England it largely was, argued Blackstone – but there were blemishes due to not rooting out primitive survivals. Blackstone encapsulated the eighteenth-century struggle between conservative moral absolutist, and liberal pragmatic and minimalist, conceptions of crime and punishment.

The criminalization of private (im)morality debates

Jurisprudential and criminological debates about the normative sources and limits of criminal law continued through the nineteenth century, with utilitarian and liberal perspectives gradually displacing more openly moralistic ones. Perhaps the most familiar argument about alleged overreach of criminal law concerns the criminalization of private behaviour that may be regarded as immoral. This was the subject of a legendary argument between John Stuart Mill and Fitzjames Stephen in the nineteenth century, repeated in the 1960s by the even more celebrated debate between Hart and Lord Devlin. It continues to echo today over such issues as abortion and assisted suicide, and in cases like *R v Brown* [1994] 1 A.C. 212 concerning criminalization of consensual sado-masochistic practices.

Mill vs Stephen

The starting point for these exchanges was John Stuart Mill's famous statement in his 1859 essay *On Liberty* of what has come to be known as the 'harm principle', suggesting parameters beyond which criminal law had no legitimacy.

> The sole end for which mankind are warranted, individually or collectively, in interfering with the liberty of action of any of their number is self-protection. That the only purpose for which power can rightfully be exercised over any member of a civilised community against his will is to prevent harm to others. His own good, whether physical or moral, is not a sufficient warrant. (Mill 1998 [1859]: 263)

Mill's essay is a quintessential statement of the liberal perspective on crime and punishment. The foundational premise is the paramount importance and value of the autonomy of the individual. Punishment is in itself an undesirable and harmful assault on liberty. In Mill's own words later on in the same paragraph, to compel someone's actions by punishment, even in a good cause, is 'visiting him with…evil.…To justify that, the conduct from which it is desired to deter him, must be calculated to produce evil to someone else' (ibid.).

Liberal discussions of crime tend to place a substantial burden of proof on those who propose justifications of criminalization: these must be sufficiently weighty to overcome the pains of punishment. Mill's simple 'harm to others' seems at first blush to provide a straightforward test for criminalization. It has been a powerful resource for liberals, most notably during the period following the Hart–Devlin debate in the early 1960s, ushering in the wave of decriminalization of those moralistic offences that at the time were commonly labelled 'crimes without victims' (Schur 1965).

The problem that only became appreciated much later was the need to specify more clearly the ambit of the deceptively simple notion of 'harm'. The complex issues in defining what counts as harm were anticipated by Mill himself in the later parts of his essay. Not all conduct that hurts others is to be punished, but only actions that injure 'certain interests, which, either by express provision or by tacit understanding, ought to be considered as rights' (Mill 1998 [1859]: 322).

Mill does not spell out in principle the interests and rights that are to be protected from harm by criminal law. However, he gives several examples or 'applications'. These indicate a surprising range of activities where, in Mill's view, penal intervention was justified on the 'harm to others' principle.[3]

Although Mill's own interpretation of the 'harm principle' was hedged in with considerable complexity, it aroused the ire of conservatives. The best known was Lord James Fitzjames Stephen, an eminent judge, who vigorously championed legal moralism, justifying the promulgation and enforcement of criminal laws to protect traditional morality. Stephen clearly pitched his position against Mill's 'harm principle': 'there are acts of wickedness so gross and outrageous that, self-protection apart, they must be prevented as far as possible at any cost to the offender, and punished, if they occur, with exemplary severity' (Stephen 1967 [1873]: 162). Nonetheless, 'law and morals are not and cannot be made co-extensive, or even completely harmonious' (Stephen 1883: 75). However, the core of criminal law, the 'gross offences...murder, rape, arson, robbery, theft, or the like' derived completely from morality, and the role of criminalization was to indicate unequivocally society's censure and revulsion. The 'sentence of the law is to the moral sentiment of the public in relation to any offence what a seal is to hot wax', and criminal punishment 'proceeds upon the principle that it is morally right to hate criminals' (Stephen 1883: 80–1). Legal punishment was a legitimate way of expressing the public desire for revenge and retribution (Stephen 1967 [1873]: 152).

Wolfenden

One hundred years after Mill's *On Liberty*, the argument between his 'harm principle' and Stephen's legal moralism was rerun in a high profile dispute between H. L. A. Hart, the Oxford professor of jurisprudence, and the distinguished judge Lord Patrick Devlin. The historical context is important for understanding why the argument became so celebrated. The Hart–Devlin debate was largely a reaction to the controversy sparked by the publication in 1957 of the Report of the Committee on Homosexual Offences and Prostitution, chaired by Sir John Wolfenden (Wolfenden 1957).

The Wolfenden Report adopted liberal premises echoing Mill's 'harm to others' test. It noted first that 'there appears to be no unquestioned definition of what constitutes or ought to constitute a crime. To define it as "an act which is punished by the State" does not answer the question: What acts ought to be punished by the State? We have therefore worked with our own formulation of the function of the criminal law so far as it concerns the subjects of this inquiry' (Wolfenden 1957: para. 13). It declared that the function of criminal law was 'to preserve public order and decency, to protect the citizen from what is offensive or injurious, and to provide sufficient safeguards against exploitation and corruption of others' (ibid.).

Wolfenden's formulation of the 'harm' principle emphasized the notion of privacy as a limiting condition for the reach of criminal law. 'It is not, in our view, the function of the law to intervene in the private lives of citizens, or to seek to enforce any particular pattern of behaviour' (1957: para. 14). In its most cited section, the Committee criticized legal moralism and argued that privacy limited the legitimate ambit of criminal law. 'Unless a deliberate attempt is to be made by society, acting through the agency of the law, to equate the sphere of crime with that of sin, there must remain a realm of private morality and immorality which is, in brief and crude terms, not the law's business' (1957: para. 61).

Applying these principles, the Report recommended that prostitution should not in itself be illegal, although it suggested strengthening the laws against soliciting, being involved in a brothel or living off the earnings of a prostitute (Recommendations xix–xxx). These proposals were largely implemented in the 1959 Street Offences Act.

The Report's most controversial recommendation was its first one: 'That homosexual behaviour between consenting adults in private be no longer a criminal offence' (Recommendation i). Ultimately, after a decade of argument, this was achieved by the Sexual Offences Act 1967. The 1967 Act was part of a wave of decriminalizing statutes under the Labour government in the late 1960s that are collectively seen as part of the 'permissive society', or as Roy Jenkins, the home secretary at the time, spoke of it, the 'civilized society' (Newburn 1991).

Hart vs Devlin

The Hart–Devlin debate was a crucial aspect of the public controversy sparked by Wolfenden, which culminated in the 1967 Act and the other decriminalizing statutes of the late 1960s. Devlin entered the fray first, with a lecture to the British Academy delivered in 1959 under the title 'The Enforcement of Morals' (published in Devlin 1965 [1959]). His arguments ran together many strands that should be distinguished. He combined a defence of the legitimacy of criminal law enforcement of communal moral values, expressions of disapproval of what he thought of as immorality, assertions about the need to respect the prevailing moral standards in a community, and consequentialist claims about the deleterious impact of immorality in practice.

Devlin's starting point was an attempt to rebut the very enterprise on which Mill, Wolfenden, Hart and others were embarked: the specification of principled limits to legitimate criminalization. 'I think, therefore, that it is not possible to set theoretical limits to the power of the State to legislate against immorality. It is not possible to settle in advance exceptions to the general rule or to define inflexibly areas of morality into which the law is in no circumstances to be allowed to enter' (Devlin 1965 [1959]: 12–13).

Devlin expressed disapproval of homosexuality as 'addictive' and a 'miserable way of life' (Devlin 1965 [1959]: v).

However, his main arguments were not based on personal attitudes but his construal of the prevailing sentiment. In his view, although the encouragement of tolerance is desirable, nonetheless if conduct aroused strong feelings of indignation and disgust in the average person – the 'juryman' or 'the man on the Clapham omnibus' – this justified criminalization (ibid.: 16–17). Devlin's view of communal morality was relative, however, rather than absolutist. By 1967, he had changed his mind sufficiently to be a signatory of a letter to *The Times* advocating decriminalization.

Devlin's crucial argument, however, was not pitched in terms of protecting the average person from offence. It is a particular version of consequentialism, based on his claim that a society's morality was the essential glue binding it together. Conduct challenging morality was a fatal social threat requiring criminal law as protection. 'For society is not something that is kept together physically; it is held by the invisible bonds of common thought. If the bonds were too far relaxed, the members would drift apart. A common morality is part of the bondage. The bondage is part of the price of society; and mankind, which needs society, must pay its price' (Devlin 1965 [1959]: 10). This entitles it to 'use the law to preserve morality in the same way as it uses it to safeguard anything else that is essential to its existence' (ibid.: 11). On this line of argument, the flaw in the Wolfenden claim that the criminal law should not penalize 'private' conduct is that actions that take place in private may still have public consequences, weakening social order.

Hart's celebrated reply to Devlin carried the day at the time and was able to take advantage of the changing cultural climate. Hart mounted a withering attack on what he called the 'disintegration' thesis, that a society's moral code, especially on sexual matters, was crucial to its survival, and thus deviation from it was the equivalent of treason (Hart 1968). Beyond that, however, he vigorously defended Mill's 'harm to others' principle as generally staking out limits to what it was desirable or sensible to criminalize. He argued, however, that in its sharp and absolute form it could be criticized. Sometimes, for example, there might be justifications for a degree of paternalism to prevent people harming themselves

– which Mill himself recognized in the final section of *On Liberty*.

Hart emerged the clear victor over Devlin in relation to the specific issues of decriminalizing consenting adult homosexual activity. However, there has been an increasing volume of critique of Hart's formulation of the more general principles governing criminalization (e.g. Dworkin 1999; Harcourt 1999, 2014). In the light of the normative turn in criminal law theory to be discussed below, it is hardly surprising that the position that *in principle* acts regarded as immoral should not be criminalized has been questioned. There may of course be many reasons, principled and pragmatic, to restrain the use of criminal law. But it is a matter for debate issue by issue. As Gerald Dworkin argues, for example:

> Perhaps it is a good idea, in general, for the state to restrict the amount of condemnation in which it engages. These questions, however, seem to be matters of good judgement and prudence, not matters of principle. The criminal law is an institution whose central rationales include making it less likely that acts that ought not to be done are not done and serving as a vehicle for condemning those who do what ought not to be done. The existence of principled reasons for ruling out (in advance) the criminal process as a means of discouragement therefore seems quite implausible. (Dworkin 1999: 944–5)

He suggests that liberals should not have argued that consensual adult homosexuality ought to be decriminalized because the law had no business punishing private immoral conduct but, more robustly, because such relations are not immoral (Dworkin 1999: 946).

More generally, the 'harm' principle has been subject to considerable debate, even from commentators broadly in sympathy with it. In essence, the problem is that 'harm' is as elastic a concept as 'morality', and can be used in diverse and conflicting ways. The language of 'harm' has increasingly been taken over by conservatives to criminalize conduct they regard as immoral, extending rather than restricting the ambit of criminal law (as pointed out by Harcourt 1999). Anti-abortion activists, for example, often seek to document the harms abortion causes, rather than deploying arguments based on traditional morality. As we saw above, Devlin himself tried to defend the criminalization of homosexuality by suggesting it was as harmful as treason. On the other hand, liberals and radicals, who had generally opposed the extension of criminal law, have engaged in 'progressive criminalization' (Aharonson 2010; Aaronson 2014). Given that criminalization has become the main currency of condemnation, radical groups have argued for more extensive criminal law enforcement against such harms as hate crimes.

The normative 'counter-reformation' in criminal law theory

As seen in the last chapter, the prevailing perspective on criminal law in the twentieth century was positivist and formalist. Identifying what the law *was* could, and should, be sharply distinguished from normative evaluation. The sheer variety of criminal laws precluded any explanation of content other than the circular: a criminal law was one which, if breached, could result in criminal proceedings aimed at punishment. Pascal remarked long ago that 'what is truth on one side of the Pyrenees is error on the other', and to the legal positivist this applied also to morality and crime.

Although this is still articulated by textbooks as at least an initial definition of criminal law, an increasing number criticize it. As a leading current text argues: 'But to define criminal law only in these procedural terms fails to shed any light on a more fundamental problem: why does the distinction between criminal and other law matter?...We need to identify the distinguishing features that also justify treating crimes as a separate body of law' (Simester and Sullivan 2013: 1–2).

The poverty of purely procedural and positivist definitions of criminal law has come to be seen as problematic by many legal theorists. In the words of one leading scholar: 'Such process-driven definitions of crime...said nothing about what kinds of conduct should, or should not, be followed by "criminal" proceedings' (Horder 2014: 5). Frustration with this resulted in 'the emergence of what might be called a "counter-reformation" in criminal law scholarship', which has taken the form of 're-moralising the idea of criminal law' (ibid.: 2).

Many contemporary theorists have sought to develop normative approaches delimiting the scope and content of criminal law. To some extent, the arguments echo the exchanges in the criminalization of private morality debates. However, they do so over a larger canvas, looking at how criminalization can be justified in general. There is also a growing literature on such contemporary trends as preventive criminalization (Ramsay 2012; Ashworth and Zedner 2014), the proliferation of offences with pragmatic regulatory purposes but not requiring a substantial element of fault if any, together with a broader dilution of requirements for conviction, such as a greater acceptance of evidence of bad character (Redmayne 2015). Why has the ambit of criminal law expanded, and to what extent are such developments acceptable?

Most recent normative theoretical analyses of criminal law start from a quite explicit liberal perspective (Roberts 2014). This was also true of many theorists in the earlier generation of positivist and formalist definitions, but the latter primarily adopted consequentialist, utilitarian justifications of criminalization and punishment. These were always subject to challenge by moralist standpoints such as those of Stephen or Devlin, and of course consequences had to be implicitly evaluated as harmful or promoting happiness. However, as we have seen, positivists like Hart tried to keep sharply distinct the issues of identifying the criminal law from its moral assessment. In terms of the legitimate ambit of criminal law, Hart and other consequentialists argued against the criminalization of conduct purely on the grounds of its immorality. Ethical judgement of the law was vital, but it was distinct from the question of its validity.

Moral considerations also played a crucial part in some positivist theories of punishment, in addition to the practical arguments for or against different penal regimes. Hart, for example, saw the fundamental justification in systems of punishment as being their possible harm-reducing consequences. However, punishment could only be applied fairly to particular individuals if they had committed morally culpable acts, and not just to promote the general welfare (Hart 1968).

Others have also argued in similar fashion for dual theories of punishment, combining consequentialist justifications of penal institutions with moral criteria added in as necessary conditions for criminalization and the application of punishment to individuals. For example, Braithwaite and Pettit have argued that 'only persons who are morally culpable for a proscribed encroachment upon the dominion of others should be convicted' (Braithwaite and Pettit 1990: 99). Thus even primarily consequentialist theories can, and indeed usually do, include some moral considerations, at least as constraints on the distribution of punishment.

Recent 'counter-reformation' theories of criminal law, however, are more directly based on deontological versions of morality. They see crime and punishment as justified by intrinsic culpability for violations of moral, as well as legal, rules and duties. In this, they reflect a broader normative turn in political and moral philosophy, associated above all with the seminal influence of John Rawls's theory of justice (Rawls 1971).

Some recent theories of criminal law have harked back (albeit with more sophisticated philosophically based arguments) to the purist moralism of Stephen or Devlin. They see morality as the basic justification for declaring types of conduct criminal, as well as for punishing individual perpetrators on the grounds that they intrinsically deserve retribution. Moore, for example, claims that the prime function of criminal law is to achieve retributive justice by punishing 'all and only those who are morally culpable in the doing of some morally wrongful action' (Moore 1997: 35). In principle, moral wrongdoing supplies both necessary and sufficient reasons for a presumption in favour of criminalization: 'all and only moral wrongs should be criminally prohibited' (ibid.: 662). However, that presumption can be defeated by other moral considerations about the impact of criminalization on other values. For example, due respect for individual liberty may outweigh the case for actually criminalizing some wrongful conduct (ibid.: ch. 18).

However, most contemporary theorists of criminal law operate from a clear liberal framework. A major concern is how to reconcile criminal law and punishment – which seem by their nature to be restricting, censuring and delivering pain – with the fundamental liberal sensibility that is 'at its heart...concerned with prioritising individuals' *liberty*...treating the individual as the primary unit of ethical concern' (Roberts 2014: 331). In the words of one of the pre-eminent such theorists, 'by a liberal theory of penal justice I mean one that derives legal constraints on punishment from an idea of what reconciles penal force with the freedom and inviolable worth of the individual agent' (Brudner 2009: ix).

Primarily consequentialist perspectives, notably utilitarianism (which also claimed to be 'liberal', especially in J. S. Mill's version), could overcome this issue by a dualistic analysis. The purpose of criminalization was to curb activities that threatened overall happiness and well-being. However, the application of pain to those who violated the rules was justified only if they satisfied the required standard of personal culpability. This glosses over the empirical reality of power differences in the ability to shape law, the unequal pressures to deviate on people of different class and in other positions in the distribution of social advantages and the gross inequalities in the actual delivery of criminal 'justice'. Neglect of the wider issues of social justice remains largely true of contemporary deontological versions of liberalism. Only a few contemporary legal theorists seriously consider the implications of socio-economic and political contexts for analytic and normative understanding of criminal law (exceptions include Lacey et al. 2003; Ramsay 2012; Melissaris 2012a, 2012b; Norrie 2014).

Contemporary theorists are generally sensitive to the neo-Kantian Rawlsian critique that 'classical utilitarianism fails to take seriously the distinction between persons' (Rawls 1971: 27). They seek to honour the axiom that one should 'Act in such a way that you treat humanity, whether in your own person or in the person of any other, never merely as a means to an end, but always at the same time as an end' (Kant 1993 [1785]: 30). This enjoins people to 'Act only according to that maxim whereby you can at the same time will that it should become a universal law without contradiction' (ibid.). Criminal laws can only accord with this if they satisfy certain criteria about their formulation, intended functioning and application to specific people who are accused of breaching them.

There are many subtly different attempts to address these issues in contemporary scholarship. I will set out below a broad-brush indication of the lines of argument that have been proposed, though this doubtless does violence to the important differences between individual theorists.

How can criminal laws formulated to coerce people into adhering to codes of conduct, on threat of the pain of punishment, possibly respect their individual autonomy? One commonly invoked answer is the notion of the social contract: the idea that people have – or more plausibly can be treated as if they had – agreed to rules governing their coexistence in order to secure mutual protection from threat of interpersonal harm.

The original Hobbesian version suggested that people in a postulated state of nature, fearing a 'war of all against all', agreed to cede some power to a sovereign in exchange for a measure of security. As was seen earlier, the notion of a social contract was the prime justification of criminal law and punishment in Beccaria, the key figure in the eighteenth-century classical school. Versions of contract theory (formulated explicitly as thought-experiments) remain important ways of legitimating criminal law, criminal justice and punishment (Matravers 2000, 2011).

A related approach is imaginatively to construct the criminal laws and security institutions that would be agreed to in conditions of dialogic equality and fairness, along the lines of Habermas's ideal speech situation (Loader and Walker 2007). Like thought-experiment versions of contract theory, such reconstructions involve explicit assumptions about human organization, needs, interests, welfare, perceptions, decision-making processes, capacities and limitations that are argued for on a basis of empirical evidence and a priori normative assertion.

Probably the most usual argument for reconciling coercive criminal law and notions of human autonomy is that political democracy implies at least some measure of consent, even from those who suffer the pains of policing, prosecution and punishment (Lacey 2014). This is supported by the historical coincidence of the long march of democratic citizenship from the late eighteenth century onwards with the gradual reforms of criminal law, policing, prosecution and punishment (Reiner

2010b). This process of social inclusion makes it possible to represent the core of criminal justice as at least approximating to standards of due-process legality.

The contractual, dialogic-community and democratic-citizenship interpretations all coincide in suggesting a roughly similar justification of criminal law, seeing at least its general part, and the core specific offences, as respecting, perhaps even emanating from, liberal notions of individual autonomy. At the same time, lurking in the shadows of such interpretations is fear of some contemporary trends that threaten liberal ideals. These include: regulatory offences dispensing with individual liability requirements, pre-emptive offences that may in effect penalize thought not conduct, punishments imposed without full criminal trial rights, all resulting in an explosion of imprisonment and other forms of punitiveness. Indeed, much current theorization is driven by primary concern with such illiberal threats, so the attempt to define the purposes of criminalization is aimed at limiting the spread of punishment, rather than the criminal conduct itself.

The primary purpose of criminal law in these theories remains a version of the 'harm' principle. Most generally, for example, the American 'Model Penal Code', claims that: 'The general purposes of the provisions governing the definition of offenses are...to forbid and prevent conduct that unjustifiably and inexcusably inflicts or threatens substantial harm to individual or public interests [s. 1.01(1)]'.

A couple of contemporary examples from leading criminal law theorists illustrate such harm-based definitions, clearly offered in a context of concern to limit the ambit of criminal law. In an influential book criticizing the trend towards what he calls 'overcriminalization', Douglas Husak suggests four principled constraints on the scope of criminal law. These are: 'the *nontrivial harm or evil* constraint, the *wrongfulness* constraint, the *desert* constraint, and the *burden of proof* constraint' (Husak 2008: 55).

More recently, in a book critically analysing the proliferation of preventive offences penalizing preparatory acts or even thoughts, two leading Oxford criminal law scholars suggest similar criteria that must be met if criminal laws are to be warranted. Criminalization is justified when 'certain wrongs are so serious that they should be condemned as criminal and should be able to result in punishment... to warrant criminalization, the conduct should amount to a moral wrong, should be (potentially) harmful and should be brought about culpably, and... there must not be strong countervailing considerations such as the creation of unwelcome social consequences, the curtailment of important rights, and so forth' (Ashworth and Zedner 2014: 17). They sum this up as 'The "harm plus culpability" model', described as 'the paradigmatic form of the most serious criminal offences' (ibid.: 96; Simester and von Hirsch 2011 propose a similar analysis).

The reference above to the 'most serious' offences is significant because a key aspect of recent criminal law is the proliferation of what have been described as crimes 'outside the core' (Husak 2004). As William Stuntz expressed it, criminal law has become 'not one field but two. The first consists of a few core crimes... The second consists of everything else. Criminal law courses, criminal law literature, and popular conversations about crime focus heavily on the first. The second dominates criminal codes' (Stuntz 2001: 505). Most normative criminal law scholars have regarded this as problematic because the 'non-core' offences (a modern euphemism for the idea of *mala prohibita* – wrongs criminalized by the state that were not *mala in se*, wrong in themselves) threaten punishment for conduct (or in many cases non-conduct) that does not satisfy the criteria of serious harm, wrongfulness and individual moral culpability.

The 'harm' principle offered as the justification of criminalization is clearly also intended to constitute a hurdle limiting its ambit. In the final section of this chapter, I will consider how the notion of harm has been used by some recent criminologists in the opposite way, as pointing to activities that are not penalized but inflict at least as much damage as conduct that is criminalized.

What both usages point to is the problematic character of the notion of 'harm' (Feinberg 1984–90; Harcourt 1999). The idea of 'harm' has as much elasticity as the concept of crime which it purports to elucidate and is at least as much an open invitation to conflicting interpretations. As indicated earlier, there are many attempts to pin down the moral principles underlying the notions of harm, wrongness and culpability (such as Kantian or Hegelian ethical philosophy, or

Rawlsian and other contract theories). More often, they are just assumed as given by the common-sense of specific cultures, if not as timeless essences.

Value commitments are ultimately existential choices. They can be argued for more or less convincingly but not finally established in knock-down ways that would be capable of converting even all well-intentioned people. The philosopher Richard Bernstein characterized the history of modern theories of knowledge as a variety of attempts to allay what he called 'Cartesian anxiety' (Bernstein 1983). The twin harbingers of the modern – the Renaissance and the Reformation – had undermined the foundations of knowledge provided for medieval Europe by Catholicism. Descartes offered the prototypical example of a modern philosopher seeking a rational first principle, an Archimedean leverage point that would relieve anxieties about the foundations of knowledge, dispelling doubts that our cognitions were the misdirections of an evil demon. Descartes offered his argument *cogito ergo sum* as a purportedly indubitable axiom to fend off the spectres of cognitive chaos and relativism.

Anxieties about the foundations of knowledge are multiplied in the realms of ethics and politics. I would propose the notion of 'Hitlerian anxiety' as the normative counterpart to the Cartesian variety. Given time in a locked room with Hitler, how could one persuade him of the wrongness of genocide and mass murder? Is there some way out of moral relativism, or is it inevitably 'liberalism for the liberals, cannibalism for the cannibals'? (Lukes 2003, 2008). Perhaps the most that can be found is some 'overlapping consensus' between 'reasonable' people, with the need somehow to 'contain' the unreasonable (Rawls 1993: xvii).

There is arguably such an 'overlapping consensus' that can be traced between the attempts to ground the liberal egalitarianism espoused (in different ways) by the various normative groundings of criminal law. The egalitarian mutuality encapsulated for example in Kant's categorical imperative, or in Rawls's principles of justice, has deep and ancient roots, and recurs in most influential conceptions of justice in moral philosophy and theology. It is the conception that I have dubbed 'reciprocal individualism' (Reiner 2007: 18–20). It must be contrasted with the 'egoistic individualism', encapsulated notoriously in Mrs Thatcher's assertion that '[T]here is no such thing as society...and people must look to themselves first. It's our duty to look after ourselves and then, also to look after our neighbour' (Keay 1987).

Thatcher explicitly inverted the biblical golden rule, 'Love your neighbour as yourself' (Leviticus XIX: 18), which is the 'golden thread' running through the various expressions of liberal egalitarianism, and ethical or democratic socialism. In her version, neighbours have to wait in line whilst we look after ourselves first. But the golden rule places its bedrock value on the welfare of *all* individuals, whose interests have to be balanced on the basis of fundamentally equal concern, including oneself ('as yourself') but not only oneself. Indeed, the Talmudic sage Ben Azzai specifically related the golden rule in Leviticus to the earlier statement in Genesis I: 27, that all people were created in the image of God, i.e. that individuals share in a common basis for equal concern and respect (using the terminology of Dworkin 2002, 2013).

This derivation not only makes clear that the golden rule is universalistic, applying to all people and not just literal 'neighbours'. It also introduces an element of objectivity into the concrete obligations of care that flow from the injunction to 'love'. They should be based on a notion of the common 'image' of humanity, not my subjective preferences. If I am a masochist, I don't fulfil the injunction by flogging my neighbour. The negative version of the biblical golden rule, 'don't do to others what you don't want done to yourself', perhaps provides a clearer basis for deciding what should count as 'harm' in liberal theories of criminal law. Culpable wrongdoing is inflicting harm on others, defining harm as consequences that most people would not wish for themselves and culpability as failing to see others as equally worthy of concern. Failure of equal or reciprocal concern may result from an intention to do harm, negligence about it or indifference, turning a blind eye.

Critical criminology and the normative critique of criminal law

Critical criminologists have frequently argued that criminal law fails to define or enforce as criminal very serious wilful harms that are committed by the powerful, in particular by states and corporations (cf. chapter 4). The argument has been crystallized by the recent claim that criminology should be replaced by 'zemiology', the study of serious culpable harms (Hillyard et al. 2004; Davies et al. 2014). The question of whether harms are proscribed by criminal law would be a crucial issue for zemiological analysis.

The definition of 'harms' is, of course, morally and socially contentious, as we saw in the earlier discussion of the harm principle in criminal law theory. The zemiologists opt for it because they see it as having greater ontological reality than crime, but achieving objective measures of harm is a project (Hillyard et al. 2004: 268–9) and it is beset by different evaluations of suffering. Nonetheless, zemiology opens up discussion of what should or should not be sanctioned, and in what ways, rather than foreclosing these issues by a mask of objectivity as in positivist theories of law that shield the value judgements and biases embodied in law and its enforcement.

Critical criminologists have demonstrated many times that the monetary and human value of the harms inflicted by the crimes of the powerful are immensely greater than those caused by the routine thefts and offences against the person that are the predominant business of the criminal justice system. 'The cost of bailing out a single savings and loan institution surpassed the total losses of all the bank robberies in American history' (Rosoff, Pontell and Tillman 2010: viii). No wonder corporate crime has been described as 'the looting of America' (ibid.) and the 'theft of a nation' (Barak 2012).

Nor is corporate crime just about property. Many well-known cases have involved colossal loss of life: the 1988 Alpha oil-rig explosion, the Chernobyl nuclear plant disaster, Bhopal, the drug thalidomide, the Dalkon shield contraceptive, the dangerously inflammable Ford Pinto, the P&O ferry sinking and the Hatfield rail crash are just some of the most notorious. These potential exhibits in a 'black museum' of corporate crime are but the most prominent instances of a much larger number of routine threats to life and limb (Tombs and Whyte 2015: ch. 2).

A distinction between the violence that is straightforwardly understood as crime and work-related fatalities is that the former inflicts immediate, face-to-face injury. Occupational deaths usually involve complex chains of causality that make the attribution of moral responsibility more ambiguous. The serious injuries leading to death may not be seen immediately or at all by those who commit the culpable actions (say, deliberate violation of safety requirements and tests as in the recent revelations about Volkswagen in the United States [BBC News 2015]) that predictably produce fatal results (Slapper 1999; Wells 2001). Similarly, the difference between a terrorist suicide bomber on the ground and a war hero in the air may be a plane and an altitude of 3,000 feet. Seen or unseen, their victims are blown to bits all the same.

The most vivid deconstruction of the morally tenuous, if not arbitrary, differences between the harms constructed as crime and those that are hidden by the complex chains of causality in modern social relationships, facilitating denial of responsibility, is J. B. Priestley's play *An Inspector Calls*, which has been unjustly neglected by criminology. Priestley used the narrative structure and conventions of the Agatha Christie cosy whodunnit to show the moral similarity of the intentional harms perpetrated by the powerful and privileged and what is more commonly regarded as crime. An inspector calls on a respectable bourgeois family who are celebrating their daughter's engagement to a man from a more established wealthy background. The inspector is investigating the lonely, anguished death (from swallowing an acid disinfectant) of a poor young woman. He painstakingly establishes that each person present contributed something to the tragedy by a legal but thoughtlessly cruel action that they saw as justified and normal (sacking her for orchestrating industrial action; arranging for her dismissal from another job in a shop because of apparent rudeness; seducing, impregnating and abandoning her; refusing her charitable support when she was pregnant and destitute). Only the daughter and son of the family come to recognize their responsibility for the girl's homicide. The paterfamilias smugly denies it: 'I can't accept any responsibility. If we were all responsible for what happened to everybody we'd had anything to do with, it would be very awkward, wouldn't it?'. The inspector's parting shot draws the appropriate riposte:

> One Eva Smith has gone – but there are millions and millions . . . still left with us, with their lives, their hopes and fears, their suffering, and chance of happiness, all intertwined with our lives, with what we think and say and do. We don't live alone. We are members of one body. We are responsible for each other. And I tell you that the time will soon come when, if men will not learn that lesson, then they will be taught it in fire and blood and anguish. Good night. (Priestley 2001 [1947]: 207)

The criminal law, reflecting the outcomes of power struggles and moral panics and political exigencies over many centuries, scarcely maps in even a rough and ready way the boundaries of human infliction of serious pain and harm on others or the moral responsibility for this. The normality of deviance and law breaking, and how criminal law and criminal justice invert the hierarchy of harm and responsibility, will be elaborated in the next three chapters.

3

Everybody's Doing It: Social Conceptions of Crime and Deviance

Many criminal acts are statistically and culturally 'normal'. Tax evasion, cannabis use, driving while using a mobile phone (and many other examples) are commonly committed criminal offences. Other behaviour may be legal but stigmatized – e.g. the 'romps' of football stars, politicians and other celebrities that flourish on the *Sun on Sunday*'s front page. This chapter will consider the relationship between social conceptions of deviance and criminal law, examining how they vary between and within cultures and over time.

Durkheim's famous attempt to provide a sociological definition of crime suggested that 'Crime shocks sentiments which, for a given social system are found in all healthy consciences…an act is criminal when it offends strong and defined states of the collective conscience' (Durkheim 1973 [1893]: 73, 80). This is as positivist and tautologous a definition as the standard criminal law textbook's, albeit emphasizing social/cultural rather than legal construction. As Durkheim himself recognized, conceptions of the criminal vary considerably between and within societies, and over time. Crime in this view is whatever happens to be reacted to as seriously wrong in a particular culture, with no objective standpoint for analysis or critique. 'Liberalism for the liberals, cannibalism for the cannibals', as Martin Hollis ironically depicted this relativist tendency (Lukes 2003).

What is actually treated as criminal in particular cultures differs not only from the law but also from professed moral beliefs. Respectable middle-class people who see themselves as staunchly law abiding, and who stoutly condemn crime, commonly engage in practices that constitute theft, such as padding insurance claims or paying cash for services, thus conniving in tax evasion (Karstedt and Farrall 2004). They will defend themselves from a self-perception as 'really' criminal by similar 'techniques of neutralization' of moral guilt to those used by the street criminals from whom they distance themselves. For example, they might 'condemn the condemners', arguing that the insurance companies are ripping them off as clients through extortionate premiums or unfair conditions such as extravagant household security requirements.

What is typically sanctioned as deviant in social practice will vary from the formal definitions of law or of professed morality, and different groups will treat different conduct as truly criminal. An occupational hazard for a criminologist at parties is to deal with irate demands to explain why the police and courts harass the speeding or drinking motorist instead of 'real' criminals. Is drink-driving socially deviant? It is in most circles nowadays but was not in England until some three decades ago, and even then was regarded as deviant, in Scandinavia for example. We have yet to see whether driving under the influence of mobile phones will go the same way.

'It is a salient characteristic of "crime" in public perception that it is committed by "others"' (Karstedt and Farrall 2004: 65). Dominant characterizations of 'crime' see it as conduct associated with 'inferior' classes, as the etymology of labels for offenders indicates. The online *Oxford Dictionary* states that 'villain' derives from the medieval French for feudal tenant or low-born rustic, and 'rogue' from the Latin for beggar. By contrast, 'propriety' and 'property' share a common root, indicating a connection between privileged economic class and conceptions of 'good' behaviour. Inequalities in the administration of criminal justice, a perennial source of liberal concern, are rooted deep in cultural perceptions and hierarchical social structures that represent crime as the conduct of disadvantaged and dangerous outsiders. As the 'well-bred young man-about-town' Gerald Croft remarks in *An Inspector Calls*, 'After all, y'know, we're respectable citizens and not criminals'. To which the inspector replies, 'Sometimes there isn't as much difference as you think. Often, if it was left to me, I wouldn't know where to draw the line' (Priestley 2001 [1947]).

This chapter will explore the relationship between deviance, legally defined crime and different moral positions about what is wrong and harmful. It will begin by discussing the problematic notion of deviance itself and move on to document the evidence that most people are self-confessed deviants – and that the rest are almost certainly liars. This, however, raises the question of why only some acts of deviance and some deviant actors come to be openly regarded as such, either by law and criminal justice or by informal social sanctions. This patterning is intimately related to the unequal and unjust structures of social advantage, status and power. The massive, yet usually unacknowledged and largely ignored, harmful behaviour and culpable wrongdoing of the powerful will be documented in the next chapter. In this chapter, we will see that much the same applies to deviance. The rich do wrong, and the poor get censured and stigmatized (paraphrasing Reiman and Leighton 2012).

What deviance? Whose normal?

'Departing from usual or accepted standards' is how the online *Oxford Dictionary* defines 'deviant'. This immediately points to a key ambiguity in the notion of deviance. In the same dictionary, the 'normal' from which the 'deviant' is divergent is itself defined ambiguously: 'Conforming to a standard; usual, typical, or expected.' Are the 'norms' against which 'deviance' is contrasted *statistical*, the central tendency of a social distribution? Or are they *evaluative*, 'normative' in the sense used by the moral philosophies discussed in the last chapter?

The subject matter of the sociology of deviance is predominantly the latter, the breaking of rules purporting to regulate boundaries between what is judged to be good and bad behaviour. 'At its simplest, the sociology of deviance is the systematic study of social norm violation that is subject to social sanction' (Henry 2009: 1). As all texts on deviance go on to show, these simple definitions raise a maelstrom of problems.

A recent book of essays on a range of contemporary 'shades of deviance' illustrates this complexity (Atkinson 2014). It offers no fewer than 56 chapters on a fascinating variety of practices that may in some way be seen as deviant. The topics include: jaywalking, prostitution, nudity, begging, vandalism, protest, public sex, tattoos, drugs, graffiti, fire starting, speeding, joyriding, video gaming, hacking and cybercrime, sexting and cyberbullying, sadomasochism, euthanasia, binge drinking, squatting, smoking, welfare dependency, tax avoidance/evasion, stalking, pornography, disability, homophobia, migration, homelessness, mental health issues, ecocide, gangs, terrorism, human trafficking, war crimes, corporate crime and much else.

Clearly, some of these behaviours are against criminal law in 'the books'. However, the enforcement of the 'law in action' against these varies, as a result of ambiguities of definition, formal policy and, above all, who commits the offences, and how visibly and egregiously. Most of the list encompasses practices that are not criminalized by law but which may often involve or stray into accompanying conduct that is. Many of the chapters in Atkinson's book cover behaviour that is statistically common, sometimes universal. Others are the subject of raging moral culture wars about their wrongfulness and about whether they should be criminalized.

The concept of crime encapsulates many meanings, as shown in previous and subsequent chapters of this volume. This diversity is 'anchored' in a relatively clear and explicit set of laws 'in the books', breach of which may be attended by formally delivered painful consequences. The idea of 'deviance' is both broader and much more amorphous. Nonetheless, the sociology of deviance has a long-standing and distinguished pedigree, stretching from Durkheim through to many contemporary researchers and theorists. The most scholarly and sophisticated text on the subject distinguishes a considerable number of sometimes conflicting, sometimes overlapping approaches, referred to by the authors themselves as a 'Tower of Babel' (Downes and Rock 2012: 1). Their chapters cover a variety of theoretical traditions in the analysis of deviance: the 'Chicago School', functionalism, anomie, culture/subculture, symbolic interactionism, phenomenology, control theories, radical criminology, feminist criminology and more pragmatic concerns with social policy applications.

What is seldom discussed explicitly is the relationship between the ideas of deviance and crime. The list of theoretical perspectives on deviance in the previous paragraph includes a couple of varieties of 'criminology', and most contemporary texts speak of the sociology of crime *and* deviance almost as if they were identical twins. In the early days of sociology, Durkheim used the terms in an essentially interchangeable way. When he defined crime as that which shocks all healthy consciences (cited at the start of this chapter), or argued that crime is inevitable and universal (discussed in the previous chapter), he clearly does not mean the legal notion. Durkheim is fully aware that there is controversy about the content of criminal law, and that modern legal systems are not ubiquitous. He is using 'crime' as a virtual synonym for 'deviance'. In most analyses, crime is an aspect of deviance, distinguished by authoritative formulation and buttressed by formal penal sanctions. Durkheim's own definition quoted at the start of this chapter itself implies this when it says 'an act is criminal when it offends strong and defined states of the collective conscience', although this takes for granted a consensus view, in which criminalization is the crystallization of collectively shared specifications of the worst offences against common-sense views of right and wrong.

Nowadays, the concepts of crime and deviance are usually understood as part of a spectrum of rule-breaking conduct, in which out of the vast array of deviant behaviours some get labelled and occasionally processed by the formal mechanisms of law making and enforcement. However, for much of the history of modern sociology the term deviance was used as a more or less explicit alternative to crime. This was for theoretical reasons that are analogous to the arguments of some positivist criminologists for rejecting the term 'crime' as a valid base for the discipline (although the sociology of deviance has been dominated by constructivist and interpretative perspectives that are the antithesis of positivism). Sociologists of deviance and positivist criminologists shared a common problem with the concept of crime as the foundation of their analyses, despite their huge differences in ontology and epistemology: their conceptions of the social world, and how it can be known and understood.

The shared problem is that the predominant concept of crime is legally defined. As discussed earlier, this encompasses a bewildering, unsystematic and largely unprincipled miscellany of formally prohibited acts, varying considerably between time and place. How could such a devil's brew of poisonous elements be characterized and explained in an intellectually disciplined, 'scientific' way, whether by positivistic and quantitative, or interpretative and qualitative, methods? So both sociologies of deviance and positivistic criminologies have sought to construct their own alternatives to the legal notion of crime in order to provide a coherent object of analysis. Lombroso, for example, conceived of the 'born criminal' as the subject matter of criminology, not the unfortunate array of misfits actually found in the convict population.

Deviance was adopted as the fundamental concept by many sociologists in order to provide a hopefully universal subject matter that was defined by the discipline – the breaking of rules. Thorsten Sellin, for example, argued that violations of 'conduct norms', rather than legally defined crime, should be the basis of sociological and criminological analysis. His view (and Sutherland's celebrated extension of criminology to the study of white-collar crime) were the subject of critique by Paul Tappan and others, arguing that only the legal category of crime offered a sufficiently clear-cut definition. 'But law has defined with greater clarity and precision the conduct which is criminal than our antilegalistic criminologists promise to do' (Tappan 2001 [1947]: 31). Classic texts from the ongoing debate between the advocates of legalistic and other definitions of the subject matter of criminology or sociology of crime can be found in Henry and Lanier (2001), especially part I, with a penetrating introductory commentary by the editors.

Is deviance dead?

Conceptualizations of deviance in the last two decades have been haunted by the so-called 'death of deviance' debate, sparked by Colin Sumner's stimulating and provocative 'obituary' for the sociology of deviance (Sumner 1994). At one level, it is clear to everyone, Sumner included, that the study of deviance is in rude health. Courses on it, and textbooks catering for these, abound in the United States, the United Kingdom and elsewhere, usually as parts of more general degree programmes in social science, criminology or criminal justice. However, this does not necessarily mean anything but a kind of zombie existence. As Joel Best has put it, 'Deviance may be alive, but is it intellectually lively?' (Best 2004). The appearance of several monographs and volumes of essays on deviance by vibrant young researchers and theorists suggests that, in the words of one collection, the 'death' of deviance has been followed by its 'resurrection' (Dellwing, Kotarbe and Pino 2014). Indeed, there has been something of a rapprochement or synthesis of positions, as suggested by Sumner himself in a recent essay subtitled 'Beyond the Death of Deviance Debate' (Sumner 2012). Much of the flourishing enterprise of 'cultural criminology' recognizably bears the spirit of aspects of deviance theory, as does the 'ultra-realism' developed over recent years by Steve Hall, Simon Winlow and Rowland Atkinson, amongst others (Hall, Winlow and Ancrum 2008; Hall 2012; Hall and Winlow 2012; Winlow and Atkinson 2012; Atkinson 2014; Hall and Winlow 2015).

Whilst the concept of deviance has arguably survived or been resurrected in some form, the thesis advanced by Sumner in his 2004 'obituary' remains important (useful assessments can be found in Roberts 1996, Moxon 2011, 2013, Banks and Moxon 2013 and Horsley 2014). The book is a complex, detailed and nuanced critical and contextual history of the sociology of deviance, from its origins in Durkheim, through its efflorescence in the Chicago Sociology Department of the 1920s and 1930s, to its most influential theoretical formulation by Merton's version of Durkheimian anomie theory and the subcultural perspective that developed from it. Sumner traces the self-questioning of the tradition by David Matza, and the labelling critique of the 1960s pioneered by Becker and Lemert, developing into the broader radical and critical criminologies of the 1970s and 1980s.

For all the complexity and variations in these approaches, the essence of Sumner's analysis is that the perspective taken was the pursuit of the causes of deviance, and the desire to reduce, if not eradicate, them. Implicit in the sociology of deviance, even in its critical versions, was the assumption of a dominant moral order from which some deviated. In Sumner's view, deviance theory was intellectually and normatively allied with the 'New Deal' and European social democracy, which shared the project of uprooting social evil. This remained true to some extent even of the labelling perspective, despite its explicit call for sociologists to ask 'whose side are we on?', and to see the roots of deviance not as something lacking in deviants or their environment, but rather in the oppressive moral entrepreneurs and agencies that labelled them (Becker 1967; recently reassessed in a valuable collection of essays, Cowburn et al. 2013).

What was foreshadowed in the labelling critique of the 1960s was the increasingly problematic nature of the assumption of a consensually accepted normative order. The culture wars that began in that decade (with harbingers in the later 1950s), and which have become ever more intense with the explicit relativism of 'post-modernism', render increasingly untenable the assumption of clear-cut lines of moral normality and deviance. Sumner's 'obituary' was part of a project he had been developing since the mid-1970s, advocating the replacement of the sociology of deviance and the avowedly Marxist 'new' criminologies of the time (the Marxist credentials of which had been questioned by some theorists, notably Paul Q. Hirst) with a sociology of 'censures'. This was explicitly an application of broader Marxist theories of ideology to the subject matter of crime and deviance. 'Censures' are 'negative ideological categories with specific historical application' (Sumner 1990: 26).

Censures, like ideologies in general, are pervasive, and have a double face. Whilst in an unequal society conflicts between groups about what practices to censure are tilted towards the dominant powers, to become hegemonic they must make sense of aspects of the life situation of other less powerful groups, too, rather than being imposed from above.

> According to Sumner, all groups of people develop censures, but in class societies, the economically dominant class will have the greatest capacity to assert its censures, for instance

> through the legal system and through its control of media and communication... The sectional censures of the dominant class can therefore become social censures, widely accepted and internalized even by subordinate classes. (Moxon 2011: 108)

What gets to be generally regarded as deviance, and a fortiori what comes to be officially censured as crime, is the subject of an unequal political struggle. Concepts of crime and deviance are produced by:

> a series of normative divides or ideological cuts, cuts made in social practice – and the dominant cuts in our society are those made by the rich, powerful and authoritative.... It is their distinctions, forged in the heat of driving interests and conflictful practical enforcement, in the practice of conquest, domination and possession, which divide the world up into the positive and the negative, right and wrong, normal and deviant. (Sumner 1994: 299)

In the decades since Sumner pronounced the 'death of deviance', culture wars about what is to be censured as deviant – or whether such 'judgementalism' is itself to be censured – have raged ever more fiercely, a paradoxical consequence of the embedding of the ideological hegemony of economic neo-liberalism. As Marx and Engels prophesied a century and a half ago, the free market erodes traditional ways of life and beliefs:

> The bourgeoisie cannot exist without constantly revolutionizing the instruments of production, and thereby the relations of production, and with them the whole relations of society... All fixed, fast-frozen relations, with their train of ancient and venerable prejudices and opinions, are swept away, all new-formed ones become antiquated before they can ossify. All that is solid melts into air, all that is holy is profaned. (Marx and Engels 1998 [1848]: ch. 1)

In Sumner's more recent revisiting of the debate, he argues passionately for the need to reinvigorate a moral code to restrain the destructive actions of the economic super-elite whose wrongdoing precipitated the crash of 2007–8. 'We need protection from business: the censure and punishment of the bankers could be the starting point of a new moral order or at least the recognition of the idea and reality of the moral economy' (Sumner 2012: 178). Deviance as the violation of a supposed consensual moral order may have had a near-death experience, according to Sumner, but it needs resuscitation on the basis of an ethics that reflects the interests of the majority rather than those of the dominant class.

We are all guilty: the normality of deviance

As discussed above, the notion of deviance assumes a substantial measure of normative agreement about the rules that deviants fail to follow. It further implies that the normatively deviant are also statistically deviant – that deviance is abnormal in the double sense of unusual as well as censured. This should be true a fortiori of crime, the most formally crystallized and enforced parts of deviance. The plausibility of the idea of a shared consensual normative order has been stretched almost to vanishing point as, on the one hand, official tolerance of cultural diversity has increased, but on the other there have flourished culture wars between liberals and an increasingly vocal counter-revolution of moral conservatives, represented for example by the Tea Party in the United States and UKIP in the United Kingdom. What meaning, if any, can be given to the concept of deviance in what Jock Young called 'the vertigo of late modernity' with its shifting structures of tolerance (Young 2007)? Young himself plausibly argued that the modern world was intolerant of cultural or normative *diversity*, which it attempted to convert and assimilate into the mainstream more or less forcefully, but was relatively tolerant of *difficulty*, of people experiencing trouble in conforming because of individual or social problems, who were seen as a challenge to rehabilitate and reform. The late modern world, however, celebrates *diversity* and *difference*. Its intolerance is reserved for *difficult* people and *dangerous* classes, on whom it pours scorn and against whom it builds elaborate exclusionary defences (Young 1999).

There is, however, plentiful empirical evidence that, even in the supposed heyday of moral consensus, many, probably most, people deviated in practice from the supposedly dominant moral norms, as well as from criminal law, and this continues today even amongst the apparently most respectable and conformist sections of society. The clearest evidence of the ubiquity, perhaps universality, of deviant behaviour comes from what are known as 'self-report' studies. These ask samples of the population questions about their offending behaviour, in conditions of anonymity, in order to map their 'hidden' deviance.

An influential early study, based on a 49-item mail questionnaire to 1,698 adults in New York, found that 99 per cent of adults admitted at least one offence, and even ministers of the church admitted an average of eight offences each. It concluded that: 'Unlawful behaviour, far from being an abnormal social or psychological manifestation, is in truth a very common phenomenon…the solid truth remains that there is a large chance element in our administration of justice and it's the unlucky ones who are caught' (Wallerstein and Wyle 1947: 111–12). The universality of admitted deviance in the pioneering Wallerstein and Wyle study (the 1 per cent who did not admit any offences at all were probably lying!) owes much to the inclusion of very minor technical offences, as they themselves noted.

The method of self-report studies has subsequently become increasingly sophisticated and, whilst they reveal that offending is common, they also show that more serious and frequent crime is not. However, the studies have predominantly focused on young people, and on the kinds of crimes (predatory street crimes) that are the main ones processed and measured by formal criminal justice (see chapter 5). As will be shown later, many serious crimes and forms of harmful wrongdoing are excluded from these measures and are likely to be widespread, in particular amongst sections of the population hardly touched by criminal justice.

Self-report studies have focused on two issues:

(a) analysing the relationship between the class, ethnicity, gender and other demographic features of those who are formally labelled as offenders and the pattern found in self-reports in order to assess discrimination in criminal justice (Maguire 2007: 286–9; Phillips and Bowling 2012: 379–81);

(b) tracing the sources of offending behaviour, especially through longitudinal studies probing the factors associated with higher rates of self-reported offences (Farrington 2007; Smith 2007; McAra and McVie 2012).

They continue to demonstrate the high prevalence of crime and deviance. The Cambridge cohort studied by Farrington and others showed, for example, that by the age of 32 around half the sample admitted to shoplifting, and about one-fifth to burglary (Farrington 2001: 37). Only one in 40 of the self-reported shoplifting offences and 41.7 per cent of the burglaries resulted in a conviction. Between 2003 and 2006, the Home Office conducted several sweeps of what they called the 'Offending, Crime and Justice Survey'. This found that 49 per cent of their sample of young people admitted committing at least one of the 'core offences' asked about: assault, criminal damage, selling drugs, thefts ranging from the minor to burglary and robbery (Hales et al. 2009: 7). The study also probed drug use and anti-social behaviour, and 72 per cent of the sample admitted to at least one of these (ibid.: 8).

Conduct deviating from supposed norms (even of criminal law) is thus statistically normal on the evidence of self-report studies. So why and how do norms that most people at least occasionally violate become authoritatively promulgated? And why are other serious harms never defined as offences even in principle? Why is some harmful wrongdoing largely ignored by the criminal justice system and indeed by public opinion and political debate?

Explaining criminalization and the construction of deviance

In itself, the widespread commission of deviant acts and crimes does not necessarily signify rejection of the law in principle, or of the moral norms defining conduct as deviant. Rule-breakers, whether juvenile delinquents, sex offenders or perpetrators of the most egregious war crimes, including genocide, typically apply to themselves 'vocabularies of motive' that act as 'techniques of neutralization' (Sykes and Matza 1957; Taylor 1972; Cohen 2000). These function to exempt their conduct from the opprobrium that they often agree should attach to violations of the rules in general. Most thieves, for instance, are not anarchists who proclaim with Proudhon that 'property is theft', even as they themselves steal in circumstances that they feel exculpate their conduct.

David Matza's seminal work showed the tenuous and complex relationship between rule breaking and rule rejection. A classic paper, drawing on interviews with incarcerated delinquents, showed that most accepted the moral validity in general principle of the norms that their behaviour deviated from. However, they exonerated themselves from accepting full culpability by a variety of 'techniques of neutralization' (Sykes and Matza 1957). As they were convicted, by definition the courts had not accepted their arguments. Nonetheless, they invoked familiar tropes used by us all to draw the sting of shame or guilt from our peccadilloes. They include: denial of responsibility (I was drunk, overcome with desire or rage, or in other ways not fully capable of self-control); denial of injury (the big stores don't feel the loss from shoplifting; she enjoyed what I did to her, it was just a playful fight – no harm was done); denial of the victim (they had it coming; they shouldn't have dissed me); condemning the condemners (the real crooks in our society are the cops, the banks, the politicians, who are all hypocrites); appeal to higher loyalties (my baby was hungry; I couldn't let my mates down).

In a later paper, Sykes and Matza developed the argument by pointing out that the motives underpinning much deviance were expressions of 'subterranean' values in conventional culture (pleasure or thrill seeking, the excitement of what contemporary cultural criminologists call 'edgework', cf. Matza and Sykes 1961; Lyng 1990; Ugwudike 2015: 211). The difference between those who come to be labelled as deviant and those who don't is the appropriateness of time and place for hedonistic expression. What might be appropriate in a club or a bar is carried out on the streets because of differences in opportunities.

Given the statistical normality of law breaking, and the variety, complexity and ambiguity of the norms defining deviance, how can the construction of law and censure be explained? This was a major theme of early critical criminology, which devoted considerable attention to studies of the emergence of legal rules and dominant norms. The classic text pioneering the labelling perspective, for example, devoted much attention to analysing the role of 'moral entrepreneurs' in the construction of rules defining deviance, focusing on a case study of the criminalization of marijuana (Becker 1963: chs 7–8). A standard feature of the many readers on critical criminology in the 1960s and 1970s was a section of papers offering models and case studies analysing the processes by which deviant categories and criminal laws emerged (e.g. Chambliss and Mankoff 1976).

A key theme of these critical criminological analyses of the emergence of criminal law was the advocacy of a 'conflict perspective', as opposed to the 'consensus' perspective attributed to traditional studies. As seen earlier, Durkheim exemplifies the consensus model, at any rate in his definition of criminal law. In his earliest book, he argued that 'social solidarity is a completely moral phenomenon which, taken by itself, does not lend itself to exact observation or indeed to measurement...We must substitute for this internal fact which escapes us an external index which symbolizes it...This visible symbol is law' (Durkheim 1973 [1893]: 64). This is a clear statement of a view of law as reflecting social and moral solidarity and the 'conscience collective'.

A common negative target of the conflict perspective in critical analysis of the emergence of criminal laws was Radzinowicz's magisterial history (Radzinowicz 1948–1986). For all its rich complexity of detail and meticulous scholarship, it was often characterized as embodying a straightforward consensus model of criminal law as the progressive unfolding of English national character. An example is Radzinowicz's account of criminal law reform in early nineteenth-century England:

> The development of social consciousness in the penal sphere was slow but steady and once aroused it did not allow itself

> to be stifled. In England, in Buckle's words 'so soon as public opinion is formed, it can no longer be withstood'. Once the many doubts concerning the criminal law had impressed themselves upon the public mind, its reform became a matter of national concern. (Radzinowicz 1948: 39)

Although, as discussed in the previous chapter, criminalization has become a key theme of contemporary criminal law theory, it is primarily focused on the normative question of delimiting what should or should not be criminalized. Given the huge variety and proliferation of criminal laws in the last couple of decades, contemporary theorists usually call into question the possibility of explaining this miscellany by any simple model. The Law Commission has estimated that more than 3,200 new offences were added to the statute books in the ten years after 1997 (Law Commission 2010: 5). 'Untrammelled expansion of the criminal law is a cause for concern not least because it has the potential to limit individual autonomy and expand the power of the state to exercise its most coercive powers over more and more aspects of daily life' (Lacey and Zedner 2012: 174). The sources of this process are complex, and only partly accounted for by serious new security concerns (and much of the new legislation is scarcely if ever invoked in practice). Partly, it is attributable to a proliferation of regulatory agencies, partly to expansion of the criminal justice net to encompass preparatory acts, and partly to the quasi-criminalization of lower-level anti-social behaviour (ibid.: 173–6). As discussed in the last chapter, this has produced a plethora of normative critique from liberal criminal law theorists.

What is clear is that no simple model is capable of explaining criminal law emergence in general. Criminal law is in large part a contingent outcome of highly complex interactions between a miscellany of actors and agencies, and variable specific local and time-bound factors (Lacey 1995). A major factor is the huge variety of criminal laws, emerging at different times and places. These cover a spectrum from serious culpable harms to people's bodies or personal property that are criminalized in some form in all jurisdictions (Hart 1961: 189–95; Stuntz 2001; Cowling 2008: ch. 2), through many offences that are contested and controversial, to regulatory offences that may be seen as necessary to coordinate complex modern societies but in many jurisdictions are formally distinguished from core crimes (Lacey and Zedner 2012: 175).

Nonetheless, in formal terms I would suggest it is possible to construct a more complex model that indicates the requirements for analysing specific cases of legal emergence and development. It can be summed up in Marx's well-known aphorism: 'Men make their own history, but they do not make it just as they please; they do not make it under circumstances chosen by themselves, but under circumstances directly encountered, given and transmitted from the past' (Marx 1852: 1). This is a pithy expression of the dialectical relationship, the web of interdependence, between human action and interaction, and the social structures constructed out of that which in turn shape future actions. An application of this to the explanation of the emergence of criminal law can be seen in Marx's own analysis in *Capital* of the origins and development of the English Factory Acts (Marx 1976 [1867]: ch. 10).

In Marx's analysis, class struggle is built into capitalist relations of production. Competitive pressure drives the owners of the means of production to seek to maximize the extraction of surplus value. This means trying to lengthen the working day, and/or increase the intensity of effort within it, as much as possible. Workers for their part will seek to resist the continuous extension or intensification of their working day, so there is perennial potential for conflict.

The legislative history of the early nineteenth century presents a puzzle for that analysis, as Parliament passed a series of Factory Acts aimed at protecting the hours and conditions of work of the labour force. This was a parliament elected entirely by the upper and middle classes: workers only began to be enfranchised in gradual stages after 1867. Marx's polemical claim in the *Communist Manifesto* that the state was 'but a committee for managing the common affairs of the whole bourgeoisie' was literal description as well as critique (Marx and Engels 1998 [1848]: 37). So how could it come about that the parliament of the capitalists came to enact a series of measures restricting their exploitation of workers? (This puzzle was accentuated for later Marxists by the proliferation of 'welfare state' policies in all capitalist countries in the century after Marx's death, and his account of the Factory Acts provides a paradigmatic explanation.) Marx's analysis blends elements of structuralist and humanist perspectives to explain the seeming paradox of laws acting against the interest of the classes that dominated the legislature.

Marx's primary explanation of the emergence of the Factory Acts is structuralist. The function of law, argues Marx, is to reproduce capitalism as a mode of production. It thus benefits the capitalist class as a whole but, in order to achieve this, the law may have to act against the interests of individual capitalists. The remorseless pressures of competitive markets drive individual capitalists to exploit workers ever more intensively, but this undermines the viability of the system as a whole because the health of the labour force is threatened. Laws limiting the permitted hours of work relieve the pressures of competition facing capitalists and preserve the fitness and hence productivity of labour. Individual capitalists in a competitive environment could not achieve this without legislation because, if any would allow their workers to work less intensively, their profitability and hence their survival would be threatened. This was not due to the malice of capitalists, nor could it be changed by their benevolence. It required legal change to ensure that a reduction in working hours (which the more perspicacious capitalists pressed for) did not affect the viability of most firms.

The logic of this argument is analogous to many conservative analyses of law, which see its function as being to curb individual freedom for the long-run benefit of all. Marx's account sees law as essentially operating at two levels. Law satisfies the conditions of existence of any viable system of production, thus achieving the common interests of all. However, law particularly benefits the dominant class in the system that it reproduces.

Whilst Marx's primary explanation of the emergence of the Factory Acts is that they mitigated the destructive consequences of undiluted competitive pressure, this could only be achieved by human action. Marx's account examines in detail the political and class struggles that brought about the structurally required legislative changes. His points exemplify some key themes of later sociological analyses of law.

Marx emphasizes that the Factory Acts had an important *symbolic* as well as practical role, implying that the law was concerned with the welfare of the working class. The Acts passed in the early part of the nineteenth century (before the 1833 Factory Act) had no impact at all in practice, and were only of significance symbolically. In the face of growing labour unrest in the form of Luddism (machine breaking) and combinations (incipient trade unions), five Acts were passed to improve working conditions, an illustration of the use of reforms to head off wider discontent, claims Marx. But 'Parliament...was shrewd enough not to vote a penny for their compulsory implementation' – a nice example of what the legal realists were later to call the gap between the 'law in the books' and the 'law in action'.

The 1833 Act, however, established a Factory Inspectorate to enforce the limits on child and other labour that it ordained. From then on, the story largely becomes a running battle between the Inspectorate and the factory owners, who developed a series of techniques of avoidance whereby they could operate within the limits of the law whilst maintaining the intensity of labour in their enterprises. As the inspectors succeeded in closing loopholes by new legislation, so the factory owners in turn developed new avoidance techniques.

In 1844 and 1847 the Inspectors succeeded in getting Acts through Parliament that brought the maximum hours of labour down to ten and enhanced their powers to curb abuses. In part this was due to tireless campaigning by the Inspectorate (in many ways the heroes of Marx's narrative). Marx argues, however, that the inspectors were able to succeed only because the balance of forces in the class struggle had tilted towards labour in the 1840s. The capitalist class became increasingly split into two factions, the landowners and the manufacturers, provoked by conflict over the Corn Laws (protectionist measures to keep up the price of domestic corn by restricting imports, supported by agricultural interests, but opposed by industry as it raised the cost of living for urban workers). This was a major political fault line of the period, with ramifications for all other legislation as well. The landowners used the issue of factory conditions as a weapon to discredit the industrialists, and (in Marx's words) 'thundered with philanthropic indignation against the "nefarious practices" of their foes'. For their part, the manufacturers promised the Ten Hour Act as a way of gaining working-class support. In addition, the Ten Hour Act was used to reduce mounting pressure for wider and more radical reforms, notably Chartist agitation for extending the franchise to the working class.

After 1848, however, the balance of power shifted back towards capital, as the Chartist movement collapsed under repression. Fear generated by the 1848 revolutions on the European mainland united the English bourgeoisie. Manufacturers began to exploit loopholes in the Factory Acts in a new atmosphere less conducive to rigorous enforcement. This in turn increased working-class resistance. The result was a compromise. A new Factory Act in 1850 lengthened the permitted hours of work for adult labour from ten to ten and a half hours, but also made abuses easier to control.

After the 1850 Act, there was rapid extension of its principles throughout industry. Marx attributes this to a variety of factors. Partly, it was due to the manifestly beneficial results of a healthier and hence more productive workforce. In addition, there was an autonomous process of legal rationalization once the general principle of regulation of work conditions was established. The legal profession, with a financial interest in litigation, was a key interest developing the ambit of the legislation as it was interpreted in case law. Finally, the Acts themselves strengthened the power of the working class in a variety of ways, providing a springboard for further reforms.

The general conclusion drawn by Marx himself from this narrative was that the law was an arena of struggle in which the principle of equality before the law *could* be built on to achieve reforms that benefited the working class. Achieving legal rights that practically benefit the working class requires effective organization and tactics, concluded Marx. The success of these is not purely a function of human ingenuity and tactical skill. There are also structural conditions that can make working-class struggles for reform more or less effective. Perhaps the most fundamental is the one Marx stressed at the outset of his analysis: whether or not reforms on behalf of the working class are beneficial for the social order, for the mode of production as a whole (as distinct from the interests of individual members of the ruling class). There also may be specific historical circumstances more conducive to reform. The possibility of achieving reforms is more likely when they are seen as a way of damping down pressures for more radical or revolutionary change. Whilst recognizing that legal equality is not only compatible with considerable factual inequality but may act as an ideological smokescreen, nonetheless Marx clearly saw the achievement of legal rights for the mass of the population as a desirable advance both in itself and as a platform for other changes (similar to Thompson's celebrated but controversial argument a century later that 'The rule of law . . . seems to me to be an unqualified human good': Thompson 1975: 266).

Thus the emergence of criminal laws must be seen as a complex dialectic between structural requirements of social order (both in general and in particular social contexts) and the largely autonomous interpretations and interactions of the actors and agencies concerned about specific issues. The majority of contemporary criminal laws, which are primarily concerned with regulating the quotidian operations of complex societies, pass without much controversy or attention from the wider public. Some criminal laws are controversial, however, and become sites of struggle between different ideologies and interests. The playing field for such conflicts is not usually even but reflects the balance of social power between classes and other dimensions of disadvantage and inequality. Law predominantly embodies the interests of the powerful and privileged, but at the same time reproduces the conditions of existence of society as a whole. Because of its claims to impartiality and universality, on occasion legal institutions may act against the interests of specific members of the elite.

Perhaps even more important than how laws come to embody the interests of the powerful, however, is the way they tend *not* to criminalize the harms done by them. As indicated at the end of the last chapter, the harmful practices of the upper echelons of society systematically evade criminal sanctions, as critical criminologists have documented. In the next chapter, I will analyse the crimes of the respectable and powerful and the sources of their relative impunity. The chapter will consider car crime, middle-class offending, and corporate and state crime. It will conclude by asking why these do *not* typically figure in official statistics and are largely not subject to criminal justice processing. Chapter 5 examines the crimes that are processed officially by the criminal justice system, the crimes of the poor and powerless who become police property.

4

How Do They Get Away With It? The Non-Criminalization of the Powerful

The overwhelming majority of people who are criminalized – stopped by police, arrested, prosecuted, punished – are from the poorest and least powerful parts of society, as chapter 5 will document in detail. In the United States today, a vastly disproportionate number of poor African-American and Hispanic men account for the bulk of the mass incarceration epidemic of the last four decades. Almost 40 per cent of the 2.2 million US prisoners are African-American males. A US judge comments:

> In many respects, the people of the United States can be proud of the progress we have made over the past half-century in promoting racial equality. More haltingly, we have also made some progress in our treatment of the poor and disadvantaged. But the big, glaring exception to both these improvements is how we treat those guilty of crimes. Basically, we treat them like dirt. (Rakoff 2015)

Imprisonment has become the 'new Jim Crow', perpetuating the segregation of most black people as second-class citizens, despite the achievements of civil rights legislation (Alexander 2012).

In the United Kingdom, racial disparities in the criminal justice system are also substantial. 'In 2011/12, a person aged ten or older who self-identified as belonging to the black ethnic group was six times more likely than a white person to be stopped and searched' (Ministry of Justice 2013).

There is little reason to believe these disparities are the result of different propensities to commit crime (Western, Travis and Redburn 2015: 50 shows this for the United States). In the United Kingdom, too, a thorough review of the evidence concludes that whilst 'black people...are over-represented in arrest and prison statistics...self-report studies...contrast sharply with their indication that offending is no more common among the black population than the white population' (Phillips and Bowling 2012: 380).

The massively disproportionate criminalization of the poor and the powerless raises the question of the dog that *didn't* bark in the night. How do the rich and powerful get away with it? What are the politics of immunity, of *non*-criminalization? Why do the very substantial harms of the top echelons typically evade the criminal law's reach? Why does an inspector seldom call on respectable bourgeois families like the Crofts, portrayed in J. B. Priestley's play *An Inspector Calls*?

The predominant view pervading political and media discourse is that the majority of people, in particular the 'respectable' and aspirant middle classes, are law abiding, and the function of criminal justice is to protect them against victimization by 'others', the 'dangerous classes' of the indigent and excluded. 'Politicians refer to them as the "law-abiding majority", ignoring the fact that the majority do not abide by the law, or at least are highly selective about when to and when not to comply' (Karstedt and Farrall 2007: 1). We will examine this in relation to the deviance and crimes of the relatively powerful and the dominant elites.

Middle-class crime

Middle-class people are normally thought of (and perceive themselves) as the acme of respectability. In political terms, they have been a bastion of support for the police and other modern criminal justice institutions throughout their history (Reiner 2010a: 53). In the colourful words of Engels:

> the law is sacred to the bourgeois, for it is his own composition, enacted with his consent, and for his benefit and protection. He knows that... the sanctity of the law... is the strongest support of his social position. Because the English bourgeois finds himself reproduced in his law, as he does in his God, the policeman's truncheon which, in a certain measure, is his own club, has for him a wonderfully soothing power. But for the working man quite otherwise!... The working man knows too well... that the law is a rod which the bourgeois has prepared for him. (Engels 2009 [1844]: 234–5)

The predatory street crime that constitutes the bulk of official statistics, and is often seen as 'real' crime in popular culture and some criminology, is the subject of respectable fear and loathing. Nonetheless, the respectable themselves *do* regularly commit culpable harms of considerable seriousness, although these are usually hidden from sight and are seldom officially recorded or processed. This section will illustrate this with examples of crime and deviance engaged in by 'respectable' middle-class and upper-class people. Edwin Sutherland's original definition of white-collar crime referred to crime committed by 'a person of high status in the course of his occupation' (Sutherland 1949: 9). As deconstructed elegantly by David Nelken, this definition (despite its discipline-transforming impact on criminology) is highly ambiguous (Nelken 2012: 629). This section will look at some examples of the everyday criminal behaviour of white-collar people. The following sections will consider the crimes of the powerful and of the organizations they direct, under the rubrics of corporate and state crime.

Car crime

Driving offences are widespread throughout the social hierarchy. Many are 'subsumed in subordinate legislation of regulations and orders, but all driving offences are crimes under road traffic law that is separate from criminal law though an integral part of it' (Corbett 2010: 904). Despite the considerable harm caused by driving offences (which will be documented below) they are generally not seen as 'real' crime (Wells 2011). They are certainly not subject to the same scale of penalties or stigma as the majority of property or violent offences recorded in the officially labelled crime statistics.

The definitive texts on the topic document the origins of this in the era when motoring began, when the only owners of these potentially lethal weapons were wealthy. 'These affluent drivers were soon in conflict with the traffic police and government at their unwarranted "criminalization" from enforcement of the traffic laws.... On one occasion, police were exhorted by the Home Secretary not to treat motorists who might be "persons of the utmost respectability of character and position" as "possible criminals"' (Corbett 2010: 904). The rise of mass car ownership did not change this. The normalization of car offending perpetuated techniques of neutralization and denial that can be traced back to the car's origins as the prerogative of the propertied.

> Early vehicle owners largely comprised the elite, including MPs and judges, who may not have rushed to over-penalize 'minor' transgressions they personally might commit. This may give a clue why the public discourse around failing to comply with traffic laws has developed in the way it has. Using the word 'accident' to construct collisions as blameless and unpredictable events that could befall anyone would have suited the interests of the first car owners and illustrates how that early discourse of driving offences as 'minor' has endured to this day. (Corbett 2010: 905)

The harm done by many traffic offenders is far from 'minor'. Road deaths are amongst the largest threats to life worldwide, and unlawful driving behaviour is a major factor. Although not considered 'real' crime by most motorists, 'viewed from the perspective of victims and bereaved relatives, excess and inappropriate speed are extremely harmful and were implicated in 32% of fatal collisions and 20% of serious injury collisions as contributory factors in Great Britain in 2006' (Corbett 2010: 905). Most drivers admit speeding in self-report studies (Wells 2011). 'Two thirds (67%) of drivers admit they speed on the motorway, a 2% rise on last year and a 4% rise compared to 2012' (RAC 2014: 61).

By contrast with speeding, relatively few drivers drink and drive nowadays.

> The Road Safety Act of 1967 introduced the first legal maximum blood alcohol (drink-driving) limit in the United Kingdom. Since then, the number of motorists driving under the influence has fallen dramatically. In 1979, which is the first year for which accurate records of drink-drive attitudes, behaviour and casualties are available, 28 people were killed or seriously injured every day in drink-driving accidents on British roads. By 2009, this number had fallen to just four a day – a seven-fold reduction. (RAC 2014: 69)

However, criminalization is far from a guaranteed way of changing risky driving behaviour. In 2003, driving whilst using a handheld mobile phone became illegal, and more than a million drivers have been convicted of this since. The RAC estimates that drivers are four times more likely to crash if using a phone. Yet it seems to be a widespread practice, although not one that most drivers will admit to (RAC 2014: 54).

The demographic pattern of those convicted of road offences, especially serious and repeated ones, is similar to that for other offenders (Corbett 2003, 2010). They are disproportionately male, young and are more likely to have convictions for other offences. The question is, however, whether these groups are the 'usual suspects' and thus more likely to be apprehended (for 'driving whilst black', for instance), or is it that they actually commit more offences? Self-report studies suggest that many types of road offences are widespread (even if disapproved of), whilst others have become deviant in the double sense of statistically uncommon and stigmatized.

Certainly, there are well-known causes célèbres of, on the one hand, elite people being subject to severe penalties for road offences and, on the other hand, scandals where they have been treated with spectacular leniency. An exceptionally egregious example was reported in 2013. 'A North Texas teen from an affluent family was sentenced to probation this week after he killed four pedestrians when he lost control of his speeding pickup truck while driving drunk, a punishment that outraged the victims' families and left prosecutors disappointed.... A psychologist called as an expert defense witness said the boy suffered from "affluenza"' (*Huffington Post* 2013).

Everyday tales of law breaking by respectable people

Some twenty years ago, a book by Thomas Gabor, a Canadian criminologist, claimed that 'everybody does it!' (Gabor 1994). More recently, a major study of middle-class crime in Britain and Germany analysed the increasing involvement of 'respectable' people in crime as a consequence of the fundamental changes in political economy and culture associated with neo-liberalism (Karstedt and Farrall 2004, 2006, 2007). It also showed that some criminological theories usually deployed to explain officially labelled criminal behaviour have equal purchase on the deviant practices of the apparently 'law abiding', notably the ideas of anomie, opportunity and techniques of neutralization.

The authors traced how a variety of economic, situational, regulatory and cultural aspects of neo-liberalism eat away at the traditional attachment of respectable people to strong clear norms of right and wrong, creating an increasingly anomic situation that they wittily dub 'the moral maze of the middle class' (Karstedt and Farrall 2004). The result is a proliferation of criminal acts contemplated and often committed by the majority of people in the most mundane settings of everyday life, not by deviant 'outsiders'.

> These are the 'crimes' and illegal and unfair practices committed at the kitchen table, on the settee and from the home computer, from desks and call centres, at cash points, in supermarkets or in restaurants. They are committed by people who think of themselves as the 'respectable', who are, as citizens and consumers, members of the middle classes, and who would definitely reject the labels of 'criminals' and 'crimes' for themselves and their actions. These 'crimes' are not committed by those who are in vulnerable positions in the modern market society (e.g. those excluded by unemployment), but

> rather those who are at the *centre* of modern societies in two respects: they are the centre of its normative consensus, and at the centre of its social space. (Karstedt and Farrall 2004: 65)

The data for these conclusions were gathered from surveys of random samples (almost five thousand in all) of the population aged 25–65 in England and Wales and in Germany, as well as in-depth interviewing of fraud experts and ordinary citizens (Karstedt and Farrall 2004: 73–4). These sources revealed widespread illegality or dishonesty, including:

> not paying TV licence fees; making false insurance claims; claiming refunds one is not entitled to; requesting and paying cash in hand in order to avoid taxes; and claiming benefits and subsidies one is not entitled to. Not all behaviours are strictly illegal but, in general, all are seen as morally dubious by both victims and offenders. We call these types of behaviour 'crimes of everyday life' to signify that these activities are not unusual or events of an outstanding nature. (Karstedt and Farrall 2007: 2)

The surveys revealed widespread experience of victimization by fraudulent practices, but also widespread commission of such acts. Of the England and Wales sample, 61 per cent admitted committing at least one of the following offences: paying cash in hand to avoid taxation; keeping the money when 'over-changed'; taking something from work; avoiding paying TV licence; wrongly using identity cards for own gain; claiming for refunds they knew they weren't entitled to; not disclosing faulty goods in second-hand sales; asking a friend in a bureaucracy to 'bend the rules'; padding an insurance claim; deliberately misclaiming benefits for own gain (Karstedt and Farrall 2007: Table 2). The German surveys also revealed a widespread propensity to commit such offences (Karstedt and Farrall 2004: 80).

The motivation for dishonest practices was not related to absolute economic pressure. Within the samples, higher income and security of employment were associated both with more victimization and greater readiness to carry out offences, a pattern also found in US research (Karstedt and Farrall 2004: 79). The motivation and the purported justifications for dishonest or illegal practices came from a fundamental restructuring of the markets in which people were implicated, due to the embedding of neo-liberalism since the 1970s. This had profound consequences for the 'moral economy' underpinning markets, borrowing the concept developed by E. P. Thompson in his seminal studies of crime and law in eighteenth-century England (Thompson 1971, 1975). 'First, economic citizenship was transformed into active self-advancement and neo-liberal policies were directed at maximizing the "entrepreneurial comportment" of the individual... Second, consumers were declared "sovereign" and urged to take responsibility and risks. Simultaneously, markets were deregulated, thus creating a new "risk environment" with little oversight or regulation... Finally, citizens were urged to become "consumers"' (Karstedt and Farrall 2007: 4–5). These processes generate increasing disrespect for law and rules, and readiness to violate them if the opportunity arises to do so with impunity. 'The law-abiding majority not only do not abide by the law, they also do not believe in the value of laws and rules, shrugging them off in pursuit of their interests and desires. They even regard law-abidingness as a disadvantage' (ibid.: 7). The data suggest a growing moral darkness at the heart, the very epicentre, of neo-liberal society, although media and political concern focus on 'crime in the streets' and, to a lesser but growing extent, 'crime in the suites'. The crimes of the powerful and their organizations are the focus of the following sections.

Corporate crime

News stories about financial crime were prominent during the week at the end of May 2015 when this section was drafted, an unusual concurrence as upper-world crime rarely features in the mainstream media. The most publicized concerned FIFA, which:

> has been plunged into an unprecedented crisis by the arrest of senior officials in dawn raids in Zurich following a long-running FBI investigation, while Swiss authorities

> simultaneously launched an inquiry into bidding for the 2018 and 2022 World Cups. A dramatic day for football's world governing body...concluded with a damning press conference in Brooklyn at which the director of the FBI and the US attorney general accused senior Fifa executives of presiding over a 'World Cup of fraud'. (Gibson and Neate 2015)

Considerable attention was also given to the start of the trial of some traders in London for rigging the LIBOR rate. LIBOR, the London Interbank Offered Rate, is the average interest rate estimated by leading banks in London for borrowing from other banks and underlies many of the rates charged in everyday transactions. The bankers who rigged it stood to gain large amounts of money whilst disadvantaging the mass of people whose loans would be affected by it. As the deputy governor of the Bank of England stressed, the LIBOR and the forex (foreign exchange) rates underpin the everyday financial transactions of ordinary people, as 'they permeate almost all of our economic transactions...these markets really matter to us all' (Shafik 2014: 3).

In addition, there was prominent reporting of the latest round of huge fines levied on major banks for rigging the forex rate.

> Loretta Lynch, the US attorney general, said [...] 'The penalty these banks will now pay is fitting considering the long-running and egregious nature of their anticompetitive conduct. It is commensurate with the pervasive harm done. And it should deter competitors in the future from chasing profits without regard to fairness, to the law, or to the public welfare.' [...] Andrew McCabe, FBI assistant director, said: 'These resolutions make clear that the US government will not tolerate criminal behaviour in any sector of the financial markets.' (Treanor and Rushe 2015)

These cases are widely seen as examples of long-established and deeply ingrained criminality in major corporate institutions. As summed up by leading economic commentator Will Hutton:

> The world's biggest banks had been steeling themselves for months before the US Department of Justice's rulings on

> manipulation in the foreign exchange markets. [...] Crucially, the banks also admitted that what they had done was criminal. [...] Put bluntly, the world's most prestigious banks had brazenly and systematically ripped off their clients. It was the crime of the decade. (Hutton 2015)

Another news story that week revealed that illegal and predatory behaviours were pervasive, according to a survey of financial service professionals. Despite attempts at regulatory change, the major scandals since the 2007–8 crash and the negative media publicity encapsulated, for example, by Martin Scorsese's 2013 film *The Wolf of Wall Street*, the data suggested that malpractices had increased, becoming the new normal.

> The wolf is still on Wall Street. According to a report released on Tuesday a third of financial executives who said they made more than $500,000 annually 'have witnessed or have firsthand knowledge of wrongdoing in the workplace'. A quarter would conduct insider trading if they were guaranteed $10m – and knew they would get away with it.
>
> [...] 'Nearly one in five respondents feel financial service professionals must sometimes engage in unethical or illegal activity to be successful in the current financial environment.' (Rushe 2015)

Such prominent attention given to stories of financial crime is a novel phenomenon. Media crime news stories tend to focus almost exclusively on serious violent crimes, as shown in chapter 6. The relatively few studies of media reporting of financial and corporate crime find that only the rarest cases, exceptionally egregious scandals or celebrity angles for example, feature in anything but the specialist finance pages of newspapers or the specialist press (Levi 2006), and often the language of crime or the criminal is avoided (Machin and Mayr 2013). As with crime stories more generally, the main concern of news media is with the supposedly abnormal pathological behaviour of a few 'bad apples', with much less attention given to the cultural, institutional and wider structural roots of harmful and wrongful practices (Burdis and Tombs 2012: 280).

There are growing signs of change in official discourse. For example, Baroness Shafik, deputy governor of the Bank of England, recently criticized the 'one bad apple' framework. 'The initial argument that it is just the case of a few bad apples is no longer credible... Perhaps there is something also wrong with the barrel?' (Shafik 2014: 4). The stories cited earlier indicate at least some discursive departure from established patterns, probably due to increased public concern especially since the financial crash of 2007–8. One feature of this is greater readiness to frame narratives in the discourse of crime, as indicated in the stories cited. Indeed a plethora of commentators across the political spectrum have remarked on the dearth of criminal prosecutions of individuals following the credit crunch, as summed up in a recent book by Brandon Garrett, *Too Big to Jail* (Garrett 2015; Rakoff 2015; cf. also Rakoff 2014).

The increased salience of news about corporate crime in the media does not establish that the problem has worsened. The pitfalls of crime statistics (discussed in the next chapter) are multiplied in this area: where there is no regular official recording process, definitions are much more ambiguous and secrecy rife. Consequently, 'the "dark figure" of white-collar crime remains even more unquantifiable than that pertaining to "street" crime' (Burdis and Tombs 2012: 280).[1] Overall, the standard methods for studying street-level crime and criminal justice – ethnography, surveys, interviewing, etc. – have been almost entirely absent from the criminology of corporate (or state) crime. This is largely because of access problems, funding opportunities and career pressures that combine to make criminologists focus almost entirely on the crimes of the powerless, not the powerful (Walters 2003, 2009; Hillyard et al. 2004; Scraton 2007). In effect, they become what the American social scientist Leon Baritz described long ago as 'servants of power' (Baritz 1960). Nonetheless, there has emerged over the years a formidable body of criminological literature analysing the crimes of the powerful, despite the complex conceptual difficulties (Levi 1987; Punch 1996; Slapper and Tombs 1999; Croall 2001; Nelken 2012; Ruggiero 2015), and the fact that information about higher-level wrongdoing is gathered mainly from serendipitous case studies arising from scandals and 'muckraking' journalistic exposés, rather than systematic data collection about routine, mundane behaviour, attitudes and practices (Burdis and Tombs 2012: 279–83).

Since Edwin Sutherland's celebrated 1939 presidential address to the American Society of Criminology introduced the concept of white-collar crime to the discipline, the concept has been subject to much criticism. Intellectually, it has been criticized for its ambiguities, vagueness and complexity (Nelken 2012: 628–31; Ruggiero 2015: ch. 2). Politically, it has been attacked both for its moralistic radicalism in going beyond strictly legal definitions (Tappan 2001 [1947]) and for the conservatism of sticking to the notion of criminality rather than broader ideas of harm or human rights violations (Schwendinger and Schwendinger 1975; Hillyard et al. 2004). Nonetheless, Sutherland's fundamental claim, that the actions of powerful people and organizations wreaked far greater harm than the mundane street crimes which fill the criminal justice system, was impossible to deny and has inspired generations of empirical and theoretical development (Gobert and Punch 2003: ch. 1; Tombs and Whyte 2015: 131–6). Sutherland's impact is indicated above all by the efforts of the large corporations whose wrongdoing he documented to suppress his findings, so that the unexpurgated edition of his book, naming the malefactors, only appeared in 1983, more than three decades after its censored version (Sutherland 1983).

The literature on corporate crime is now so vast that it can only be briefly indicated here, although a recent book does an admirable job of synthesizing the most important information in a provocative and sophisticated theoretical framework (Tombs and Whyte 2015). As with crime in general, the concepts of white-collar and corporate crime cover a very diverse range of harms and wrongs, monetary and personal. Some are clearly violations of criminal law, others arguably so, whilst some are serious wrongs or anti-social harms that particular analysts argue should be regarded as crimes. This does not mean that it is argued they ought be treated as crimes in the sense of being subject to the current menu of criminal punishments. A problem for those who argue that many corporate misdeeds should be regarded as criminal, in that they are seriously harmful and culpable wrongs, is that the predominantly liberal or Left theorists who claim this are rightly dubious about the value or justice of conventional punishments for any crimes.

In the treatment of corporate crime, two major legal issues militate against the viability of successful prosecution, indeed cloud the perception of such wrongs as crimes, even if the harm done is considerable. The first is the core role of individual responsibility, *mens rea*, in the modern concept of crime (Tombs and Whyte 2015: 86–99). The second related issue is the complex chain of causation between individual power holders in large organizations and the harms their decisions produce on the ground. This has seriously inhibited the long-standing efforts to develop an effective law of corporate homicide (Slapper 1999; Wells 2001; Tombs and Whyte 2007). Corporations are regarded as persons in law, separate from the flesh-and-blood human beings that are employed in them.[2] As such, they can be convicted of crimes, but they cannot be construed as forming intentions analogous to those of individual actors, nor can they be subject to the same punishments, notably imprisonment. So the offences that they are charged with are predominantly strict liability ones, not requiring evidence of *mens rea*. These are a scandal to liberal conceptions of criminal law, are often handled by regulatory agencies and processes other than criminal courts and are consequently widely perceived not as 'real' crime, however substantial the damage done.

The complexity of causation behind the harms perpetrated by corporate activities (even if the harm itself is gross and transparent) raises another dilemma (which also bedevils notions of state crime). The lower-level employees who are closely connected with the harmful actions may be shielded somewhat by the claim that they 'were only carrying out orders', following normal procedures (even if they fall short of compliance with safety and other regulations). On the other hand, the directors of the organizations were only 'giving orders', creating procedures at some remove from the actions or omissions that actually caused harm. All along the line, nobody *intended* harm, the *mens rea* prerequisite for murder, and they may not even have been reckless or strongly negligent. In most cases, the last thing they wanted or had in mind was the harm that transpired as a result of policies and actions or omissions that were not sufficiently safe. Cutting corners, not following safety procedures in full and so on, resulted from a concern with the profitability and efficient running of the organization, of which the broken or dead bodies resulting were collateral damage. What they were really guilty of was *indifference*, failing to consider the possible consequences of routine actions. Some analysts have argued that this should be a ground of culpability, but it only approximates to current legal criteria if it can be construed as negligence (Pemberton 2004, 2015).

The consequence is that even in the cases of 'accidents' and 'disasters' that stemmed from corporate failures or wrongdoing, resulting in considerable death or injury, such as the 1987 capsizing of the *Herald of Free Enterprise* ferry in Zeebrugge when 193 people died, convictions are hard to achieve. The official inquiry found that three of the crew had responsibility for sailing without closing the bow doors, but it also held that their inaction resulted from a network of sloppy and illegal management practices going all the way to the top of the organization that owned the ship. Consequently a coroner's inquest returned a verdict of unlawful killing. Seven individuals working at different levels of the organization were charged with gross negligence and manslaughter, and the operating company, P&O European Ferries (Dover) Ltd, was charged with corporate manslaughter. However, the trial collapsed after the judge directed the jury to acquit the company and the five most senior individual defendants. Similar sagas of individual ground-level errors, made possible or even likely by policy and management failures originating in commercial pressure, privatization and government deregulation, are found in fatal train crashes, such as the 1997 Southall crash in the United Kingdom when seven people were killed and 139 injured. The passenger-train driver was initially charged with manslaughter, but the case was dropped. His employer, Great Western Trains, was fined £1.5 million for not having a system that ensured high-speed trains did not undertake long journeys with the automatic warning system inoperative (Gobert and Punch 2003: 31–4).

Growing concern over such cases eventually resulted in the 2008 Corporate Manslaughter and Corporate Homicide Act.

This specifically excludes individual directors from conviction for 'aiding, abetting, counselling or procuring an offence of corporate manslaughter' (s. 16), and has thus had little impact. Individuals can only be convicted if their connection to the deaths resulting from corporate action or omission is sufficiently close that they can be held to be directly negligent or reckless, which so far at any rate has only been found in cases involving very small companies (Tombs and Whyte 2015: 96–7).

Tombs and Whyte demonstrate that, in addition to the 'monster' cases of huge financial loss or substantial injury and loss of life that make headline news, corporations are culpable of wide-ranging and cumulatively substantial 'routine, everyday harm' (Tombs and Whyte 2015: 37). They document this with respect to four key areas: corporate theft and fraud (especially in the retail financial services sector); crimes against consumers (notably food safety matters); crimes against workers (workplace safety crimes); and crimes against the environment, notably air pollution (ibid.: 37–50). All involve similar mixes of substantial economic loss and death or serious injury or ill health, attributable to corporate malpractice. Only a small fraction of cases has resulted in criminal convictions and penalties, usually of low-level individuals, or of corporations for regulatory breaches that have normally been dealt with outside the criminal courts. Elites are thus shielded from the stigma of criminal status by a corporate veil (ibid.: 91–9). Criminalization remains the monopoly of the lower strata of society, the 'usual suspects' from the 'dangerous classes'. As singer-songwriter Woody Guthrie once said, some will rob you with a six-gun, some with a fountain pen.

State crime

As discussed in chapter 1, the contemporary concept of crime developed hand in hand with modern states and capitalism. The dominant, 'anchored' conception of crime is violation of state-defined, enforced and penalized law. Nonetheless, even within this positivist definition, 'the emergence of so-called international criminal law... especially in the last half century, represents... a transnational arena of criminalisation in which some states (or at least their agents) have potentially become subjects (rather than controllers) of criminal justice' (Cotterrell 2015: 13). The key source of this emerging jurisprudence is the founding 1998 Rome Statute of the International Criminal Court (ICC), and the Court's interpretations of offences. The roots of the ICC lie in particular in the Nuremberg trials of Nazi war criminals after the Second World War as part of the reaction to what is generally seen as the greatest crime of all time, the Holocaust (though scarcely analysed by criminologists; cf. Cohen 2000; Morrison 2006: ch. 8; Brannigan 2013). Subsequent ad hoc tribunals for massacres in former Yugoslavia and the Rwandan genocide were the ICC's immediate progenitors.

Human Rights Watch (2008) reviewed the Court's first decade positively: 'The ICC's establishment sends a strong signal to current and would-be perpetrators that complete impunity for the worst crimes will not be tolerated.' Their assessment also indicated some of the limitations of the positivist conception of state crime that is embodied within the emerging international criminal law structure. The focus is on the most egregious examples of war crimes and crimes against humanity where there is little ambiguity about the harm done or its immorality. Even so, as with crime in general, it is essentially only the offences perpetrated by relatively small fry that do not have impunity in practice. It is noteworthy that all the cases cited by the Report involve very poor African states, lacking any pretensions to being democracies, some hovering on the fringe of being 'failed' states (although trials have involved leaders as well as foot soldiers). It is inconceivable that war crimes perpetrated by powerful nations would end up at The Hague. The United States initially signed up to the Treaty under President Clinton, but then President Bush notified the ICC he would not ratify it. India and China, along with numerous smaller Asian and African states, have not even signed the Treaty.

The problems of researching state crime are similar to those facing the study of corporate crime, notably the capacity of the powerful to resist scrutiny. Nonetheless, there is an impressive and rapidly growing empirical and theoretical literature (Tombs and Whyte 2003; Green and Ward 2004, 2012; Whyte 2009; and Chambliss, Michalowski and Kramer 2010 offer invaluable guides), with researchers finding highly innovative, often ingenious (not to say sometimes perilous) ways of finding information (Green and Ward 2012: 730–5; Whyte 2012). Journalism investigating major scandals is a key resource, as are the leaked data released by WikiLeaks, Edward Snowden and other whistle-blowers since 2009 (Green and Ward 2012: 733–4).[3]

The above sources all establish that the volume and gravity of state crime, in terms of both monetary and physical harm, far outstrip the mundane criminal offences occupying the criminal justice system. This section cannot discuss state crime exhaustively but will focus on just two important types: first, some spectacular scandals, including truly heinous war crimes perpetrated by major western powers; second, the mundane horrors of neo-liberal governance, notably the routine but tragic and numerous deaths resulting from state-imposed policies of austerity.

A sensitive and thought-provoking exploration of the moral dilemmas of criminology notes that 'War crimes and massacres are tangential to the subject matter of criminology. There are historical reasons for this, relating to the circumstances of criminology's birth and its dependence on state patronage... But there are no good *intellectual* reasons for it. War crimes are moral abominations, but they are also of course *crimes*' (Cottee 2013: 6). Cottee's chapter begins with a long and harrowing quote describing the notorious My Lai slaughters during the Vietnam War.

> The massacre had begun just after eight o'clock on the morning of 16 March 1968... By the time Calley and his men sat down to lunch, they had rounded up and slaughtered around 500 unarmed civilians. Within those few hours, members of Charlie Company had 'fooled around' and laughed as they sodomised and raped women, ripped vaginas open with knives, bayoneted civilians, scalped corpses... Other soldiers had wept openly as they opened fire on crowds of unresisting old men, women, children and babies. At no stage did these soldiers receive any enemy fire or encounter any form of resistance save fervent pleadings. (Bourke 1999: 160)

There cannot be any debate about the horrific events being anything but serious crimes on all the dimensions considered in this book: legal, moral, social, officially labelled and prominently condemned by media and political discourse. Sadly, however, they are not unique in their heinousness. The book from which the above passage is drawn, Joanna Bourke's *An Intimate History of Killing*, comprises more than five hundred pages of such cases in the twentieth century, depicting '"ordinary" men and women rejoicing as they committed grotesque acts of cruelty' in the British, American and Australian armed forces.

What makes the My Lai massacre almost unique is the huge media attention it received, the rather unusual fact that fourteen officers (including a major-general) were court-martialled and that one, Lieutenant Calley, was convicted of more than twenty murders and sentenced to life imprisonment (though he was released after three and a half years, spent mainly under house arrest). The case clearly raises some of the most difficult and contentious issues in the understanding of state crime. Calley was convicted because of clear evidence of his personal involvement in killings, as well as those by his men. His defence that he was 'following orders' was rejected. His immediate superior officer, Captain Medina, was acquitted because the court accepted his claim that his shooting of a civilian was because he (wrongly) thought the man was armed. It also rejected the claim that he gave orders directly leading to the atrocities (this was the flip side of the verdict rejecting Calley's defence of following orders) and denied any notion of 'command responsibility'.

In her book on the case, Mary McCarthy sees Medina as 'a transition figure between the war makers and the "animals"...and his acquittal halted a process that might have gone up the ladder of responsibility' (McCarthy 1972: 168). The lines of responsibility are complex, ambivalent and contentious. Calley was regarded as a hero by a large swathe of the US population (who bought sufficient copies – nearly 2 million – of the 1971 top-40 hit 'The Battle Hymn of Lieutenant Calley' to make it a gold record). They presumably accepted the accounts found in numerous statements by soldiers at My Lai about the overall context. These stressed that the soldiers had been indoctrinated into a view of the war as a righteous struggle for freedom, and they had direct experience of combat, reinforcing the official depiction of the Vietcong as dangerous and constantly threatening. The case 'shows how problematic are the connections between theories ("they were just obeying orders", "they were part of the system") and assessments of responsibility, culpability, blameworthiness, or guilt' (Cohen 1988 [1979]: 124). Even amongst the perpetrators at ground level, there were considerably different types of involvement. As the passage above shows, whilst some seemed to revel in butchery and brutality, others wept as they shot women and children. The end of the slaughter began with the heroic actions of Warrant Officer Hugh Thompson and his helicopter crew. They landed their aircraft repeatedly when they saw the killings, stepping between soldiers and civilians and rescuing a child. Thompson and his crew were decorated for their heroism, but on their return home they also received anonymous death threats (Goldstein 2006).

My Lai not only poses the fundamental criminological conundrum of explaining the different reactions of offenders, bystanders and rescuers to similar circumstances. It also raises the acute issues of attributing moral responsibility at different levels of large organizations and systems, when chains of command and direct causal connection are complex and interwoven, a fundamental problem for corporate and state crime. As Mary McCarthy put it in her contemporary analysis:

> Logic here is unpersuasive: the deliberate individual killing of unresisting people *is* more repugnant than the same result effected by mechanical means deployed at a distance and without clear perception of who or what is below. Even those who profess to see no distinction in Vietnam between the crime of war and single acts of homicide would be hard put to deny that distance does not seem to count in diminishing responsibility. Demonstrators shouting 'Hey, hey, LBJ, how many kids did you kill today?' were logically right in viewing Johnson as the final cause, insofar as that could be targeted in one person, but humanly they failed to convince, since he was not the proximate cause and could not even be said to have *intended* the slaughter of Vietnamese children in the sense that Hitler intended the annihilation of Jews in the gas ovens. (McCarthy 1972: 35)

Against this powerful rhetoric, however, there are some counter-arguments that cloud the issues. Whilst the culpability of the face-to-face killers is plain, the responsibility of people up the line of command, all the way to the top, is also significant, and in some ways greater. It may lack the manifest visceral cruelty of the face-to-face shooter or violator of a pleading child, but the higher-level decision makers are responsible for quantitatively greater harm, and they make their decisions in apparently rational and coldly considered ways, not the hot-rush, red mist of fear and adrenalin in combat. This is not to excuse the actual killers – but it is to implicate the command levels at least as significantly.

The more recent wars involving the United States, Britain and other western allies, notably in Iraq (in 2003), Afghanistan and Libya, encompass just as strong a set of charges against the governing elites of those states (as well as some combat troops). All were wars of choice and, especially in the case of Iraq, the legal, moral and indeed pragmatic justifications seem elusive and controversial, to put it mildly. Many, probably most, international lawyers deny these wars' legality, and they do not seem to satisfy the ethical criteria for just war (as expressed by Walzer 2006, for example). There is a strong case for saying some major western states' leaders are guilty of waging aggressive war, although for evident reasons of global power they are unlikely to be in the dock of the ICC at The Hague any time soon. There is also evidence of a variety of violations of the principles of *ius in bello*. Examples include the abuse and torture of prisoners, most notoriously at Abu Ghraib for which several soldiers were imprisoned and senior officers were demoted and sanctioned. There is now plentiful evidence that these violations of human rights and international law were based on 'enhanced interrogation techniques' authorized by the US government, and, more broadly, the launch and conduct of the invasion involved many legal and ethical violations (Sands 2006, 2009). Beyond the illegal violence associated with the Iraq war itself, the 'systematic corruption of the reconstruction economy…is a major and ongoing humanitarian crisis that has created human suffering on a staggering scale' (Whyte 2010: 134). The collaboration of the military occupation and plundering corporations is a prime example of state-corporate crime, leaving millions without adequate food, water, health services, power supplies or education (Whyte 2007, 2010: 134–5).

There are countless other cases of spectacular illegality by 'democratic' western states. A major book, for example, documents how the British government response to the 'Troubles' in Northern Ireland since the 1970s involved decades of illegal violence, including death squads, interrogation techniques and intelligence gathering (Punch 2012). This is not a unique example of counter-insurgency slipping into criminality. Similar techniques and processes have been documented in South Africa, Chile, Argentina, Brazil, Spain and elsewhere (Brogden and Shearing 1993; Osiel 1997, 2008; Chevigny 1998; Huggins 1998, 2002; Hinton 2005; Marks 2005; Punch 2010).

Crime by states is not just a matter of the overt use of illegal violence in war or counter-insurgency. The consequences of economic and social policy are often severely harmful and even fatal. Can these be considered crimes by the state and/or individual ministers and officials? Almost certainly not in terms of any prospects of legal sanctions. However, they may be seen as such in normative conceptions of crime as serious harm or as violations of human rights, including social and economic security.

States are not monolithic entities but constellations of institutions exercising (more or less) legitimate power over a territory. They are sites of struggle between different interests and ideologies, although that contest is not between equal parties. In general, states are dominated by the rich and powerful, even when they function fundamentally to safeguard the system rather than particular interests or groups, and may well initiate policies protecting the less privileged, as shown by Marx's analysis of the Factory Acts discussed earlier.

In the first three-quarters of the twentieth century, and especially in the three post-Second World War decades, the state in western democracies operated Keynesian, welfare state economic and social policies that fostered overall growth and security which were widely shared. The displacement of this by the growing neo-liberal hegemony since the 1970s has involved increasing attacks on state-sponsored social support and welfare. In the wake of the 2007–8 financial crisis and subsequent economic downturn, this has been magnified hugely by policies of 'austerity', pursued especially vigorously in Europe. The purported justification is to reduce the deficits in public finance, although paradoxically these resulted from the state bail-outs of the financial institutions, wherein the crisis originated.

Under 'austerity', the wealth of the rich has ballooned, but the cost is borne primarily by the mass of the population, especially the poorest sections. 'Socialism for the rich, capitalism for the poor' – the aphorism first popularized by Michael Harrington's study of poverty in the United States (Harrington 1962: 170) – is an apt characterization of the impact of austerity policies. The British and other governments' defence of austerity as an inevitable necessity is challenged by the majority of economists, as shown by a survey by the Centre for Macroeconomics (Centre for Macroeconomics 2015). Many leading economists have demonstrated cogently that austerity exacerbates the deficits it purports to tackle because of the negative effect on state finances of falls in tax revenue and increases in welfare expenditure as growth slows (e.g. Wren-Lewis 2013, 2015; Skidelsky 2014, 2015; Krugman 2015; Sen 2015; Stiglitz 2015). Indeed, the slight post-2012 recovery in Britain resulted from a tacit switch towards limited Keynesianism, returning in practice to the path adopted by Labour before 2010. Nonetheless, the Coalition and the Conservative governments' narrative that the prime cause of the economic recession was profligate spending, and that austerity is the cure, is dominant in the media and, it seems, in public opinion (Seymour 2014, Blyth 2015 and Mendoza 2015 are critical analyses). This is an eerie confirmation of the Right's superior capacity to manoeuvre 'shocks' and disasters to its advantage (Klein 2008) and to *Never Let a Serious Crisis Go to Waste* (Mirowski 2014).

The key point for a discussion of state crime is that austerity policies have clear, well-documented, extremely harmful effects, which render them potentially criminal if they are unjustified economically as the above arguments suggest. There is plentiful empirical evidence, both in the United Kingdom and worldwide, that austerity 'bites' (O'Hara 2015) and, in the extreme, 'kills' (Stuckler and Basu 2013). This adds to the large body of accumulating evidence about the fatal consequences for the health of populations that are caused by inequality (Wilkinson 2005; Wilkinson and Pickett 2009; Dorling 2015). These books contain a wealth of statistical evidence demonstrating the extensive deaths and disease stemming from austerity and the poverty and inequality it exacerbates.

In many cases, death seems to be a predictable and fairly direct result of tougher welfare policies, stemming from austerity economics. In the United Kingdom, one of the most dramatic was the death of a 59-year-old ex-soldier: 'Clapson, of Stevenage, Hertfordshire, who worked for 29 years, died three weeks after his £71.70 weekly allowance was stopped. When his body was found by a friend, his electricity card was out of credit, which meant the fridge where he kept the insulin on which his life depended had not been working' (Wintour 2014). This was widely reported, and at a subsequent House of Commons Select Committee Inquiry, the Labour MP for Oldham suggested that there were potentially hundreds of thousands of such cases. A website, 'Black-triangle', has tried to list these deaths. According to a report, 'The Department for Work and Pensions (DWP) has admitted that 10 of the 49 benefit claimants whose deaths were subject to secret reviews had had their payments sanctioned' (Pring 2015). Sadly, an internet search reveals hundreds of such stories since 2010. As the friend of a mother-of-three who committed suicide after her benefits were cut put it: 'this government's got blood on its hands' (Chakrabortty 2015). In a later case, a coroner's official verdict attributed a man's death to benefit cuts (Chakelian 2015).

There can be no doubt that such cases do not amount to murder – even the most impassioned critic of the UK Coalition and Conservative governments would not imagine that ministers actually intend or wish for such tragic consequences. However, in the light of the clear warnings from expert charities and other bodies with experience in the field, and the accumulating file of cases, a plausible argument could be made for *mens rea* (negligence, perhaps recklessness), judged by the standard of reasonable foreseeability.

The rich get richer, the poor get the blame

If crime is part of the lifestyle of the rich and powerful, how is it that the criminal justice system primarily processes the poor and powerless? A large part of the answer is that although crime is committed throughout the social structure, and the harms committed by those higher up the scale arguably have more serious harmful effects, 'those types of crimes which are handled by the police' (Braithwaite 1979: 62) and filtered into the criminal statistics and the criminal justice process are predominantly committed by the poor (Maguire 2007: 288).

Why are the serious harms of the powerful normally hidden from criminal justice processing? Victor Jupp and his colleagues have probed the features of the construction of 'invisibility' for some harms rather than others in two major books (Jupp, Davies and Francis 1999; Davies, Francis and Jupp 1999, 2014). They suggest that 'invisibility' of serious harm typically arises out of seven absences: no knowledge (of the harm committed); no statistics (official methods of regular data collection do not feature these harms); no theory (there is little criminological or other social science analysis of these issues, because positivism and liberalism focus on legally sanctioned wrongs); no research (epistemological, methodological and practical barriers – access and funding issues – frustrate research); no control (little attention from the main criminal justice agencies especially the police, and a dearth of specialist regulatory agencies); no politics (the politics of law and order are focused on the rare symbolic assailants threatening immediate face-to-face violence and harm); and no panic (media concentration on exceptional folk devils means few moral panics about upper-world crime). The work of Jupp and his associates offers detailed insight into the construction of invisibility shrouding the serious harms perpetrated by the respectable and the elites.

The ultimate sources of these 'absences' can be traced to four fundamental ways in which power affects the definition and the sanctioning of harms. These are the ability to shape:

- *Crime definitions*: corporate and political elites have the capacity to shape laws to fit their interests.

- *Structural shaping of criminal justice operations*: policing, the entry point into the criminal justice process, is shaped by private property. Police powers apply primarily to public space.
- *Stereotyping*: police tactics largely focus on 'rounding up the usual suspects': together with other criminal justice agents and the public, they tend to stereotype criminals as young, underclass, ethnic-minority male. This becomes a self-fulfilling prophecy affecting all stages of the criminal process.
- *Power to influence process*: materially, it is predominantly elites who have access to the law, especially since the severe cuts in legal aid. Culturally, they benefit from the politics of credibility that advantage the testimony of the apparently respectable. They wield the 'influence of affluence' (Gilens 2012), powerful social connections (Jones 2014) that can operate as a shield and a sword. All of this gives a degree of leverage against those who seek to investigate them, for example if they threaten to complain about the police. Finally, they have the means to try and directly corrupt legal and criminal justice agents (Punch 2009; Whyte 2015).

These four basic processes, whereby economic, cultural and political power shape the conception of what is subject to criminalization, underlie the relative immunity of elites and the respectable. The other side of this is stigmatization of the poor and powerless, which will be examined in the next chapter.

5
The Criminal Justice Process and Conceptions of Crime

The criminal justice process is a crucial source of the conceptions of crime that dominate popular and political discourse. As we saw in chapter 1, criminal law has been characterized as the set of rules whose infraction gives rise to the possibility of criminal proceedings. The operations of criminal justice agencies are also the prevailing basis for official statistics on the patterns and characteristics of crime and criminals. These data purport to offer authoritative assessments of their extent, nature and trends, and of the degree of success of policy and practice.

The direction of influence is not one way, however. The criminal justice system and its official statistics are indeed a pivotal source of practitioners', politicians' and public images of crime and criminals. But, in turn, the operation of criminal justice agencies, and the statistics they generate, are largely shaped by inputs from the public. The relationship between popular conceptions of crime, and the officially processed and measured patterns, is a dialectically interdependent one.

In its official pronouncements, the criminal justice system purports to deal with crime effectively and fairly. 'The purpose of the Criminal Justice System (CJS) is to deliver justice for all, by convicting and punishing the guilty and helping them to stop offending, while protecting the innocent. It is responsible for detecting crime and bringing it to justice' (UK

Government 2014). This optimistic gloss masks the huge amount of crime that is *not* tackled by criminal justice, and a fortiori the wrongs and harms that are not criminalized even in principle. It also sanitizes the massive biases in the processing of various sorts of crimes and different classes of people.

The deviation between the criminal law in principle and in practice is not only huge. It is also systematically biased against the poor and powerless, who are the predominant population processed by all criminal justice institutions. The 'law in action' – the officially processed pattern of crime – differs massively from what either criminal law texts – the 'law in the books' – or popular and political discourse suggest. This cavernous gap is far from innocent. The criminal justice system is a prodigious engine for injustice, even if (a big if) it is perfectly fair in all individual cases. And apart from the immediate social (and all too often individual) injustice of criminal 'justice', the cultural and political effect of the distorted imagery of crime conveyed by official data is to shore up ideologically the broader social structures of inequality and oppression.

This is summed up succinctly in the title of a classic critical criminology text: *The Rich Get Richer and the Poor Get Prison* (Reiman and Leighton 2012). But in addition to massively disparate exposure to the pains of prison and other penal sanctions, the poor (and other relatively powerless groups) also endure the lion's share of criminal victimization, as the Left realists of critical criminology have demonstrated (Lea and Young 1984; Matthews 2014). This disproportionality of suffering is no accident, Reiman and Leighton suggest. The apparent failure of modern criminal justice systems to have much impact on crime levels over the last two centuries[1] is perpetuated because of its latent ideological functions. The recurrent spectacle of menacing folk devils from the underclass diverts anger from the powerful victors in an increasingly unequal social order.

This chapter will unravel the conceptions of crime generated by the criminal justice process. These are conveyed primarily in the regularly published official statistics about crime, criminals and criminal justice agencies. The next section will review the well-known problems of these statistics. Following these health warnings, we will consider what the data suggest about the shape, trends and patterns in offending.

The (mis)measurement of crime

Criminal statistics are notoriously riddled with pitfalls. Changes in the recorded figures may often be due not to changes in offence levels but to fluctuations in reporting by victims or in recording by the police or in the counting rules. However, very substantial steps have been taken in recent decades to alleviate these problems by developing alternative measures and by tightening the procedures for the police-recorded data.

Nonetheless, there have been several serious scandals concerning the official crime statistics recently, as well as mounting criticism from various governmental bodies. These include Her Majesty's Inspectorate of Constabulary (HMIC), the House of Commons Public Administration Select Committee (PASC) and the UK Statistics Authority (UKSA) – which in January 2014 stripped the police-recorded crime statistics (produced since 1856) of their Kitemark as officially designated National Statistics.

What are the crime statistics?

Any attempt to measure crime is of course bedevilled by all the conceptual issues in defining crime that are explored in this book. Official crime statistics are part and parcel of the administrative processes of the state and are based on a legal conception of crime.

HMIC is explicit about this in its account of the Home Office Counting Rules (HOCR) for compiling police-recorded statistics.

> To determine whether an incident is a crime, the HOCR state that: 'An incident will be recorded as a crime (notifiable to the Home Secretary) for offences against an identified victim

> if, on the balance of probability: A. The circumstances as reported amount to a crime defined by law (the police will determine this, based on their knowledge of the law and counting rules), and B. There is no credible evidence to the contrary.' (HMIC 2014: 35; ONS 2014: 21)

The list of 'notifiable offences' (those which the police have a statutory obligation to record for the Home Office) comprises more than 1,500 types of criminal offence which have been criminalized over the centuries by common law and statute.

Until the early 1980s, all political and media debate about the 'crime rate' referred to one long-running series of statistics based on police records, officially collated and regularly published by the Home Office. Since then, there has been an additional set of statistics compiled and published by the Home Office: the British Crime Survey (its complex origins are analysed in Castelbajac 2014). The BCS, now known as the Crime Survey for England and Wales (CSEW), is based on interviews with samples of the population. The Home Office published an annual volume *Crime in England and Wales* (as well as quarterly updates) of both the police-recorded crime and BCS figures until 1 April 2012, when the Office for National Statistics (ONS) took over publication. *Crime in England and Wales: Year Ending September 2014*, was published on 22 January 2015.

Problems of interpreting crime statistics

Police-recorded crime statistics

Criminologists and statisticians have long been aware that the official crime statistics suffer from many problems, making their interpretation hazardous. Nonetheless, tabloid newspapers presented the police-recorded statistics as if they were accurate measures of crime, at any rate until the recent scandals culminating in their losing their status as national statistics. What the tabloids unabashedly called the 'crime rate' is labelled tautologously as 'Crimes Recorded by the Police' in

Home Office/ONS publications. This designation is accurate if taken literally: by definition the number of crimes recorded by the police is the number of crimes recorded by the police! But the question is: do the figures recorded by the police really measure the rates and patterns of crime?

The 'dark figure' The police-recorded statistics are problematic above all because of the so-called 'dark figure' of unrecorded crime. Many crimes occur that are not recorded by the police, for a variety of reasons. In a well-worn metaphor, the recorded rate represents only the tip of the iceberg of criminal activity, and at issue is what we can learn about the totality from what is visible. There is much evidence that the police statistics have always been 'supply-side' driven, reflecting the changing exigencies of Home Office policy makers and police bureaucracies as much as the activities of offenders and victims (Taylor 1998a, 1998b, 1999).

If we could be confident that the recorded rate was representative of the whole, it would at least be a reliable guide to trends and patterns. But a fundamental problem is that the recorded statistics are not only incomplete. They are biased, as empirical evidence and analysis of their process of construction by the police has shown. Some crimes and some criminals are much more likely to enter the records than others, with clear patterns of class, age, ethnic, gender and area disproportionality.

Events that violate criminal law do not automatically enter official statistics. For an incident to be recorded as crime, it must get over two hurdles: (1) it must get to be known to the police; (2) it must be recorded by the police.

Hurdle 1: Getting 'known to the police'

There are two ways crimes can become known to the police: report by a member of the public, usually the victim; or discovery by the police of crimes without individual victims, often through proactive policing. The Home Office and the ONS call this latter category 'offences against the state' (ONS 2014: 21–2). This does not of course mean they are 'political', or at any rate no more so than any other offence that is prohibited by statutory processes. The ONS examples are 'the possession of drugs, carrying a weapon, and public order offences that have no victim'. The distinction turns on whether there is a specific identified victim, as distinct from the public at large who are purportedly represented by the state.

How a crime comes to police attention depends on whether or not there is a victim who is aware of it. This has crucial implications for the likelihood of different offences reaching the statistics.

Crimes with aware victims If the crime has a victim who is aware of their victimhood, they may decide to report the crime to the police – although, for a variety of reasons, many do not. The decision whether or not to report turns on a more or less explicit cost – benefit assessment. About three-quarters of victims who do not report a crime tell the BCS/CSEW that this is because the offence was too trivial, or involved no loss, and the police would not or could not do anything about it. Such pragmatic reasons for non-reporting are most commonly stated in the case of property crimes. For violent crimes, however, other factors, such as regarding the matter as 'private', or a fear of reprisal, are important. Trends in overall crime reporting are highly sensitive to fluctuating practical considerations such as the prospect of making an insurance claim and the convenience of reporting (Where is the nearest police station? Can crimes be reported by phone or online?).

Crimes without aware victims Many crimes involve victims who, for a variety of reasons, are unaware of what has happened to them:

(a) There may be crimes with individual victims who do not realize the nature of what has happened. The victims may be children who are aware of their suffering, but not that what was done to them was a crime reportable to the police. Or they may be adult victims of frauds that are so successful that the victim does not realize that they have been deceived or even hard done by (e.g. the mis-selling of PPI). Victims of theft may think they have lost the property involved or not be sure.

(b) Many crimes do not have recognizable victims at all. These include 'consensual' offences, such as drug taking, and 'vice' offences, such as those relating to prostitution, pornography and gambling. People involved in these activities may paternalistically be regarded as harming themselves or others, but the putative victims are often willing participants. The 'victim' of other offences may be the public at large: examples include tax evasion, smuggling, pensions or mortgage mis-selling, insider trading and other financial crime, motoring offences, public order offences and treason.

The common element in these examples is that they only come to be known to the police by chance, or through proactive policing work (e.g. surveillance of 'hot spots', undercover work, raids on pubs and clubs for drugs, analysis of financial transactions for fraud or other crimes, searches of travellers at customs). Mapping and analysing these aspects of the 'dark figure' is much more problematic, and any estimation of trends and patterns can only be tentative and fragmentary.

Hurdle 2: Getting recorded by the police

What surprises many people is that, even if 'known' to them, the police do not necessarily record incidents as crimes. Indeed, the scandals that in January 2014 led the UK Statistics Authority to withdraw the police-recorded statistics from the designated 'official national statistics' turned precisely on this issue (HMIC 2014: 29).

This is neither a recent nor a marginal phenomenon. Observational and historical studies of policing have long shown that the police frequently exercise discretion not to record crimes that they have witnessed or received reports about (Banton 1964; Chatterton 1976; McCabe and Sutcliffe 1978). 'Crimes known to the police' should perhaps be relabelled 'crimes the police wish to make known'.

The first BCS estimated in 1981 that the police recorded only 62% of all crimes reported to them, and 'less than half of those involving violence' (Hough and Mayhew 1983: 12).

By 1995, the overall proportion of victim-reported crime that the police recorded had fallen to 50%. Following a 1998 change in the counting rules, this increased to just below 60%. A Home Office Research Study that monitored the outcome of calls to the police found only 47% of crime allegations were eventually recorded as crimes (Burrows et al. 2000: ch. 5). In 21% of cases where a crime was recorded, it was classified differently from the initial allegation.

These findings prompted the introduction of a National Crime Recording Standard (NCRS) in 2002. This had 'the twin aims of ensuring proper focus on the victims of crime and consistency in crime-recording in all 43 police forces... based on applying legal definitions of crime to victim reports' (HMIC 2014: 33–4). The NCRS had a considerable initial impact, and by 2003–4 the proportion of victim reports recorded by the police was more than 90 per cent. Within a decade, however, this had slipped back to 70 per cent (Flatley and Bradley 2013: 9). For a comprehensive review of the evidence about police recording practice and the attempts to reform it, see Mayhew (2014).

Although increasingly tightly structured by the 1998 revisions to the HOCR and the NCRS, police officers inevitably exercise some de facto discretion not to record all crimes reported to them, or about *how* to record them. Police exercise such discretion for reasons varying from benign (for example, if there is genuine doubt about the truthfulness or accuracy of a victim's report) to completely corrupt (for example, in return for a bribe). But probably the main sources of police failure to record offences actually known to them are a variety of bureaucratic pressures. These range from resource constraints to more or less explicit sanctions to achieve performance targets.

Earlier versions of the HOCR, dating back to the 1920s, used to leave the initial decision as to whether to record a crime largely to the police themselves. A study by a former senior officer gave a vivid insider's account of the various devices used by police to avoid recording crimes (Young 1991: ch. 5). The tightening of counting rules and procedures since then has made this strategy more difficult. The 1998 reform of the Home Office Counting Rules began a process of tightening them to ensure that victims' perspectives were prioritized. This has culminated in a 2015 revision that makes this unequivocal.

> 2.2 An incident will be recorded as a crime (notifiable offence) for 'victim related offences' if, on the balance of probability: (a) the circumstances of the victim's report amount to a crime defined by law (the police will determine this, based on their knowledge of the law and counting rules); and (b) there is no credible evidence to the contrary immediately available. (Home Office Counting Rules for Recorded Crime 2015)

This constrains the police exercise of discretion, although they still have to decide the issue of whether a legal crime has occurred and whether the person reporting an incident is indeed a 'victim'.

The major revisions in recording procedures, represented by the 1998 HOCR and the 2002 NCRS, aimed *inter alia* to prioritize the victim's perspective. But legal and organizational pressures tend in the opposite direction. Increasing emphasis on performance measurement and results makes spinning the figures more desirable to police officers. The recent reports by HMIC, PASC and ONS are united in criticizing the perverse incentives that followed the increasing concern with scrutinizing efficiency, effectiveness and economy by ever more complex target setting pursued by both Conservative and Labour governments from the mid-1980s to 2010.

The British Home Secretary Theresa May stated in a speech on 2 March 2011: 'I've scrapped the last remaining national police targets, and replaced them with a single objective: to cut crime.' This is itself of course a target and, other things being equal, could lead to police focusing efforts on bringing crime down overall, without attention to seriousness and other priorities – the 'low-hanging fruit' problem. It was precisely to counter this that more complex performance measures were developed. Moreover, the last set of targets introduced by Labour, concerned with measuring public confidence, was intended to mitigate the risks of concentrating on crime figures at all costs. In any event, the central plank of Conservative police reform, the introduction of an elected police and crime commissioner for each force, in practice runs counter to the declared objective of altering the target culture.

As the Public Administration Select Committee states: 'In recent years, central Government has sought to shift the emphasis away from the use of centrally-imposed targets as a means of assessing police performance, but this is not reflected in the attitudes, systems and processes of individual police forces and their governing authorities, Police and Crime Commissioners' (PASC 2014: 26).

As empirical observational research and historical experience suggest, it is impossible to close off all avenues for discretion. Certainly, there have continued to be scandals about deliberate manipulation of statistics since the reform of procedures, in both the United Kingdom and the United States (Davies 1999, 2003a, 2003b; UKSA 2013; PASC 2014: ch. 3; HMIC 2014; Eterno and Silverman 2012 show similar processes at work in New York City).

The police failure to record all crimes reported to them by victims is indefensible in principle, however time-honoured a practice it is. Nonetheless, it is puzzling that the scandal about this has blown up so recently when research over decades has demonstrated the existence of the issue. Moreover, the Home Office's own BCS, since its 1981 inception, has actually charted the extent of the gap between victim reporting and police recording, usefully dubbed the 'grey figure' of unrecorded crime (Hope 2013: 49). The eruption of the current scandal was triggered above all by increasing concern about the shamefully poor treatment accorded by police to women who have suffered sexual violence, highlighted by recent causes célèbres and whistle-blowers (PASC 2014: 14–17). This chimes with much evidence arising over many years about how traditional police culture and practice result in a massive police failure to deal with crimes against women in a fair and effective way (Heidensohn and Silvestri 2012; Dick, Silvestri and Westmarland 2014). More generally, the 'grey figure' indicates a considerable degree of poor service to victims of crime.

What is rather less defensible is the conception of crime that animates the recent reforms. As was seen earlier, the fundamental notion of 'notifiable offences' is stated in purely legal terms, ignoring all the problems with this conceptualization that were discussed in earlier chapters. This may be understandable in the collection of statistics that are part of the state's official governmental procedures, geared increasingly to managerial concerns. Nonetheless, it leaves completely out of account any serious wrongdoing or harm that is not unambiguously and formally criminalized. Even within the legal conception of crime, however, the recent official critiques of police statistics invoke an unattainable chimera of 'a full and accurate account of crime' (PASC 2014: 5), as if this were feasible.

The official critiques do recognize that in practice not all crimes can be recorded, even if the 'grey figure' of police non-recording could be minimized, because many offences are not reported by victims (as charted by the BCS and other victimization surveys). But the truly 'dark' and unknowable figure is the extent of crime without individual victims who are aware. This is both conceptually and pragmatically a difficult area to estimate. The claim that crimes occur which have not been formally judged as such by an official recording process is contingent and probabilistic. It is an assertion that certain behaviour *would* have been recorded as a crime had it come to the attention of the relevant authorities. This relies upon presuppositions that are dubious, so the 'true' extent of crime is a metaphysical conundrum known, if at all, only by Mephistopheles. In addition to this theoretical issue, there is no way of calculating the extent of crime that may occur without the knowledge of victims or authorities. But, as it includes much corporate, financial and state crime, it is likely to massively outstrip in extent and seriousness either victim-survey or police-recorded statistics.

Technical recording problems

In addition to the 'dark figure' of crimes not reported to or recorded by the police, there are many technical issues that affect the validity and reliability of crime statistics and which must be borne in mind when interpreting them (Maguire 2007). Many questions are involved in moving from allegations and incidents to numbers recording them, and different decisions, whether made in good faith or bad, will produce very different counts of crime. The key questions concern the range of offences eligible for the statistics and the way that incidents are translated into numbers.

The coverage of recorded statistics

The 'notifiable offences' that police are required to record mainly consist of 'indictable' offences, i.e. those that must or may be tried in a Crown court. It thus includes most of what would generally be regarded as the more serious crimes, but excludes summary offences, triable by magistrates. No official records are kept of the number of these, only of those convicted or formally cautioned. This amounts to well over a million cases per annum. From time to time, most recently in 1998 when common assault and assault on a police constable were added, changes are made by the Home Office in the range of 'notifiable offences'. However strong the case for this in terms of seeking to take account of changing conceptions of seriousness, it necessarily introduces problems of comparison before and after the alteration.

In the United Kingdom, the Home Office tally of 'crimes known to the police' excludes offences that are recorded by other public police forces, such as the British Transport Police, the Ministry of Defence Police, the Royal Military Police and the UK Atomic Energy Constabulary Police. Other enforcement agencies, for example HM Revenue and Customs or the Health and Safety Inspectorate, investigate and sometimes prosecute offences, but they primarily work through administrative procedures. Their cases will enter the Home Office criminal statistics only in the rare event that the police are involved and define an occurrence as a criminal violation.

How many and which offences to count?

Another important set of technical issues arises in the translation of incidents into numbers. There are two main problems here: how many crimes should be counted in particular situations; and which offences should they be classified under? If an offender attacks a series of targets in a short time (say, s/he lets down the tyres of every car on a street), is that one offence or as many as the number of objects damaged? In many situations, there is also ambiguity about what offence has occurred. For example, the scene of an alleged attempted burglary may contain no physical evidence at all, or only of criminal damage (a broken window or scratch marks around a lock). Should the recording be guided by the possibly lurid perceptions of the anxious householder, or only by what the physical signs suggest? At a much more serious level, how many crimes were committed on 11 September 2001 or 7 July 2005?

There are no categorically right or wrong answers to any of these questions. The HOCR and the NCRS seek consistency in the way that crimes are quantified, and they mandate a more victim-oriented approach. Each victim counts as a separate crime, and the victim's version should be accepted in the absence of contrary evidence.

Nonetheless, there remains much scope for defining crime up or down, according to what is most credible to, and convenient for, the police. However desirable in themselves, moreover, such reforms always introduce problems of comparison before and after the change. The published statistics therefore carry appropriate health warnings.

Dimensions of the 'dark figure'

To get some sense of the extent to which recorded crime figures are incomplete it is salutary, if somewhat shocking, to consider the depiction of what the Home Office calls the 'attrition rate', the disappearance of cases at different stages of the criminal justice process. Figure 5.1 below shows the attrition rate for 1998, as published by the Home Office (it has not been revised since, but earlier versions during the 1990s showed a similar pattern). The figure presents a baseline that is described as 'offences committed'. This is taken from the BCS total of crimes reported by victims in its sample and is at best only an estimate of those crimes with individual-aware victims. Completely absent from this

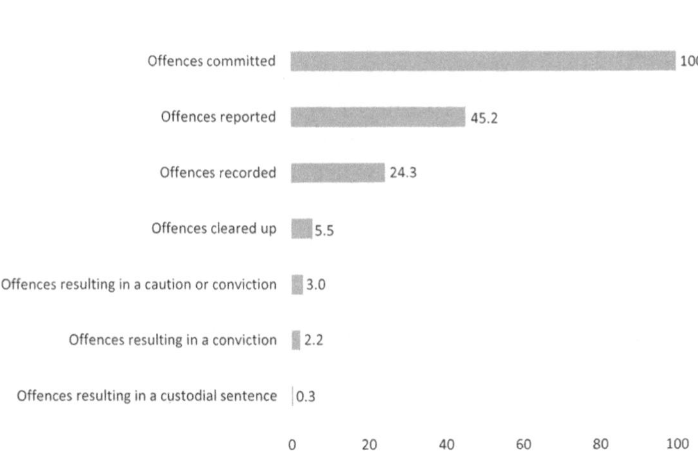

Figure 5.1 Attrition in the criminal justice system
Source: Barclay and Tavares 1999: 29.

baseline of '100 per cent' of 'offences committed' is the truly 'dark figure' of crimes without individual victims who could – at least in principle – report the incident in a survey. This *dark* 'dark figure' encompasses offences that could involve very serious harm to persons or property, but which are not uncovered by the police or other enforcement agencies. They include vice offences, most major frauds, financial crimes, smuggling, tax evasion, breaches of safety standards that could lead to death or serious injury and many other examples.

Given that they exclude all offences not reported in the BCS, the attrition rates shown in Figure 5.1 understate the real dimensions of non-recorded crime and of the failure of the criminal justice system to deal with offences. Even with that qualification, fewer than half of BCS-recorded offences are reported to the police by victims. Less than a quarter of BCS-calculated victimizations are recorded by the police (although this 'grey figure' has diminished somewhat since the post-1998 reforms of counting procedures). Only 5.5 per cent are 'cleared up' by them (i.e. cases where the police have some reason to believe they know the identity of the perpetrator but do not charge them). Only 3 per cent of

BCS-known offences end with a formal identification of guilt (a caution or a conviction), and only 2.2 per cent in a conviction. Just 0.3 per cent result in a custodial sentence. Thus the officially recorded figures for levels of crime, and for identified offenders, relate to only a very small proportion of all crimes known about and, a fortiori, of crimes committed.

Recorded crime statistics are not just incomplete but biased. Some crimes, some criminals, are much more likely to appear than others. This has been demonstrated by a plethora of studies showing the influence of class, gender, ethnicity, age and other dimensions of social inequality on victims and suspects at all stages of the criminal justice process. A clear example is provided by Table 5.1, which compares the characteristics of people in prison with those of the general population.

Table 5.1 shows that people in the prison population are a highly skewed sample of the overall population. It is based on 1991 figures, the last time a national survey of the prison population detailing these socio-economic data was published. More recent Ministry of Justice figures, based on a survey of newly sentenced prisoners, confirm the general pattern (Hopkins 2012): 91% were male; 15% black or other ethnic minority; 69% were unemployed at the time of arrest (although 20% had been employed at some point in the year before that); 49% of

Table 5.1 Prison and general population compared

	Prison population (%)	General population (%)
Under 25	40	16
Male	96	49
Ethnic minority	16	5
Semi-skilled/unskilled occupation	41	18
Unemployed	33	8.7
No permanent home	13	0.3
Left school before 16	40	11
Frequent truancy	30	3
Lived with both parents until 16	62	83
Taken into care before 16	26	2

Sources: Walmsley, Howard and White 1992; *Social Trends* 1993.

those who had been employed worked in 'routine or semi-routine' occupations, and only 5% in managerial/professional, compared with 22% and 34% in the general population; 64% had received benefits in the year prior to incarceration, compared with 14% in the general population (ibid.: 5–10). The pattern was similar to that found in a Social Exclusion Unit survey of ex-prisoners (SEU 2002) and in a recent report in the House of Commons Library (Berman 2012).

The prison population remains overwhelmingly male, and ethnic minorities are considerably over-represented.[2] Prisoners are drawn predominantly from the most marginal economic groups in the population: most prior to incarceration were either unemployed or employed at the lowest occupational levels. Many were homeless when arrested. They have extremely poor educational backgrounds and histories of family disruption.

The incompleteness and bias of official crime statistics mean that apparent trends and patterns may be quite misleading, with devastating consequences for the assessment of crime trends and for constructing explanations of the sources of criminality from study of the prison population (as so many theories, past and present, have done). Changes in recorded crime levels or patterns may be the product of fluctuations in the balance of the 'dark figure' of unrecorded offences relative to the rest, rather than changes in offending. Until relatively recently, these problems could be identified, but no light could be shed on their possible dimensions. However, in the last four decades research instruments have developed that cast some light on the 'dark figure' of crimes not recorded by the police.

Alternatives to the police statistics

Growing awareness of the limitations and biases of police-recorded crime statistics has prompted the development of a variety of alternative measures since the 1960s. Victimization surveys (like the BCS) are by far the most significant because they have been supported on a large scale in several countries, offering an alternative measure of trends over time. They also provide insights into reporting and recording processes that enable better understanding of the police statistics themselves. Other measures, such as self-report studies, can be used to assess the relationship between the characteristics of offending that they reveal and the pattern of crimes and offending shown in police and criminal justice statistics. However, they are not usually constructed so as to assess overall trends through time, an exception being the self-reported drug use questions used by the BCS in recent years. Another interesting measure that has been developed recently is the use of data from hospital accident and emergency departments to assess trends and patterns of injuries sustained as a result of violence (Shepherd 1990; Sivarajasingam et al. 2012). This offers a useful alternative source of data capable of mapping trends in interpersonal violence.

The advent of the BCS in particular has led many commentators to think of it as something like a 'true' measure of crime. It is commonly referred to as 'authoritative' or 'reliable', in contrast to police statistics with all their pitfalls. But *all* measures of crime have limitations that are inevitably associated with their particular protocols and techniques of construction, even if they are conducted with impeccable methodological rigour. It is only with a reflexive awareness of these limitations that interpretations can be made with any degree of safety.

The proliferation of alternative measures is, nonetheless, a boon to the understanding of crime trends and patterns. When the different measures point in the same direction (as they did in the 1980s and early 1990s and have again since the mid-2000s), we can be much more confident that this corresponds to what is happening to offending and victimization. Even when they diverge (as for much of the 1990s and early 2000s) it is possible to understand some of the reasons for this and to make appropriate allowances in interpreting each series of statistics.

Crime surveys

Victim surveys began during the 1960s in the United States with three exploratory studies for the 1967 Presidential

Commission on Law Enforcement. In 1972, a programme of annual national surveys (now the National Crime Victimization Survey [NCVS]) was instituted by the US Department of Justice. In Britain, limited surveys of victimization began in the 1970s. The General Household Survey (GHS) included a question about domestic burglary during 1972–1982. A pioneering survey in London was instrumental in the development of the methodology of later studies (Sparks, Genn and Dodd 1977).

As alluded to earlier, despite its regular appellation as 'authoritative', the BCS (and all other crime surveys) has many limitations, even if conducted with faultless methodological rigour. These are succinctly identified at the very outset of the report of the first BCS (Hough and Mayhew 1983: 3–4). First, there are the thorny conceptual issues about how to define crime – and whose definition should prevail in a conflict. A victimization survey will necessarily be limited to what can be gleaned from a putative victim's perspective. For example, what the interviewed 'victim' may see as an assault may be regarded by the supposed aggressor as self-defence or a playful push – and it is entirely possible that the latter's perspective would prevail if the matter came to the attention of the criminal justice system.

Secondly, victim surveys by definition can only measure crimes with crime-aware individual victims. Entirely beyond their ambit are whole swathes of offences, for example: crimes against business and other institutions; public order offences; successful frauds against unknowing victims; smuggling and tax evasion; offences with willing participants such as drug taking or trafficking; and most 'vice' offences. Murder, generally seen as the most serious crime of all, cannot be included in a victim survey (for obvious reasons). These are not small exceptions. Each year, the police record well over a quarter of a million thefts from shops, just under half a million burglaries other than from dwellings, and more than a hundred thousand drug offences. None of these are within the scope of the regular surveys – but they are just a fraction of what is likely to be a huge 'dark figure' of unrecorded crime.

Thirdly, as with all other surveys, there are sampling issues. The BCS began with interviews of a random sample of 11,000 households in England and Wales, and 5,000 in Scotland. (There has been a separate Scottish Crime Survey since the late 1980s.) It expanded over the years to more than 46,000 interviews in England and Wales in 2012, when the ONS announced a reduction to its current size of 35,000 and a name change to the Crime Survey for England and Wales to reflect its actual geographic coverage. Certain groups are not included in the population sampled. The BCS was originally a survey of adults, so did not measure the victimization of children under 16, but since 2006 there have been surveys of victimization in the 10–15 age group (current sample size 3,000), despite the formidable methodological issues (CSEW 2014: 103–9).

Since it is a household survey, it does not cover crimes against the homeless (Newburn and Rock 2005). The initial sampling frame used was the electoral register (Hough and Mayhew 1983: 4), but this became increasingly problematic as non-registration mounted during the 1980s, leading to a switch to the Postcode Address File. The response rate has been about 75 per cent – very respectably high by most survey standards but still allowing the possibility that non-respondents may have different experiences from respondents.

As with all surveys, the accuracy of results is only as good as the honesty and memory of respondents, despite the care taken with the construction and administration of questions and interviews. These issues are most acute with regard to the gravest interpersonal offences, especially violent and sex crimes, where willingness to confide in a strange visitor from the Home Office is likely to be problematic, although improvements in methodology, such as the use of computer-assisted self-completion techniques for such questions (to ensure respondent confidentiality), have been introduced over time.

The BCS/CSEW is a valuable additional source of data but not a definitive calculation of crime rates. We must always bear in mind the issues of whether changes in the police-recorded figures are likely to be due to changes in victim reporting or local police-recording practices, or Home Office and police policies. But trends in the BCS/CSEW may sometimes be due to changing sample coverage or other methodological problems. There can never be certainty about any of this, but triangulation of different data sources allows more informed attempts at interpretation. In the next section, I will try and describe recent trends and patterns in crime, interpreting the statistics with due caution in the light of the many problems discussed above.

Trends in crime

The most apparent trends in crime since the Second World War are: the spectacular overall rise in recorded offences from the late 1950s until the mid-1990s; and the sustained downturn since the mid-1990s, returning to the levels of the early 1980s when the BCS was launched. In the early 1950s, the police recorded less than half a million offences per annum. By the mid-1970s, this had risen to 2 million. The 1980s showed even more staggering rises, with recorded crime peaking in 1992 at over 5.5 million; but by 1997 recorded crime figures had fallen back to 4.5 million. The major counting rule changes introduced in 1998 and 2002 make comparison of the subsequent figures especially fraught but, on the new rules (which undoubtedly exaggerated the increase), just below 6 million offences were recorded by the police for 2003–4. This has now fallen back again to 3.7 million in 2013–14 (ONS 2015a: 15–17).

Contrasting the police-recorded statistics with victim surveys suggests a more complex picture. Figure 5.2 pinpoints Thatcherite neo-liberalism as the accelerant behind a crime explosion in the 1980s and early 1990s, with a sustained decline since 1995 (apart from a brief period of increasing police-recorded crime from 1998 to 2004, due to counting rule changes). Three distinct phases can be distinguished since the mid-1950s.

1955–83: recorded crime rise

Until the 1970s, there was no measurement of trends apart from police statistics, which began to chart a virtually continuous rise after the mid-1950s. In the absence of any other measures, it is impossible to know how much of this was

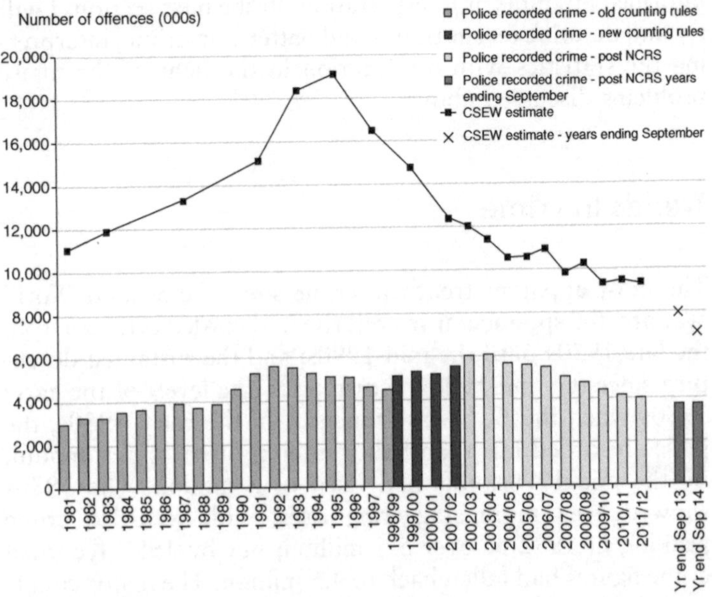

Figure 5.2 Trends in police-recorded crime and CSEW, 1981 to year ending September 2014.
Source: ONS 2015a: 6

really due to more offending and how much might have resulted from greater reporting or recording. But during the 1970s the General Household Survey began to ask about burglary victimization, and its data showed that most of the increase in recorded burglary was due to greater reporting by victims. In the 1970s, recorded burglaries doubled, but victimization increased by only 20 per cent. Victims reported more burglaries mainly because of the spread of household contents insurance, and it is plausible to infer that this applied to property crimes more generally. So the rise of crime in the heyday of the mixed-economy, welfarist consensus was probably substantially less than the recorded statistics suggested – although, no doubt, the first stirrings of consumerism in the 'live now, pay later' era stimulated acquisitiveness and crime. As the growth of consumer credit urged people to 'take the waiting out of wanting' (the advertising slogan for Access credit cards when they were launched), those without legitimate cards were tempted to find illicit routes to the must-have glittering prizes.

1983–1992: crime explosion

The British Crime Survey, which was first published in the United Kingdom in 1982, showed huge increases in offending in its first decade, roughly in line with the police statistics. BCS crime rose 77 per cent from 1981 to 1993, whilst police-recorded crime increased by 111 per cent. On both measures, crime rose at an explosive rate during the Thatcher and early Major years. The one clearly booming industry during the decade and a half in which neo-liberalism destroyed Britain's industrial base was crime.

1993–present : ambiguously falling crime

In the early 1990s, the trends indicated by the police statistics and the BCS diverged for a decade. The BCS continued to chart a rise until 1995, but the police data fell from 1992 to 1997. Paradoxically, this was because of the extraordinarily high levels of victimization. The police recorded fewer crimes because insurance companies made claiming more onerous, thus discouraging reporting by victims. At the same time, more 'businesslike' managerial accountability for policing implicitly introduced incentives against recording. The Conservatives were certainly tough on the causes of crime *recording*.

After New Labour came to power in 1997, the two measures continued to diverge – but in the opposite direction. Survey-recorded crime has fallen rapidly since 1995 and, by 2007–8, was below the level of the first BCS, conducted in 1981. The decline has continued up to the latest figures released in October 2015, when the CSEW included cyber offences for the first time, and the overall level doubled, although the total, counting only offences that had previously been included in the survey, continued to fall (Travis 2015a). The police-recorded statistics, however, rose from 1998 up to 2004, since when they have declined again. The temporary rise in the police-recorded rate was due overwhelmingly to the two major revisions between 1998 and 2002 in police procedures for counting crimes discussed earlier and was a predicted consequence of the changes.

The BCS/CSEW is free from the particular problems that make police figures unreliable as a measure of trends. However, it is not a definitive index, as we saw earlier. The dramatic overall fall in the BCS masked increases in some of the most alarming offences. Murder and other crimes of violence have increased since the 1970s (although overall violence has declined since the late 1990s, as has murder since 2004) and are a higher proportion of all crimes than they used to be (Figure 5.3). Annual recorded homicides have roughly doubled since the early 1960s when there were around 300 per annum, although the trend has been downwards in the last few years, following a peak of 904 in 2003–4. The years 2013–14 showed the lowest recorded homicide figure since 1978 (525), but this has since increased again (to 569; Travis 2015a). In 1976, just 5 per cent of recorded offences were classified as violent but by 2014 this had increased to more than 20 per cent.

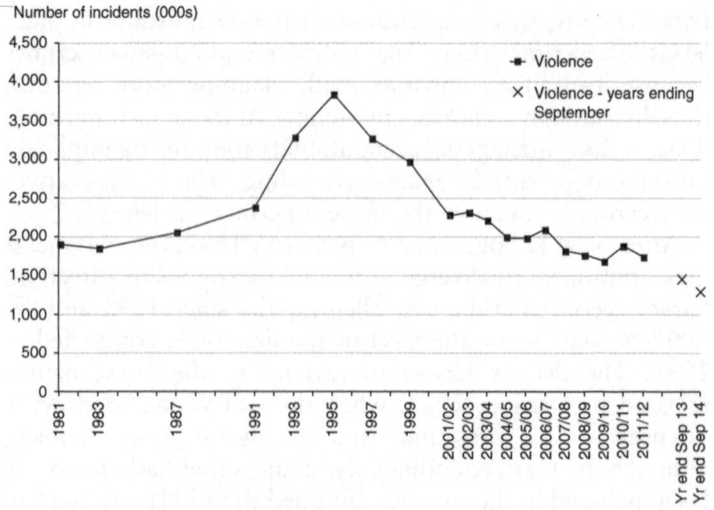

Figure 5.3 Trends in CSEW violence, 1981 to year ending September 2014.
Source: ONS 2015b: 20.

Conclusion

This chapter has analysed the conception of crime trends and patterns conveyed by the official statistics. There are well-known problems with all the major sources of crime measurement. Nonetheless, the two main data sources, the police-recorded data and the BCS/CSEW victimization surveys concur in broad outline. Both suggest a major crime explosion during the 1980s and early 1990s, followed by a drop since then.

Both series are based on crimes reported by victims to the police. The CSEW is purely an analysis of victim-perceived crime, whilst the main source of the police data is victim reports. Legally defined crimes without individual aware victims (and a fortiori social harms that are not criminalized or only ambiguously so) are a 'dark figure' that is impossible to count, but which massively outweighs any official measurements. The officially sanctioned picture of offenders represents a minuscule part of the (unknown and unknowable) total, as demonstrated by the attrition figures showing that only 2 per cent of the BCS/CSEW-recorded crimes (which are only those crimes with aware victims) result in a conviction. The characteristics of this 2 per cent of criminal justice lottery losers are well summed up by Jeffrey Reiman and Paul Leighton (2012): *The Rich Get Richer and the Poor Get Prison*. The criminal justice process is essentially an apparatus for processing some offences committed predominantly by the poorest and most powerless sections of society, mainly against victims who are also deprived and powerless. Even if every conviction was in itself just (and there are of course many miscarriages of justice), the system is a mechanism reproducing and reinforcing massive social injustice. In the next chapter, I will examine the picture of crime conveyed by the mass media and by the political process. This follows the same distorted pattern as the official statistics but to an accentuated degree, focusing only on the worst of the worst cases of the criminal justice process.

6 Media, Crime and the Politics of Law and Order

The last chapter demonstrated how the criminal justice process, and the official statistics it generates, construct an image of crime and criminals that is dominated by the predatory street crimes of the poor and powerless. The suffering inflicted by such crimes, on victims, perpetrators and society at large, cannot be denied. Nonetheless the criminal justice system's conception of crime as emanating from society's lower depths diverts fear and anger away from the even greater wrongdoing and harms of the powerful. The mass-media representation of crime and criminal justice, and the public discourse and politics of law and order that are (mis) informed by it, twist these distortions and projections even further.

Concerns about popular culture representations of crime and criminal justice have very long histories, dating back to the eighteenth-century emergence of newspapers (Rowbotham, Stevenson and Pegg 2013). Do the media undermine authority and order, a perennial conservative lament? Or do they exaggerate the risks of crime, fanning fear and encouraging authoritarian solutions, as many liberals and radicals have complained? Such competing anxieties have stimulated not only endless argument but also substantial social science research industries.

This chapter shows that there have been fundamental transformations in media discourse about crime over the last half-century, corresponding to wider changes in political economy, social structure and culture. These developments have reinforced the distortions of earlier mass media, and fanned the flames of public fear about crime, bolstering the rise of the politics of law and order.

The media crime debate

There is a long history of anxiety about criminogenic consequences of the mass media. It is pivotal to the ubiquitous 'respectable fears' about supposedly declining moral standards that Geoffrey Pearson has traced back over the last few centuries (Pearson 1983). We can dub this the 'desubordination' thesis: the claim that the media represent crime in ways that undermine authority and encourage deviance. There is also an opposing liberal/radical concern that the media distort the threat of crime, fomenting fear and stimulating public support for authoritarianism. This can be called the 'discipline' thesis.

A more complex synthesis proposes that the media are an arena of contestation between different interests, pressures and perspectives. This approach has been called 'liberal pluralism' (Greer 2003), and is suggested by empirical research on media 'effects' and on production processes, which portray a messy world of conflicting influences (Greer and Reiner 2012). The 'discipline' and 'desubordination' theses are not necessarily mutually exclusive. Rising crime and rising fear may both be in part products of media representations which feed off each other in a malign interactive loop.

The content of media representations

'Content analysis' usually refers to statistical studies within a positivist paradigm that – in the words of one practitioner – provide an 'objective and quantitative estimate of certain message attributes' (Dominick 1978: 106). There are many problems with this claim, however. The categories for counting reflect the researcher's theoretical conceptions of significance, not intrinsic characteristics of an objective structure of meaning in the media texts themselves. Items deemed identical by the analyst may have very different meanings for different audiences. Because of these problems, analyses of content must be interpreted reflexively and cautiously. Nonetheless, it is noteworthy that the many studies of the content of mass-media representations of crime and criminal justice, whether purportedly 'factual' (news and documentaries) or 'fictional', conducted at different places and times, tend to concur on certain fundamental themes (Greer and Reiner 2012).

I will call this broad convergence of the results of content analyses the 'established pattern'. A key feature of this is the perennial prominence of crime stories. News and fiction crime stories have been staples of all mass media from their birth, although there are some variations, according to medium, market and historical period, as well as cross-culturally.

The depiction of crime in most media, and at different times and places, follows what an American criminologist has aptly called the 'law of opposites' (Surette 2014). The media-portrayed pattern of crime and criminal justice is in many respects the reverse of that constructed by official statistics. Crime stories are characterized by these features:

- there is an overwhelming overemphasis on serious violent crime against individuals;
- the risks of crime are exaggerated quantitatively and qualitatively, though property crime is relatively downplayed;
- there is over-representation of older, higher-status victims and offenders;
- there is a generally positive image of the effectiveness and integrity of policing and criminal justice (e.g. most cases are cleared up), and there is little focus on corruption or abuse;
- most stories are about individual cases, not trends, analysis or policy.

Consequences of media representations

There is a huge volume of research seeking to measure the 'effects' of media representations of crime (Greer and Reiner

2012: 256–62). The dominant concern has been with testing consequences of media representations of crime for offending and violence. More recently, there has also been considerable work on the impact of the media on fear of crime (Farrall and Lee 2008; Farrall, Jackson and Gray 2009).

The bulk of research on media effects has been conducted within a positivist paradigm. The typical approach has used social psychological laboratory research: an experimental and a control group are exposed to some media content and are measured before and after to ascertain the 'effects'. This vast body of research has yielded little in return for the enormous expenditure and effort involved. An early research review remains an apposite summary of the rather unsurprising results: 'for *some* children, under *some* conditions, *some* television is harmful. For other children under the same conditions, or for the same children under *other* conditions, it may be beneficial. For *most* children, under *most* conditions, *most* television is probably neither particularly harmful nor particularly beneficial' (Schramm, Lyle and Parker 1961).

This is not to say that the media have few or no consequences for crime. The media figure in most theoretical accounts of crime as part of the causal process resulting in offending (Greer and Reiner 2012: 256–8), and 'field' studies of the introduction of new media in practice do suggest effects on crime rates (e.g. Hennigan et al. 1982, an econometric study of the spread of television in the United States in the early 1950s).

Nonetheless, the measurable *direct* effects of media on crime are small. This is because the predominant social psychological research paradigm is geared to testing a most implausible hypothesis: that media representations have universal and immediate identifiable impacts. A more plausible approach is that the media are an important dimension of cultural formation, but work interdependently with other social processes, differently for different sections of audiences and gradually over time. Thus we should 'not ask how the media make us act or think, but rather how the media contribute to making us who we are' (Livingstone 1996: 31–2). This model is hard to test, of course, and certainly cannot be the subject of laboratory experiments!

The media's exaggeration of the threat of serious violent and sexual crime has often been seen as leading to unrealistic, disproportionate, 'irrational' fear of crime (Gerbner 1995). As with research on the criminogenic effects of the media, studies of the relationship between media and fear of crime are equivocal about the strength, direction or even the existence of a causal relationship between media consumption and anxiety (Sparks 1992; Chadee and Ditton 2005).

Nonetheless, media representations are important in framing public discourse about crime and have played a crucial part in the rise of the 'politics of law and order' (Hough and Roberts 2012). They are the principal source of information about crime and criminal justice for most people, who have little or no direct experience of either, as illustrated by Table 6.1.

A more recent Ipsos MORI poll showed similar results. 'When we asked the public why they think there is more crime now than two years ago, more than half (57%) state that it is because of what they see on television and almost half (48%) say it is because of what they read in newspapers' (Duffy et al. 2008: 5). Another 15% said they based their views on the radio and 3% cited the internet. Altogether, it seems clear that most people consciously base their perceptions of crime and criminal justice issues on the media.

The media-frame debate about law and order, in conjunction with politicians' campaigning and broader shifts in culture, social structure and political economy (Silverman 2011; Dean 2012: ch. 3). It has been shown that fluctuations in public concern *follow* media and political campaigns (Beckett 1997) and are not clearly related to statistical crime trends. Fear of crime and anxiety about law and order have

Table 6.1 Sources of information about the police (%)

Newspapers	80
TV news, documentaries	80
Word of mouth	43
Media fiction	29
Direct experience	20
Other	12

Source: Data taken from Fitzgerald et al. 2002: 78.

remained strong, despite two decades of falling crime statistics, although there is some evidence of slightly declining concern since a peak in 2007–8 (Ipsos MORI 2010). The media played a central role in the politicization of law and order by Richard Nixon in the 1968 US presidential election and by Margaret Thatcher in Britain in the 1970s.

Causes of media representation

The pattern of media representation of crime is partly a direct reflection of the ideologies of media owners, producers or reporters. Most media organizations are large corporations, and their owners predominantly conservative (Conservative?). Specialist crime reporters in the past tended to be self-consciously police groupies (Chibnall 1977), working closely with detectives, but this is less true of the later breed of home affairs, legal or crime correspondents, who often have an explicitly civil libertarian or human rights perspective (Schlesinger and Tumber 1994). The old-fashioned crime reporters also had a 'watchdog' ethic, and were keen to hound out wrongdoing (they would certainly be alert to the news interest of stories of police or other official corruption). Both types of specialist crime correspondent have largely been displaced, as economic pressures on newspapers have mounted, and in their place crime stories are processed by all-purpose journalists, who are reliant on press releases and information packs helpfully provided by the burgeoning public relations departments of the police and other agencies (Mawby 2010). 'Churnalism' increasingly threatens to supplant journalism (Davies 2008), reproducing ever more faithfully their masters' voices.

Much research on the work of reporters has emphasized the importance of the professional sense of 'newsworthiness', the values that are seen as ingredients of a good story. As classically formulated by Chibnall, these are: 'dramatization, personalization, titillation, novelty' (Chibnall 1977, Jewkes 2004 and Mawby 2010 offer updated expansions of this list). The most important change is the accentuation of the entertainment values underpinning Chibnall's analysis, the increasing sway of celebrity angles, reflecting the greater commercial pressures under which news organizations now toil. The first four letters of 'infotainment' are squeezed out, as news becomes assimilated into celebrity culture. Fictional entertainment crime stories have always offered the narrative virtues of clarity and closure, as well as the thrills of vicarious danger and 'edgework', making them popular as fictional entertainment. The dividing line between overtly fictional crime stories and the presentation of crime news has become increasingly blurred, as both are governed by intensifying commercial pressures (Colbran 2014).

The underlying structural exigencies of news production are a fundamental source shaping the representation of crime and criminal justice. The police and courts are reliable story suppliers, increasingly proactive in supplying journalists' needs for ready-made news. Safety and other constraints lead to journalists becoming 'embedded' with the police when reporting on riots and other unpredictably dangerous events. The ever tighter economic pressures governing news resources constrain reporters to rely on pre-packaged sources such as PR departments in the police and other agencies. The police in particular have thus long been the 'primary definers' of crime news.

At the same time, there is a built-in tension in relations between police and press, which are perpetually threatened by the lure of highly newsworthy stories about police wrongdoing. The likelihood of such stories of police and official malpractice reaching public attention has been heightened by the growth of citizen journalism and the internet in the last three decades, which circumvent the cosy professional journalist–police nexus (Greer and McLaughlin 2010, 2011a, 2011b).

The same commercial pressures that make mainstream news increasingly reliant on police sources also affect fiction production. A pioneering study of the processes of production of TV crime and police series shows that intensifying competitive pressures lead to storylines embodying the narrative values identified by Chibnall's analysis of news: dramatization, personalization, titillation, novelty. The result is an intensification of what was described earlier as the 'established' pattern of crime stories: an exaggeration simultaneously of the threat of crime and of the capacity of tough criminal justice to contain it, bolstering the politics of law and order.

Changing content since 1945

Has the 'established' pattern changed over time and, if so, how? A historical content analysis of cinema crime films and news stories about crime (Allen, Livingstone and Reiner 1998; Reiner, Livingstone and Allen 2000, 2001, 2003) suggests it has been intensified since the mid-twentieth century. The studies analysed a random sample of crime films released in Britain between 1945 and 1991 that featured in lists of annual box-office hits and home news stories in *The Times* and *The Mirror*. This showed that the 'established' pattern was evident throughout the period, but with an intensification of the 'law of opposites' (Surette 2014): the focus on serious violent crime grew stronger. The criminal justice system became more controversial, however, with more negative representations of the integrity and effectiveness of the police in particular (the police are overwhelmingly the most commonly depicted part of criminal justice).

The prominence of crime in news and fiction stories was accentuated throughout the period since the Second World War. There was no clear trend in the proportion of films that were primarily crime stories (Allen et al. 1998). There were fluctuations from year to year, but generally about 20% of films released could be classified as crime movies. There was, however, an increase in the prominence of crime news after the mid-1960s. Until then the overall percentage of home news stories that were primarily about crime averaged about 10% in both *The Times* and *The Mirror*. Since the late 1960s, this has doubled to around 20%. The proportion of stories about the criminal justice system also increased after the late 1960s in both papers (from around 3% to 8%), corresponding to the politicization of law and order in that period (Reiner 2007: ch. 5).

The principal crimes that were the focus of the newspaper stories in the sample were documented (Reiner et al. 2003: 18–19). In both *The Times* and *The Mirror*, homicide and violent crime constituted the largest category by far in all periods, but to a slightly increasing extent. Drug-related and sex crimes also featured increasingly in news stories. The reporting of 'volume' property crimes in which there is no element of violence (by far the most common in all official statistics) diminished considerably.

This was also true of feature films (Allen et al. 1998). The majority of films featured homicide or sex crimes as the principal offence animating the plot. Property crimes have almost disappeared as the central focus of film narratives. The degree of violence depicted also intensified considerably, with considerable focus on the pain and suffering of victims.

News and fictional stories also highlight an increasing number of crimes in addition to the central one animating the narrative. Some of these are 'consequential' offences: other crimes committed as a result of the primary one (for example, to cover it up). Others are 'contextual': crimes that have no relationship to the primary one but still appear in the story (for example, the robbery in progress encountered by Clint Eastwood as Dirty Harry when he goes for a hamburger). These 'contextual' crimes signify a world permeated by a threat of crime. An increasing proportion of both fiction and news stories feature such secondary offences (Reiner et al. 2003: 17), depicting crime as a pervasive threat rather than a one-off incident.

The data also show that the media represent the police as less reliable and successful in clearing up crime and protecting victims. An increasing proportion of news and fiction stories question the integrity and the effectiveness of policing (Allen et al. 1998; Reiner et al. 2003: 22–4). In news stories, the police are overwhelmingly the most common part of the criminal justice system to be represented at all. There is a marked tendency for the police to become the central protagonists of fictional films, displacing other types of hero figure that were more prominent.

Quantitative content analysis thus shows a clear trend in the last half-century for crime to be increasingly represented as a fearful and common threat. The police, the primary symbols of crime control, are seen more negatively, in terms of both their effectiveness in providing security and their integrity and adherence to the rule of law – although they are still portrayed predominantly in a favourable light.

Qualitative analysis of news and cinema crime stories suggests even more fundamental shifts in popular media discourse about crime and justice.

The changing discourse of crime stories

The quantitative changes indicate a deeper qualitative transformation in public discourse about crime. Crime news is almost by definition bad news: it reports the occurrence of officially proscribed activity. From the late 1960s, however, crime has been presented as increasingly threatening and out of control – as symptomatic of wider social crisis, and ever more serious and pervasive in its impact on ordinary people with whom the audience is invited to identify.

Three principal themes can be discerned in this new law-and-order discourse.

Accentuate the negative

News stories increasingly represent developments in a negative way, emphasizing crime as an ever more menacing problem. One striking British example is a pair of stories reporting essentially similar changes in the official crime statistics. Both are from *The Daily Mirror*, the first on 2 May 1961, the second on 26 August 1977. The 1961 story was the first report of the annual crime statistics that we found in our sample (Allen, Livingstone and Reiner 1998). It was headlined 'Fewer sex crimes', and it reported that there had been a 'slight' fall in the recorded number of sex crimes since 1959. This was contrasted with a rise of 10 per cent in indictable offences known to the police, including a 14 per cent increase in violence. What is remarkable in retrospect is the emphasis on the *good* news, the 'slight' drop in sex offences, highlighted in the headline and the first paragraph, but the downplaying of the fairly large rise in violent and other offences. The story is written entirely without any emotional or evaluative expressions, as a straightforward report of new data.

This is in stark contrast to a report in 1977, headlined 'Crime soars to new peak'. It is a story from a period in which law and order was beginning to be politicized, emerging as a leading issue with which the Conservatives under Margaret Thatcher were attacking the Labour government (Downes and Morgan 2012). What is really striking is that the changes in the crime figures reported are mainly smaller than the 1959 ones. This time, however, every bit of bad news is stressed. The overall rise in recorded crime was 1% (by contrast with the 10% of 1959). 'The grim Home Office figures show' a 10% rise in violent crime, a 24% increase in firearms offences, a 9% rise in homicide and a 15% increase in muggings (mainly because of a 24% increase in London – the rest of England and Wales reported an 11% decline). Tucked away at the end, the story reports that 'there were 1,500 fewer sexual offences' recorded.

In short, the statistical changes reported are very similar. But whereas in 1961 the emphasis was on the good news, and the writing style restrained and descriptive, the 1977 story spotlights the bad news in a tone of panic. The contrast illustrates a number of basic trends in the reporting of crime news. Above all, it indicates the construction of crime as a major problem posing an increasing threat, in both extent and seriousness. It shows the news expressing and reinforcing the emergence of law and order as a public concern and a political issue. 'Bad news' and sensationalism have become core news values.

Victim culture: crime as a zero-sum game

Both news and fiction crime stories have become increasingly centred on the victim as the focus of the narrative. There has been a profound change in the characterization of victims and their role within crime stories. Increasingly, the harm done by crime is equated with the suffering and distress of individual victims. A potential threat to readers is implied by inviting identification with the victims through portrayals of their ordinariness, innocence and vulnerability. Whereas in the earlier part of the period studied there was also often a measure of concern for offenders, both to understand and if possible to rehabilitate them, increasingly the victim–perpetrator relationship is constructed as zero-sum: compassion for the offender is represented as callous and unjust to victims.

Two contrasting news stories illustrate this change, both involving violence against a child. On 27 February 1945, *The Daily Mirror* front page prominently featured a photo of a two-year-old girl, looking sad and in pain, headlined 'Another cruelty victim'. Even in a murky photocopy, even after more than half a century, the child's pitiful, anguished face cries out for comfort. The story is the main home news of the day. One paragraph details the poor girl's injuries: black eye, bruises, '[r]ed weal marks extended over her temple and across her cheeks.' Beyond this clinical detail, there is no attempt to spell out the trauma and suffering of the victim, or the evil of the assault. Approximately two-thirds of the story focuses on the offender, a 26-year-old Birkenhead man who lived with the girl's mother, who was sentenced to six months with hard labour. The last part of the story concentrates on his account of his own actions. He claimed that 'the child's crying got on his nerves and that he "couldn't help himself".' This was explained by the fact that 'he had been torpedoed three times and that his nerves were very bad.' What is noteworthy is the absence of demonization of the perpetrator. The story's interest in understanding from *his* point of view how he could have carried out such an act is also evident. Attempting to understand the offender is not seen as incompatible with the greatest concern for the victim, and condemnation of the act is taken for granted.

This can be contrasted with the way *The Times* reported a child-murder case on 25 November 1989. This is of course a much more serious offence: murder rather than assault. Nonetheless, the presentation of the story suggests a fundamental transformation in discourse about serious crime since 1945. The story is the lead story on the main home-news page. A banner headline reads: 'Martial arts fanatic gets life for killing daughter aged five' and a smaller headline above it tells us that the '[g]irl died from a combination of pain, shock and exhaustion after vengeful beating'. A sub-headline says that 'Social workers held many case conferences but she slipped through the safety net'. Three pictures illustrate the story: a large one of the unfortunate victim, happy and smiling; her mother weeping; and her father, the killer, looking dishevelled and menacing. The most immediately noticeable contrast with the 1945 story is the use of much more emotionally charged language to emphasize the victim's suffering and the perpetrator's evil – not only in his actions but in his essence. The assault leading to the girl's death is described in brutal detail, and the victim's pain and fear are stressed. Hammond is portrayed as essentially violent behind a facade of respectability and concern for his children. The only glimpse of the defendant's perspective offered, reporting his admission that 'he lost control and did not realise what he was doing', is undercut by its placement in the middle of a detailed, gruesome account of his actions.

The presentation of these stories is radically different in a number of ways. The 1945 *Mirror* story describes a tragic situation: a child has been assaulted but by a man who is portrayed also as a victim, rather than an essentially evil person. The injury suffered is presented in zero-degree clinical language, and no emotional or evaluative adjectives are used to colour the report. The 1989 *Times* story by contrast is replete with adjectives stressing the victim's anguish and the perpetrator's pathologically violent character. It is noteworthy that by 1989 *The Times* used more emotive styles of reporting than a tabloid had 45 years earlier. The stories illustrate a profound change in discourse about crime. By 1989, it has become a zero-sum game in which only the victim is represented as a suffering human being. Her anguish is blamed on two villains: a demonized brute who attacks her; and a negligent authority that fails to protect her. Instead of a complex human tragedy, we have a one-dimensional battle of good versus evil.

These stories highlight the key change in the discourse of crime news reporting since the Second World War. The narratives have become personalized and sensationalized. What drives them is a battle against one-dimensionally evil villains who inflict dramatic and frightening suffering on individual victims. This pattern is also found increasingly in crime fiction (Reiner et al. 2000, 2001).

It's not business, it's personal

In quantitative terms, many aspects of the pattern of crime news stories remain constant in the half-century after the Second World War and confirm the 'law of opposites'. In particular, there is disproportionate reporting of violent crime and of older and higher-status victims and offenders. Nonetheless, even in terms of the quantitative analysis, much has changed. Property crime without violence has largely dropped out of the news picture, unless there is a celebrity angle. Victims increasingly feature prominently and often occupy the subject positions of crime stories. The police are represented in a much more negative way, both in terms of effectiveness and integrity, although the predominant portrayal of them remains positive.

Crime is now portrayed as a far more frightening risk than before, not just because it is more common but also because it is represented in more highly charged emotional terms as a serious threat to ordinary people. There is much greater individualism underlying the narratives. Crime is seen as problematic not because it violates the law or other moral reference points but because it hurts individual victims with whom the audience is led to sympathize or empathize. Offenders are portrayed not as parts of social relations or structures in which the victims and the public are also embedded, but as pathologically evil individuals. Any attempt to understand them, let alone any concern for their point of view or their rehabilitation, is seen as insensitive to the suffering of their victims.

These features also testify to a decline of deference, of automatic subordination to authority. Crime is seen as wrong not because of acceptance of legality as a benchmark of how people should behave but because it causes personal harm to individuals. Moreover, whether we are concerned about this harm is constructed by the narratives as depending on our identification with the victims, as either like us or like we would wish to be, rather than because they are suffering human beings. The police and other authorities are themselves portrayed as often immoral or irrelevant. Whether we respect them or take their side is a matter not of their formal status but of their attractiveness as individuals.

Summary

The changing discourse of crime news and fiction stories is part and parcel of much broader transformations of political economy and culture, above all the hegemony of neoliberalism, the combination of free-market economics and cultural individualism that has become dominant since the 1970s. A less deferential consumerist society conceives of crime and policing not as the breaking and enforcement of generally respected laws, but as the violation of sympathetic and vulnerable individual victims. Each narrative has to construct its own moral universe in these terms: identification of characters as good or bad cannot be read off from their legal status. This contrasts sharply with the earlier narratives in which the legitimacy of law, and the evil of breaking it, could be taken for granted. Perpetrators, victims and audience shared a common humanity, and the interest of stories often turned on understanding offenders' motivations, not simply demonizing them. Following the politicization of law and order, crime stories have increasingly become an orchestration of hate and vengefulness against individual offenders, supposedly on behalf of their victims, in what sometimes amount to virtual lynch mobs.

Law and order: politics and policy

The early 1990s saw a hardening of public and political discourse about law and order, and a toughening of crime control policies, initially in the United States and the United Kingdom, but eventually in most western countries. The decline in crime since the 1990s has commonly been attributed to these tougher policies, notably rising imprisonment and 'hard cop' tactics such as 'zero tolerance' (the name given by the media to the tactic, in New York and elsewhere, of cracking down on minor street offences). This section will analyse the rise of the politics and culture of 'law and order' and assess its impact on crime control.

David Garland's 2001 book *The Culture of Control* offers a tour de force analysis that has deservedly become exceptionally influential. Garland constructed a Foucault-inspired 'history of the present', weaving together many strands of cultural, social, political and economic change. Whilst the changes in crime control result from a complex dialectic of different causes, the growing dominance of neo-liberalism in the globalizing political economy of the late twentieth century is arguably *primus inter pares* in understanding what has happened (Reiner 2007).

The origins of the politics of 'law and order' lie in the late 1960s and early 1970s. However, since the early 1990s there has been a sharp accentuation of the trend towards harder crime control discourse and policies, embedding them ever more deeply, despite some counter-trends and resistances. This is not equally prominent in all societies: some jurisdictions have restrained or at least slowed the punitive trend. The variations are closely related to the extent to which different political economies embraced neo-liberalism. Nonetheless, those states that have succeeded to date in retaining greater welfarism and social democracy face increasing pressure from global markets and from the hegemony of consumerist culture. This threatens to push them in the direction not only of more neo-liberal economic policies but of the more repressive law-and-order control policies that are their Janus face.

The rise of law-and-order politics

Until the late 1960s, criminal justice policy had not been a partisan political issue since the early nineteenth century. It did not feature in any UK party's election manifesto between the Second World War and 1970 (Downes and Morgan 2012). Nor was crime an important issue to the British public until the 1970s, at least as registered by opinion polls. Some specific aspects of criminal justice policy *were* politically controversial, notably capital punishment. Particularly spectacular or salacious crimes have always been topics of popular fascination. But the overall state of crime was not a widespread cause of concern, nor was criminal justice policy subject to political controversy and conflict.

'Law and order' first became politicized in the United States in the 1960s by the political Right, demanding that the law and its front-line troops, the cops, be unleashed. 'Law and order' was a successful campaigning slogan for Richard Nixon in his 1968 US presidential election victory, becoming a codeword for race, culture and generational backlash.

The politicization of law and order was heralded in Britain in the 1970 general election, when the Conservative manifesto said that 'the Labour Government cannot entirely shrug off responsibility' for rising 'crime and violence'. With hindsight, this was a remarkably genteel opening shot in the coming political war about law and order!

Politicization of law and order accelerated under Margaret Thatcher's leadership of the Conservative Party. During the late 1970s, in the build-up to her election victory in 1979, Mrs Thatcher blamed the Labour government for rising crime and disorder, pledging a 'ring of steel' to protect people against lawlessness. The Tory's law and order campaign was greatly helped by the emergence of the police as a political lobby, backing up the Conservative's agenda in a series of advertisements and speeches. The issue was a major factor in Thatcher's 1979 election victory, according to polls monitoring the shifts in public opinion.

The UK party political gulf on law and order reached its widest point in the mid-1980s. The key conflicts were over the policing of the urban disorders and of the miners' strike of 1984–5 (results of the economic and social dislocation engendered by the Thatcher government's monetarist policies), the Police and Criminal Evidence Act 1984 and radical campaigns for democratic police accountability. On all these issues, Labour took a civil libertarian stance, attacking the Conservative government for violating the principles of the rule of law. Labour also attacked Conservative law and order policies for increasing social divisions, aggravating rather than reforming the root causes of crime: social inequality and relative deprivation. This position proved to be an electoral liability for Labour. In the 1983 and 1987 UK general elections, the Tories attacked Labour for being 'soft' on crime because of its links with civil liberties, 'permissiveness', trade unionism (associated with disorder) and failure to develop any short-term solutions to bolster public protection (Downes and Morgan 2012).

In the late 1980s, signs appeared of a new cross-party consensus on law and order. The Conservatives, concerned about the apparent failure of toughness to stem rising crime, began to emphasize crime prevention, proportionality in penal policy and value for money (a major Thatcherite theme, of course). The new tack culminated in the 1991 Criminal Justice Act.

For its part, Labour began to try and repair some of the 'soft on law and order' image that the Tories had foisted on them, culminating in Tony Blair's legendary soundbite: 'tough on crime, tough on the causes of crime'. Blair began to tout this during 1993 in media interviews and articles, in the wake of the anguish and national soul-searching about crime and moral decline triggered by the tragic murder of Liverpool toddler James Bulger by two young boys. The slogan touched all bases, finely balancing the Left realist recognition that crime was a serious problem, with a more traditional criminological concern with 'causes'. But the main departure was rhetorical: the double whammy of toughness packed into one short, sharp sentence. Since 1993, there has developed a new 'second order' consensus on the fundamentals of law and order policy – toughness, toughness, toughness – with frenzied partisan conflict on specifics: anything you can do, I can do tougher.

In the early 1990s, Labour began to attack the Tories with some success, pointing to failures of Conservative criminal justice policies. Given the record increases in crime in the 1980s, despite burgeoning expenditure on policing and punishment, this was an open goal, as even Tory cabinet ministers conceded. Conservative Home Secretary Michael Howard fought back vigorously with his 'prison works' speech to the October 1993 Party Conference. Nonetheless, the game had changed dramatically. Labour was making the political running on what had hitherto been one of the Tories' most secure policy areas.

The period 1992–3 was a decisive watershed for the politics of law and order. Whilst during the late 1970s and the 1980s neo-liberal and neo-conservative political parties, ideas and policies became dominant in Britain, the United States and most of the western world, they were fiercely if unsuccessfully contested. On a world scale, the New Right's ascendancy was marked by the fall of the Soviet Union in 1989. But what really confirmed the global hegemony of neo-liberalism was the acceptance of the fundamentals of its economic and social policy framework by the erstwhile social democratic or New Deal parties of the West. The Clinton Democrats and New Labour, with their embrace of the 'third way' – neo-liberalism to a cool beat – marked a new, deep consensus. It sounded the death knell of the post-war mixed economy, Keynesian settlement that the Conservative parties had accepted when they returned to power in the early 1950s. An acceptance of the tougher law and order perspective previously associated with the Right was a part of the switch to 'New' Labour (and similar changes by the US Democrats).

The crime-control consensus

The post-1993 crime-control consensus had five core elements. These five elements were the obverse of the social democratic sensibility about crime and justice that had been widely shared before neo-liberalism shattered the post-war Keynesian and welfarist consensus (Reiner 2007: ch. 5, 2012a, 2012b).

Crime is public enemy number one Crime and disorder are seen as *the* major threats to society and to individual citizens, by the public and politicians. Many opinion polls have demonstrated that crime (and more recently terrorism) moved to the forefront of public concern from the early 1970s (although this prominence has receded in recent years, and law and order played little part in either the 2010 or the 2015 general elections).

Individual, not social, responsibility for crime Crime is the fault of offenders, *not* caused by social structural factors. This was expressed most bluntly in 1993 by the then British prime minister John Major: 'Society needs to condemn a little more and understand a little less.' And Tony Blair frequently echoed this.

Foregrounding victims versus offenders The victim has become the iconic centre of discourse about crime, ideal-typically portrayed as totally innocent. Crime discourse and policy are predicated on a zero-sum game: concern for victims precludes understanding of – let alone any sympathy for – offenders.

Crime control works Since the early 1990s, can-do optimism has reinvigorated confidence in tough (but smart) policing and penal policy. 'Prison works', as does 'zero-tolerance' policing, and the 'responsibilization' of citizens to take self-protective measures against victimization. Civil liberties and human rights are at best marginal issues, to be subordinated to crime control exigencies, and deeper social causes of crime are denied or played down.

High-crime society normalized Popular culture and routine activities have become increasingly focused on crime risks and the perception that we live in a 'high-crime society' (even though recorded crime has fallen since the mid-1990s). Crime prevention techniques have penetrated everyday life, paradoxically enhancing fear. The gains in security from victimization that better technology has achieved have not been accompanied by a corresponding increase in feelings of security.

Minding the reassurance gap: the puzzling politics of law and order

In the previous chapter, I discussed the crime statistics, indicating that crime as measured by them has dropped sharply since the mid-1990s. At the same time, surveys (including the BCS/CSEW) indicate the widespread public belief that crime has continued to rise. Whilst the salience of law and order as an issue seems to have diminished somewhat in recent years (and played little part in the 2010 and 2015 UK general elections), political and media discussions of crime are still framed by a politics of fear and insecurity.

Whilst trying to gain some credit because crime overall has been declining, politicians and the police have struggled to benefit from this. The evidence, from surveys and from media discussions, that public fears have not declined substantially has been labelled the 'reassurance gap' by policy makers and stimulated a 'reassurance policing' agenda to try and plug it, as if continuing insecurity was an unreasonable form of false consciousness.

There may, however, be a rational kernel to the stubborn refusal of public anxiety to decline with the crime rate, beyond blaming the messengers of the sensationalist and bad-news-addicted media. The next chapter will probe the reasons for the crime fall. It will suggest that the crime drop has not resulted from any diminution in the causes of crime but rather from better, more widespread security techniques and equipment, suppressing the crime rate but not criminality, the potential for crime to be committed. In so far as the decline in crime overall is due to more successful adoption of protective equipment and preventive routines by crime-conscious citizens, rather than any reduction in the root causes of offending, the burden of crime control falls primarily on potential victims. Whilst prevention tactics, expensive and irksome as they may be, are preferable to victimization, they may reinforce rather than reduce fear by highlighting threats. There is also good reason to fear that crime types that are not commonly recorded have proliferated (confirmed by the 2015 CSEW; Travis 2015a, 2015b).

What is required is not only reassurance that crime has been prevented but that the causes of crime have been attenuated. However, this cannot be provided so long as neoliberalism, the fundamental source of increasing criminality and of the accentuation of insecurity and law and order solutions by media and political discourse, remains triumphant.

7
Whodunnit and Why? Criminological Conceptions of Crime

Previous chapters have probed the many problems in the concept of crime and indicated the variety of meanings and images evoked by the term. This chapter will consider the history of criminological attempts to explain crime. It will then see how these can be synthesized to construct a framework for understanding contemporary trends, in particular the vertiginous rise and mysterious fall of recorded crime in recent decades.

Criminology and the explanation of crime: a crook's tour of competing theories

David Downes has pointed out that criminology is a 'rendezvous' subject: a meeting point where analysts from many disciplines converge, often briefly, to apply their particular perspectives to a topic – 'crime' – that gives it whatever amorphous and tenuous unity it has. Yet this subject matter – crime – is, as we have seen, elusive, multifaceted and contested. And many disciplines and perspectives have visited it, offering different conceptions and accounts.

Criminologies before 'criminology'

The term 'criminology' itself came into being in association with the late nineteenth-century Lombrosian version of the quest for scientific explanation of the etiology of crime. In the case of Lombroso, the science deployed was biology. However, the project of developing such an analysis using the intellectual tools of *social* science, partly to achieve policy ends of order and justice, pre-dated the label. The eighteenth-century criminologies *avant la lettre*, the 'classical' school of criminal law and the 'science of police', were both aspects of political economy. They were sidelined in the 1870s by the rise of the positivist 'science of the criminal', with its aura of scientific rigour, objectivity and dispassionate expertise.

Standard accounts of the history of criminology see its origins in the 'classical' perspective associated with Beccaria's 1764 book *Dei delitti e delle pene*, and its profound influence, via Blackstone, Bentham and others, on the Enlightenment movements for reform of criminal law and punishment. There was an intimate relationship between the broader political economy developed during the Enlightenment and the classical school's discussions of crime and criminal justice (Reiner 2012a, 2012b; Ruggiero 2013).

Political economy was intertwined particularly with the 'science of police' that flourished in the eighteenth and early nineteenth centuries but has been overlooked by criminologists until recently. The eighteenth-century 'science of police' was a vast body of work that flourished across Europe. In Britain, the leading exponent of the 'science of police' was the magistrate Patrick Colquhoun (Colquhoun 1800). Colquhoun is most commonly remembered as a pioneer of the modern British police in the narrow sense. However, he wrote extensively on political economy, crime and criminal justice, and his work can be seen as a precursor of criminology. For Colquhoun, crime and criminal justice were not independent phenomena that could be considered in isolation from broader issues of social and economic structure. His proposals for the prevention and control of crime were rooted in empirical investigation of crime patterns. Colquhoun's analysis located the ultimate causes of crime in the overall structure of economy and society, but he was concerned to unravel the social and cultural mediations generating criminality and conformity.

Overall, the analysis of security, order, crime and policing advanced by Colquhoun as the 'science of police' was more sensitive to the interplay of politics, law and justice with criminality than the later nineteenth-century 'science of the criminal'. Like the contemporaneous displacement of political economy by economics, the apparent gain in 'scientific' rigour was bought at a high price: it obscured the political and ethical dimensions of crime (and indeed of economic well-being).

Varieties of criminology

The term 'criminology' was originally associated with a positivist attempt to explain crime by criminals' biological characteristics, pioneered by Lombroso's 1876 *Criminal Man*. 'Positivism' in this context refers to the view that criminology should be modelled on a logic of analysis attributed by philosophers to the natural sciences. This aspires to construct testable objective theories explaining the general patterns found by rigorous empirical data collection. 'Criminology' has for most of its history been dominated by positivist approaches, biological, psychological and sociological, although these have been seriously challenged, especially by the post-1960s development of critical perspectives.

Positivist analyses of crime face some fundamental problems, however. Crime is not a universal, objectively definable type of behaviour, as we saw in earlier chapters. So how can we aspire to objective knowledge of it? Positivist criminology offers deterministic analyses of supposed causal relationships between variables, leaving little or no scope for human consciousness, agency or values. Throughout its history, criminological debate has been divided by fundamental philosophical and political antinomies.

Basic axes of criminological debate

Texts on criminological theory list many competing perspectives. An illustration is Vold et al.'s *Theoretical Criminology*, originally published in 1958, and now in its sixth edition (Vold et al. 2010). The book is a classic work, with a deserved reputation for sophisticated scholarship, clarity and comprehensiveness. Its chapters list the following sixteen theoretical perspectives (each further subdivided into numerous sub-schools): classical criminology; biological factors; psychological factors; crime and poverty; Durkheim, anomie, and modernization; neighbourhoods and crime; strain theories; learning theories; control theories; the meaning of crime; conflict criminology; Marxism and postmodern criminology; gender and crime; developmental theories; integrated theories. However, this rich variety of differing analytic approaches to crime are primarily permutations of certain key dimensions of debate, reflecting broader currents of argument in social science and philosophy.

Two of the most fundamental recurrent tensions are:

(a) autonomy vs determinism: To what extent is human behaviour seen as structured by causes that eliminate or reduce freedom of will and action? How much scope is there for autonomy and choice? Some analysts propose either completely deterministic or entirely voluntaristic positions, but most adopt intermediate combinations of structured choice within determined limits, according offenders a degree of responsibility but also recognizing the role of causal factors explaining criminal conduct.

    Amongst deterministic positions (total or partial), we can distinguish between those that locate the crucial causal pressures within the individual offender's biology or psyche, and those that emphasize social causation. Social theories see the individual actor's consciousness, decisions and behaviour as totally or partially structured by the social and cultural groups, networks, situations and environments within which action occurs.

    Many perspectives were originally postulated in an imperialistic way, purporting to be explanations of all phenomena relating to offending. However, the different approaches are not necessarily contradictory. They can – and indeed I would argue *should* – be seen as directed at somewhat different questions. Psychological and biological theories are primarily concerned to explain why particular individuals, rather than others, commit crime in specific situations. Social explanations are mainly intended to illuminate overall trends and patterns. Seen that way, they are not merely compatible but actually *require* each other to explain different facets of crime. An eclectic synthesis along these lines will be suggested later (pp. 158–61).

(b) conservatism vs critique: To what extent does the criminological analyst accept the perspectives, values and purposes of criminal law and criminal justice? How far does she subject them to critique and perhaps rejection? Does the theorist claim objectivity and value neutrality? If she espouses political or value commitments, explicitly or implicitly, are these identifiably conservative, liberal or radical? Whose side are we on (the question famously posed by Becker [1967] and Cowburn et al. [2013] offers a valuable discussion)? Does the analyst take the perspective of the criminal justice system or of the labelled offender?

The historical development of criminological perspectives

Historical development is never as clear cut as in the simplistic periodizations of textbooks. There is always a complex coexistence of competing perspectives. Nonetheless, some broad periods can be distinguished in terms of the relative dominance of particular theories. The ebb and flow of particular perspectives' influence relates to broader shifts in culture, political economy and social relations (as analysed for example by Garland [1985, 2001]).

1870–1960: varieties of positivist criminology

Early sociological positivism Before the term 'criminology' was coined in the 1870s to refer to a new positivist 'science of the criminal', some analysts had offered social accounts of crime. The acknowledged pioneers of *sociological* criminology were the 'moral statisticians' in 1820s France, Guerry and Quetelet. Using new national crime statistics, they showed that poor, unemployed, uneducated young men were more likely to commit offences in places where there were more wealthy people to steal from. Crime was a function both of social pressures stemming from inequality *and* of the distribution of targets and temptations. Quetelet's most fundamental discovery was the relative constancy of rates and patterns of crime over substantial periods of time, which stimulated Durkheim's later development in the 1890s of an explicitly sociological perspective.

During the 1920s, the Chicago School analysed patterns of crime in different areas of cities, seeing these as shaped by structural socio-economic pressures, mediated by interactions between people forming different cultures. In the 1930s, Edwin Sutherland synthesized social ecology and symbolic interactionism in a proposed general theory of crime: differential association. He postulated that crime was generated by a predominance of deviant over conformist meanings in a person's social world. Although he recognized an association between low social class and *conventionally* defined crime, he did not accept that crime was inherently a product of poverty. Indeed, his most significant contribution to criminology was the concept of 'white-collar' crime, which flourished in large corporations and amongst the powerful and privileged, albeit largely hidden and unrecorded by official statistics.

Robert Merton's development of anomie theory in the late 1930s remains the most influential broadly positivistic sociological theory of crime. Merton adapted the concept of anomie from Durkheim's 1897 book *Suicide*. It will be discussed further (see pp. 160–1), examining how it still illuminates contemporary issues.

1960–1975: critical and radical criminologies

During the 1960s, reflecting broader ferment in culture and social relations, the sociology of crime and criminology went through an epistemological break. There was a fundamental reformulation of its intellectual agenda, hitherto dominated by two interdependent projects: the explanation of criminal behaviour, and the application of this to improve techniques governing deviance. There was little questioning about whose interests were served by the institutions of law and order. Why were some people (predominantly disadvantaged and powerless) deemed deviant and in need of correction or punishment, whilst others were not? Whose law, what order? These questions came to the forefront during the 1960s and 1970s with the emergence of critical and radical criminologies.

Labelling theory The critical break in the study of crime that occurred in the 1960s was a shift from a subject position assuming an identification with lawmakers and enforcers to an appreciation of the position of those labelled as deviant. Howard Becker pioneered the fundamental critique known as labelling theory. Building on the theoretical foundations of social constructionism and symbolic interactionism, this problematized questions that 'correctionalist' criminology left unexplored.

> The same behaviour may be an infraction of the rules at one time and not at another; may be an infraction when committed by one person, but not when committed by another; some rules are broken with impunity, others are not. In short, whether a given activity is deviant or not depends in part on the nature of the act (that is whether or not it violates some rule) and in part on what other people do about it. (Becker 1963: 14)

Labelling theory had a huge impact, although its influence is now largely hidden, domesticated in the proliferating analyses of policing, media, and criminal justice. Although the sweeping claims of its originators are hard to sustain, its legacy lives on explicitly in contemporary cultural criminology and other qualitative, appreciative and critical approaches that flourish today (Hayward and Young 2012).

Marxism and crime Until the 1960s flowering of radical criminology, Marxists seldom referred to crime or criminal justice. It is often stated that in his mature theoretical work

Marx did not systematically address issues of law, crime, or criminal justice. *Capital* does, however, contain a lengthy historical analysis of the emergence of the Factory Acts in early nineteenth-century England (Marx 1976 [1867]: ch. 10). This constitutes a pioneering case study of criminalization and of what would nowadays be called corporate crimes (for more detailed discussion, see pp. 73–7 above).

Willem Bonger, a Dutch professor, made the first attempt to develop a systematic Marxist analysis of crime (Bonger 1969 [1916]). In Bonger's analysis, the structure of capitalism generates particular criminogenic pressures by stimulating a culture of egoism at all levels of society (Moxon 2014). This enhances the material aspirations of workers and the poor and weakens their internal controls against stealing. Bonger traced a complex multiplicity of linkages between the structural conflicts of capitalism, with its general egoism, and particular forms of crime. Attributing the root causes of crime to the larger immorality and injustices of capitalism did not remove the moral accountability of offenders. Bonger introduced many ideas that were explored in later critical criminology. He recognized that legal conceptions of crime reflected disproportionately the interests of the powerful, anticipating labelling theory, but also acknowledged the harm done by many legally defined crimes.

Macro-sociology and political economy combined with the insights of the labelling perspective in the Marxist-influenced radical criminologies that became prominent in the early 1970s. The flagship text was *The New Criminology*, with its conception of a 'fully social' theory of crime (Taylor, Walton and Young 1973: 268–80). This offered 'a political economy of criminal action, and of the reaction it excites', together with 'a politically informed social psychology of these ongoing social dynamics'.

The magisterial study of mugging and the reaction to it. *Policing the Crisis* (Hall et al. 1978), was the closest attempt at offering an analysis incorporating all these elements. Starting from the sentencing of the perpetrators of a robbery in Birmingham, the book analysed the mass-media construction of a 'moral panic' about 'mugging', and police responses to this. It then developed a wide-ranging account of British economic, political, social and cultural history since the

Second World War to explain the deeper concerns that 'mugging' condensed. The later chapters offered an analysis of the impact of transformations in the political economy on black young men in particular, and how this structured the formation of specific subcultures in which robbery was more likely. *Policing the Crisis* remains a uniquely ambitious attempt to synthesize macro-, middle-range and micro-analysis of a particular offence and the reaction to it.

1975–present: the 'realist' counter-revolutions

Left realism Left realism claimed radical criminology was in an 'aetiological crisis', as the reductions in poverty and unemployment associated with the post-war Keynesian Welfare State had failed to stop crime from rising (Young 1986). Left realists emphasized immediate steps to control crime by more effective policing and criminal justice, not the 'root causes' approach attributed to earlier 'Left idealism'. Nonetheless, when Left realists considered crime causation, they incorporated earlier sociological perspectives such as relative deprivation and anomie (e.g. Lea and Young 1984: ch. 6).

Since the 1990s, some radical theorists have returned to macro-analyses of the relationship between crime, criminal justice, and late modernity or consumer society, in combination with interpretive cultural analysis (Taylor 1997, 1999; Hall et al. 2008; Hall 2012; Hall and Winlow 2012, 2015). There has also been vigorous continuation of radical approaches in certain areas, notably the critical analysis of gender issues by feminist criminologists (Heidensohn and Silvestri 2012).

Realism rules 1975–present Since the mid-1970s, mainstream criminology, especially in the United States, has been dominated by pragmatic realism, concerned with 'what works'. This was initially based on an explicit rejection of 'root cause' theories that sought to explain crime by macro-social causes (Wilson 2013 [1975]: xv). Causal explanation was not eschewed altogether but pursued at individual (Wilson and Herrnstein 1985), situational or community levels. These are more amenable to policy interventions that do not raise questions of wider social justice or reform.

Whilst realism largely ousted macro-sociology and political economy in studying crime, it was associated with a resurgence of the economics of crime applying Chicago School neo-classical economic models (Becker 1968). There has also been a broader revival of rational choice theories based on the classical 'economic man' model of the offender, with huge influence on government crime-control policies. The two most prominent such applications are situational crime prevention and routine activities theory (Cohen and Felson 1979; Clarke and Mayhew 1980; Cornish and Clarke 1986; Felson and Clarke 1998). Both have offered policy makers and practitioners practicable policy interventions that appear to be successful in crime reduction, at any rate in the short run and in specific places, and have probably played a significant part in the post-1990s crime drop (Tilley 2005 and Crawford and Evans 2012 offer sagacious overviews).

Explaining contemporary crime trends: an eclectic model

Most of the competing perspectives on the conceptualization, commission and control of crime were formulated as imperialistic explanations, whose proponents believed they had found *the* magic bullet for the problem of order. Whilst their grand claims cannot be sustained, they do all illuminate aspects of the interlocking processes of crime and control.

The synthesis I propose is unashamedly a 'root cause' theory of the kind that was castigated by 'realists' of both the Right and the Left. It accepts the need for effective short-run policies to alleviate the problems of crime but claims nonetheless that social 'root causes' must also be addressed.

The ultimate sources of crime lie deep in social structure and culture: they are social injustice and an egoistic ethos, as suggested by many classic theorists, notably Bonger and Merton. There is a mass of evidence demonstrating that inequality, unemployment, relative and absolute deprivation, economic prosperity and consumer confidence, inflation and social exclusion are linked to property crime and serious violence, including homicide.[1]

The economic injustice–crime link does not excuse those who commit crimes (a canard proposed by conservative critics of social explanations of crime). Rather, it shows that if we are serious about wanting to protect potential victims, it is necessary to probe the deeper roots of criminality. Offenders *do* bear responsibility for the harm they inflict – but all citizens have a responsibility to get tough on crime's ultimate causes: the unjust and amoral societies we live in. The understanding of crime, whether at the macro-level of broad trends or patterns or the micro-level of specific incidents, involves a weaving together of different elements and levels of explanation. It requires recognition *both* of the choices and responsibility of perpetrators, *and* of how these are framed by political economy, social structure and culture.

Crime's complex preconditions

Several logically necessary preconditions must be met before a crime can occur: labelling, motive, means, opportunity, and the absence of control. The criminological theories discussed earlier all feed into explaining one or more of these conditions.

Labelling Apparent shifts in crime rates and patterns are frequently due to changes in criminal law or in reporting and recording incidents. In the 1970s, for example, the spread of household-contents insurance induced more victims to report burglaries, sparking an apparent surge of crime. Changes in the rules for counting offences in 1998 and 2002 drove up the police-recorded crime rate.

Motivation Detective fiction usually portrays the motives driving crime as complex, puzzling, often bizarre, requiring the sensitivity of Dostoevsky or Freud, or Poirot's little grey cells, to unravel. This is because the media focus on extremely unusual, very serious, pathologically violent, cases. Most offences are committed for readily comprehensible reasons, motivated by widely shared desires – money, fashionable goods, sex, excitement, thrills, intoxication by alcohol, adrenalin or other drugs. Most offenders are driven not by deviant values but by immersion in contemporary consumer culture (Hall et al. 2008).

The mundane aspirations and desires providing the motivation for most crime are not constant. Social, cultural and economic changes affect the attractions of those behaviours that are labelled as criminal, increasing or decreasing the numbers of people motivated to commit them.

Durkheim had suggested in the 1890s that rapid social change, such as economic downturns *and* upturns, dislocated effective cultural regulation of people's aspirations. Such social turbulence released anomic dissatisfaction conducive to suicide and other deviance. Merton developed these ideas in a brief but seminal article, which offered a framework for explaining variations in deviance both between and within societies (Merton 1938).

Despite the ritual slaying of caricatures of Merton's analysis in countless textbooks and exam answers over the decades, it remains an illuminating structural social theory of crime. It provides a classic analysis of how macro-social structures shape motivations to commit crime, varying between cultures and over time. It was developed in the 1930s to explain why the United States was then the western world's crime capital. Structurally limited legitimate opportunities generated pressures for crime, particularly in cultures that encouraged high aspirations for all, epitomized by the 'American dream' of rising from rags to riches.

Cultures that elevate monetary success above other goals generate deviance at *all* levels of society, not least – indeed perhaps above all – amongst elites. There is no terminal point for financial aspirations, and success breeds desire rather than satisfaction. Winning is all that counts. Conceptions of legitimate means get pushed aside: nice guys finish last, as the old saying has it.

These arguments have been adapted widely to understand contemporary crime patterns (e.g. Young 2003; Reiner 2007; Messner and Rosenfeld 2012). The recent British parliamentary expenses scandals, the revelations of the corrupt networks linking politicians, police and press, and, at the other end of the social scale, the 2011 shopping riots in the United

Kingdom are all testimony to the power of this 70-year-old theory.

Means of crime The commission of crime requires a variety of personal and technical resources. Changes in political economy, culture, technology and social patterns expand or contract the *means* of committing crimes. New types of crime become possible, old ones blocked off, and new ways of committing old offences created. Innovative means of exchange, most recently the internet, provide new techniques for the old art of relieving people of their money.

Cyberspace enables many new types of offence and novel ways of committing old offences, such as terrorism, piracy, fraud, identity theft, stalking, sexual offences against children, hacking security codes and racist harassment. The increased speed and extent of travel and communications signified by globalization facilitates a variety of crimes: for example, trafficking in people, drugs or arms, money laundering, terrorism.

Criminal opportunities Criminal opportunities can be expanded by a proliferation of tempting and stealable targets (for example, the spread of car ownership, televisions, videos, DVD players, home PCs, laptops and, more recently, mobile phones, iPods, iPads, each in turn becoming the hottest items for theft). Many studies have charted surges in particular kinds of theft following the development of new 'must-have' consumer goods. For example, there was a sharp rise in robberies of mobile phones from early 2000 to early 2002, tracking the rapid rise in ownership.

Controls One further ingredient is necessary before a crime can be committed – the absence of controls, formal and informal. A potential burglar, say, may be eager to find a vulnerable property in order to feed her children or a habit. Equipped with tools and know-how, she comes across a relatively secluded house, newspapers sticking out of the letter box indicating absent owners, and she spies the flashing LCDs of tempting electronic equipment through the ground-floor window. But her progress up the garden path may be arrested by an approaching police patrol car or the sound of an alarm.

Even if not, a final intervention may hold her back. On the shelf she spots a Bible, recalling the still, small voice of Sunday school scripture: 'Thou shalt not steal.' She goes home for tea and reflection.

Changes in the efficacy of *formal* criminal justice controls alter the attractions or possibility of crime. 'Crime is down, blame the police', boasted NYPD Chief Bratton (Bratton 1998); and in the United Kingdom, Conservative Home Secretary Michael Howard claimed 'prison works' (both claims are vigorously disputed, and the evidence supporting them is dubious).

Informal social controls are at least as important in interpreting crime trends. The thesis that informal controls – 'social capital': family, school, socialization, community – are the fundamental basis of order has a long pedigree and is the essence of the 'control theory' formulated by Hirschi and Gottfredson (Hirschi 1969; Gottfredson and Hirschi 1990).

Accounting for the crime trends: rising crime 1955–1995

As argued earlier (see pp. 158–9), there are no one-club explanations of these trends, nor even a simple set of factors. We have to construct a plausible narrative by considering how the five elements of crime distinguished above were affected by economic, political, social and cultural changes in each period. This draws upon what we know about the criminogenic significance of different factors on the basis of econometric, survey and observational research. The account below will apply the five-factor model to the periodization of trends in crime identified in the last chapter (for a more detailed version, see Reiner 2007: ch. 4).

Late 1950s–1970s: recorded crime rise

The initial rise in recorded crime was mainly a product of the new mass-consumer society, which reshaped the labelling of crime, enhanced motives, means and opportunities, and weakened internalized and formal controls. General

Household Survey data suggest that much of the increase was due to victims reporting more, a plausible process in a newly 'affluent' society in which high-value consumer goods were proliferating, and increasingly insured against theft. However, the culture of mass consumerism also generated higher offending levels. Most obviously, this resulted from the spread of tempting targets: cars, radios and other equipment in cars, televisions, videos and so on.

Although unemployment and inequality were at a historic low point, and general living standards rising, Mertonian anomie probably fanned motivations to steal. Consumer aspirations were stimulated by advertising's celebration of instant gratification: 'Live now, pay later'; 'Take the waiting out of wanting'. The pervasive stress on the desirability of must-have goodies for all increased the sense of relative deprivation amongst those who lacked legitimate opportunities (Downes 1966).

At the same time, the advent of youth culture and 'desubordination' reduced internalized restraints against offending. As recorded crime began to rise, pressures on the police increased, leading to lower clear-up rates and a decline in the deterrence and incapacitation effects of criminal justice.

In sum, from the late 1950s, a variety of interlinked consequences of mass consumerism fed rising crime rates. These increased the labelling of crime, and opportunities and motivations for offending, and weakened both informal and formal controls.

1980s: crime explosion

During the 1980s and early 1990s, crime reached record heights. The new BCS confirmed that the recorded crime explosion was primarily a rise in offending and victimization, not a recording change. This was primarily due to massive shifts in motivation and internalized controls.

The key driver was the brutal displacement of the post-war Keynesian, welfare-state consensus by neo-liberal monetarist policies. The result was de-industrialization and resurgent mass unemployment – indeed never-employment – for increasing numbers of young men, especially amongst ethnic minorities and in inner-city areas. Inequality deepened into a yawning chasm between the top and the bottom of the economic hierarchy, and poverty began to rise after a long historical process of increasing social inclusion. Industrial and political conflict was sparked on a scale not experienced for half a century or more, with much violent disorder.

Informal social controls of all kinds were eroded as whole communities lost the material basis of settled life. It was neo-liberalism that undermined stable family life and 'morality', not the 'permissiveness' that the Right railed against. Moral laissez-faire followed the economic. A culture of egoism, the 'me society', was stimulated under the guise of an ethic of individual responsibility. 'Greed is good' was the infamous watchword of a new 'Gilded Age'. The criminogenic consequences of unbridled turbo-capitalism in the Thatcher years far outweighed the strong state measures introduced to control it, in a Canute-like effort to stem the social tsunami. There is a plethora of evidence from more recent econometric studies of links between unemployment, inequality, business cycles, inflation and crime (cf. Introduction, note 1).

This is strikingly illustrated by a probing study of homicide trends (Dorling 2004). Between 1967 and 2002, the number of homicides in Britain rose from around 350 per annum to around 800, although it has fallen back since then. During the huge increase, however, most of the population were less at risk of murder than in 1979. The murder rise of the 1980s/1990s was primarily a phenomenon of never-employed or marginally employed young men, who constituted a new surplus population. 'Those who perpetrated the social violence that was done to the lives of young men starting some 20 years ago are the prime suspects for most of the murders in Britain' (ibid.: 191).

1992–present : falling crime, rising fear

The initial drop in recorded crime in the United Kingdom during 1993–6 was probably a recording phenomenon rather than a real decline in offending; the BCS suggests there was less reporting and recording but *more* victimization. The 'businesslike' police managerialism initiated by the

Conservatives was tough on the *recording* of crime, if not on crime itself.

However, after 1997 the BCS points to a sustained and substantial fall in victimization, returning to the levels of the early 1980s, as do the police recorded figures (after a temporary rise following revised counting rules during 1998–2002). Similar trends were apparent throughout the western world (Tonry 2014). Why this has happened is a criminological conundrum that still eludes full explanation (Marlow 2014).

The western crime drop mystery

The fall in crime since the mid-1990s presents a profound puzzle for all criminological perspectives. This is despite a rapidly growing research literature.[2] The literature on the crime drop resembles a celebrated 1976 *New Yorker* magazine front-page Saul Steinberg cartoon, 'View of the world from 9th Avenue'. The bottom half shows Manhattan from Ninth Avenue to the Hudson River, the top half depicts a heavily stylized United States, with just a sliver above the Pacific Ocean representing the rest of the world. Popular culture accounts of the crime drop focus heavily on the New York 'miracle', supposedly brought about by Police Chief Bill Bratton and/or Mayor Giuliani, with their legendary tactic of 'zero-tolerance' policing (Punch 2007).

The American-centredness of the discussion is not surprising as the crime fall started earlier there. It has turned cities, above all New York, which were watchwords for violence into much safer places. But calling New York 'the city that became safe' (Zimring 2012) isn't warranted – in 2012 it had nearly five times as many homicides as London, for instance (419 compared to 89). The US dominance of the debate is problematic because it has concentrated on explanations that are derived primarily from its experience and which are often hard to entertain when other comparable countries have sustained similar crime reductions without similar policies.

Two recent studies have comprehensively summarized the wide range of suggested explanations of the crime fall (Farrell, Tilley and Tseloni 2014: 437–9; Roeder, Eisen and Bowling

2015). Farrell et al. (2014: 438) identified the following seventeen hypotheses in the literature:

1. Strong economy
2. Concealed weapons laws
3. Capital punishment
4. Gun control laws
5. Imprisonment
6. Policing strategies
7. More police
8. Legalization of abortion
9. Immigration
10. Consumer confidence
11. Declining hard-drug markets
12. Reduction in lead poisoning
13. Changing demographics
14. Civilizing process
15. Improved security
16. The internet
17. Phone guardianship

Farrell et al. offer four evaluation tests:

1. 'the cross-national test': is the explanation one that applies to all the western countries that have experienced the crime drop?
2. 'The prior crime increase test': is the account compatible with understanding the previous decades of rising crime?
3. 'The e-Crimes and phone theft test': is it capable of explaining why some types of crime rose whilst most fell?
4. 'The variable trajectories test: is it contradicted by the timing of crime drops in different places? (Farrell et al. 2014: 439–42).

Roeder et al. (2015) group the fourteen hypotheses they identify (mostly paralleling the above list) into three distinct categories: criminal justice policies; economic factors; social and environmental factors. They also usefully divide the evaluations into two periods: 1990–1999 and 2000–2013. Some hypotheses seem to work well in one period but not the other.

Both reviews of the prevailing hypotheses reject almost all of them, at any rate as complete explanations. However, it is noteworthy that the research evaluations consist almost entirely of econometric-style statistical tests, examining whether a particular variable is associated with reductions in crime holding constant other relevant factors. This provides interesting results but not definitive conclusions. As Max Weber postulated long ago, understanding has to be both 'causally adequate' (by which he meant statistical association) *and* at 'the level of meaning'. Do the constant conjunctions that are established statistically make sense in terms of comprehensible patterns of human action (Weber 1964 [1947]: 99–100)?

Criminal justice hypotheses

An illustration of the problem with statistical testing alone is the debate between explanations of the crime drop in terms of *more* police versus *better* policing through innovative police techniques. The latter perspective itself is divided between advocates of tough zero tolerance, better management and information-led smarter policing (embodied quintessentially in the NYPD's 'CompStat'),[3] or community policing re-legitimating the cops. Claims that changing police tactics are the key source of the crime decline have been challenged by versions of the 'cross-national test'. Many police departments across the United States and in other countries never adopted any of the supposedly crucial tactical changes, and yet they experienced substantial crime decline. This argument was used to reject the innovative police tactics explanation in an influential paper, which claimed that increasing police numbers were part of the answer (Levitt 2004). Levitt suggested that 'between one fifth and one tenth of the overall decline in crime' was attributable to a 14 per cent increase in police numbers per capita during the 1990s (ibid.: 176–7).

The Brennan Center study concurs with Levitt that police numbers played a part in the US crime fall in the 1990s, when US forces increased in size, but not in the twenty-first century when they ceased growing (Roeder et al. 2015: 41–3). Farrell et al. are more sceptical (Farrell et al. 2014: 444–5). Both recognize that the resurgence of criminological confidence that more police and/or new tactics can reduce crime challenges a previous research orthodoxy that neither has much impact on crime levels (Reiner 2010a: 147–59).

What is not tackled is the reason underlying scepticism about police and crime control. It was not just a matter of empirical research findings that increasing police numbers did not correlate with lower crime. Fundamentally, the point was that, at any feasible staffing level, police resources are so stretched between a wide variety of targets for crime that more officers are unlikely to make any appreciable difference. It is difficult to see how a 14 per cent increase in numbers would make a discernible difference in itself. What is plausible is that new, smarter, intelligence-led deployment tactics (such as CompStat or 'hot spots' policing; cf. Braga and Weisburd 2010) can impact crime levels by targeting scarce resources where they are most needed. And it is plausible that this can be facilitated by greater numbers of police. However, this is 'both/and', not the 'either/or' postulated by Levitt and others. Similar issues afflict all the single-factor explanations implicitly sought by statistical techniques that aim to establish conjunction between variables whilst holding others constant.

Whilst it is plausible that policing improvements do have some impact on crime levels, and that this may have played a part in the crime fall, it remains the case that the policing changes fail the tests postulated by Farrell and colleagues and are probably not a major factor overall. Most obviously, because of the many differences in strategy in police forces within the United States itself, not to speak of the wider western world, the policing explanations are caught out by the cross-national test. The adoption of reforms also does not fit the timing of the crime decline in many places, as was pointed out by some of the earliest studies (Bowling 1999; Eck and Maguire 2000; Karmen 2000). It is also not clear why some types of street crime (e.g. mobile phone theft) have not benefited from the better tactics in the way that others are said to have done (Farrell et al. 2014: 444–5).

All these arguments apply a fortiori to other criminal justice-system explanations, notably increased imprisonment, but also capital punishment or concealed weapons and other gun control laws. The latter three hypotheses are clearly restricted to the United States and fail the cross-national test. Increased imprisonment has occurred in some other western countries, notably England and Wales, but not in others (Cavadino and Dignan 2006; Lacey 2008), although all western countries have had falling crime. Many commentators have pointed out the significant contrasts between the United States and Canada, and between England/Wales and Scotland, adjacent jurisdictions that are broadly similar. Canada and Scotland both experienced similar crime declines as their southern neighbours but without the same imprisonment booms.

Even in the United States itself, whilst there is evidence that the massive rise in imprisonment had some effect on reducing crime during the 1990s, this has largely disappeared in the twenty-first century (Roeder et al. 2015: 15–41). Partly this is because the prison boom levelled off a little. But more fundamentally, whilst increasing imprisonment may have a short-term impact by incapacitating offenders, for various reasons (such as the probability that the most prolific offenders are caught first) this is subject to diminishing returns (Reiner 2007: 158–61; Roeder et al. 2015: 15–41).

Social and environmental hypotheses

Both surveys of the hypotheses consider a miscellany of 'social and environmental factors' (Roeder et al. 2015: 55–64). These include changing demographics (fewer youth in the most crime-prone groups); immigration (which, contrary to tabloid myths, is associated with less crime; cf. Graif and Sampson 2009; Stowell et al. 2009); less lead poisoning; legalization of abortion; declining hard-drug markets; the internet; phone guardianship; the 'civilizing process'. These are all deemed by Farrell and colleagues to fail at least one of their tests, and Roeder and colleagues also attribute little if any weight to them.

Several analyses of the United States have seen a declining proportion of young people as a fairly significant factor in the 1990s drop. However, during the 2000s, the proportion of young people levelled out in the United States, yet crime continued to fall (Roeder et al. 2015: 56–8).

Whilst the Stowell et al. and Graif and Sampson papers cited above do provide some support for a connection between immigration and the crime drop (and immigration has been rising throughout the western world), there are some puzzles. Immigration was also rising in many countries in the previous decades of rising crime. It is also hard to see why it should reduce some kinds of theft but not others (Farrell et al. 2014: 446–8).

The decline in lead poisoning (which damages the brains of young people in particular) and the legalization of abortion in the United States in 1973, both about twenty years before the crime drop, are the two hypotheses that grabbed most headlines. The lead hypothesis does pass the cross-national test, as environmental controls on it proliferated in most western countries from the 1970s. Thus the cohort that benefited first from conversion to lead-free petrol reached the crime-prone age groups roughly at the time the decline in crime began. However, it is difficult to see how the lead-poisoning theory explains why crime continued to fall in age cohorts reaching their late teens throughout the 1990s and after (Farrell et al. 2014: 450–2). The abortion argument fails the cross-national test as its legalization occurred at different times in different countries and was not consistently twenty or so years before the crime fall (when foetuses would have entered the crime-prone years had they not been aborted). It also fails the cohort test: why has crime continued to fall in cohorts reaching their late teens well after any impact effect from legalizing abortion (ibid.: 445–6)?

Declining hard-drug markets as a precipitant of the crime drop has strong support from research in both the United States (Bowling 1999; Blumstein and Wallman 2000; Blumstein and Rosenfeld 2008) and the United Kingdom (Morgan 2014), the former focusing on crack cocaine, the latter on heroin. But whilst the case for an association between declining hard-drug use and falling crime is sustained for these two countries, what still needs to be explained is why the hard-drug markets have declined. It is also not a pattern found in all western countries (Farrell et al. 2014: 450).

The internet hypothesis is complex and scarcely researched, although it has given rise to much speculation. As a putative explanation of the crime fall, the argument is that young people's lifestyles increasingly revolve around staying at home, substituting virtual for physical social interaction. This reduces the opportunity for several forms of standard measurable crime, notably theft and violence. However, it does create opportunities for new forms of crime that are scarcely measured. These include various forms of cybercrime, such as cyberbullying, thefts and fraud targeting internet transactions, and grooming for under-age or other illicit sex (Jewkes 2006; Wall 2007; Jewkes and Yar 2009; Yar 2013). Timing is also problematic for the internet thesis. The crime drop generally began before the usage of the internet was sufficiently pervasive to alter lifestyles (Farrell et al. 2014: 456–7).

Cultural change: a re-civilizing process?

'The civilizing process' has been a significant factor in attempts to explain the drop in violent crime in particular (Eisner 2001, 2014; Pinker 2011). Such interpretations are inspired by Norbert Elias's classic study *The Civilizing Process*. This was originally published in German in 1939 (although mainly written in England after Elias escaped from the Nazis in 1935). It was published in English in two volumes, the first in 1969, the second in 1982 (Elias 1969, 1982). There can be no doubt that Elias was one of the great social theorists of the twentieth century. His work hardly touches on crime, although its relevance for criminology is clear. He traces in great detail the changing habits of everyday life in Europe from the late Middle Ages. He shows that norms and practices exemplified by regulation of bodily functions, table manners, sex and speech were gradually transformed. Starting from notions of court etiquette, increasing control of manners affected the expression of all bodily processes and interaction, including violence. Self-restraint, regulated by internalized shame and guilt, became idealized as 'civilized' behaviour. The second volume of *The Civilizing Process* analyses the causes: the rise of more centralized states, and greater social interdependence.

Eisner's meticulous historical work, charting the long-term decline of homicide and violence since the Middle Ages, brought Elias's account of the 'civilizing process' into the heart of criminology. The increase in violence represented by the Second World War, and the later rise in everyday criminal violence, at first appeared a challenge for Elias's perspective, so the crime decline has been hailed by Eisner, Pinker and others as a return to the long-term civilizing trajectory.

The problem is that, apart from the fall in violence and crime itself, there is little evidence of a general civilizing trend since the 1990s, when crime and violence began falling. The examples offered are a tendentiously interpreted account of some alleged normative changes since the 1960s, the culture of which is castigated as 'permissive' (in line with the condemnations of conservative politicians and right-wing criminologists like James Q. Wilson). It is salutary to remember that Roy Jenkins, the British politician most responsible for the liberalizing trends of the 1960s, labelled the 'permissive' society the 'civilized' society.

From different political and ethical viewpoints, the Pinker–Eisner interpretation of contemporary culture can be stood on its head. Pinker in particular adopts double standards in his critiques of the popular culture of the 1960s versus that of the 1990s onwards. He deploys an intimate knowledge of 1960s culture to remorselessly pinpoint the dark side of its liberalization of mores (Pinker 2011: 129–38). Almost every one of his interpretations can be challenged but, to give just one example, in these nine pages the only example of 1960s racial conflict is a brief mention of Black Panther leader Eldridge Cleaver celebrating rape as a revolutionary act (ibid.: 136–7). Martin Luther King is not mentioned, nor are any other martyrs of the predominantly peaceful struggle for justice. King is cited in the book once, some three hundred pages later, as a model for how Palestinians should conduct themselves (ibid.: 432).

Pinker's treatment of the 1960s is a one-sided caricature, to the tune of 'accentuate the negative'. Conversely, his treatment of post-1990s' youth culture uses the opposite technique, accentuating the positive. For example, citing the apparent contradiction of his re-civilizing thesis that is represented by gangsta rap and the extreme, explicit, amoral violence in many video games, films and television shows, Pinker dismisses this as 'media-savvy, ironic, postmodern' (Pinker 2011: 153–4). There is no concrete evidence that this isn't enhanced *de-civilization* rather than re-civilization, apart from the fall in crime and violence itself – a circular argument.

Economic hypotheses

The recent reviews of the crime-drop literature consider the role of some economic factors, but less meticulously than their thorough analysis of the criminal justice and social lifestyle hypotheses. Farrell and colleagues are cursory on economic hypotheses, including only two: strong economy, and consumer confidence (with inflation bundled in). The strong-economy explanation of the crime drop receives only a couple of statements, mentioning that Levitt's 2004 review had dismissed it but that, as most western countries had strong economies in the 1990s, the explanation passes the cross-national test (Farrell et al. 2014: 442–3).

Farrell and colleagues cite research linking high consumer confidence in the 1990s and early 2000s with the crime drop (Rosenfeld and Messner 2009). However, after the financial crisis in 2007–8, consumer confidence declined, and Rosenfeld turned to another economic explanation: falling inflation, which he argues reduced the market for stolen goods as new ones became cheaper (Rosenfeld 2014). Farrell and his team suggest, however, that the timing of the fall in inflation does not fit the crime drop (Farrell et al. 2014: 449–50). The Brennan Center comes to similar conclusions about the strong-economy argument, seeing it as accounting for only a small part of the crime drop (Roeder et al. 2015: 49). It also looks at low unemployment, finding that it contributed a little to the 1990s crime fall but that, as unemployment increased in the United States after 2000, it exerted upward pressure on crime levels (Roeder et al. 2015: 48–9). The data support the postulated links between lower inflation, higher consumer confidence and falling crime (ibid.: 51–4).

Entirely absent from either review is any consideration of poverty or inequality. Arguably, this is because, as both increased during the period of falling crime, they are not viable explanations for it. However, precisely for that reason they do add to the mystery and are surely relevant issues.

Strangely absent also is any systematic consideration of the major economic shift after the 2007–8 financial crisis. Roeder et al. distinguish only two periods: 1990–1999 and 2000–2013. Farrell et al. don't systematically divide the period of the crime drop, although they consider the timing of individual factors separately.

Altogether, the conventional attempts to explain the crime drop look at economic factors in isolation, if at all. They also necessarily use indicators of the economic variables that are not sensitive to the varying impact they may have in different overall social circumstances. For example, unemployment has different social meanings dependent upon wider economic, social and cultural contexts. In a flourishing economy, with plentiful jobs, unemployment can be voluntary and transitional, with no reason to link it to pressures conducive to crime. Long-term never-employment, however, signifies exclusion from the ordinarily expected ability to participate in consumption and also from the disciplining effects of work routines – a toxic criminogenic brew. If employment means pay below the living wage and irregular 'zero-hours' contracts, the benefits that work provides in terms of insulating people from the temptations of crime are enfeebled. Fluctuations in the recorded employment statistics are thus a poor proxy for changes in the seductions of crime.

In general, approaches that are restricted to correlating economic or other variables singly over time or across space are blind to the importance of macro-level qualitative change or difference. This can only be provided by political economy, rather than conventional economics or statistical modelling based on it (Reiner 2012a, 2012b; Lynch 2013). Changes in crime, now or in the past, cannot be understood without recognizing the overall qualitative shifts in political economy, social relations and culture that come as package deals, not as separable factors, but as interlocking yet unequal influences. Specifically, the rise and fall of crime must be understood as aspects of at least three distinct grand shifts since the Second World War (analogous to what economists refer to as Kondatrieff waves). These are: (i) the post-war consensus period of the Keynesian/welfarist boom; (ii) its displacement by a neo-liberal blitzkrieg from the late 1960s that was hegemonic by the late 1980s; (iii) the crisis in the neo-liberal model precipitated by the 2007–8 financial crash, the reverberations of which are still working themselves out (indicated, for example, by the continuing agonies in Greece and the eurozone).

This overall argument for a political economy approach contextualizes the one hypothesis that survives the strict tests applied by Farrell and his colleagues. This is the 'security hypothesis...that change in the quantity and quality of security was a significant driver of declining crime' (Farrell et al. 2014: 459). Farrell and colleagues quote van Dijk's succinct summary that a

> significant factor inhibiting crime across the Western world is the universal growth in the possession and use of private security measures by households and companies over the past few decades...in all Western countries, without exception, the use of measures to prevent property crimes such as car thefts and household burglaries has risen drastically over the past 15 years. (van Dijk 2006, cited in Farrell et al. 2014: 459)

The exhaustive evidence offered by Farrell and colleagues establishes clearly that the decline in volume property crime (especially burglary and car theft) fits closely in timing and spatial distribution with the proliferation of effective security techniques (Farrell et al. 2014). There can be little doubt that this is at least a proximate explanation of the greater part of the crime decline. A question mark that remains is the extension of the hypothesis to violent crime. Farrell and colleagues suggest that there are spillover effects, for example because volume property crimes are often debut offences in criminal careers that may end up including violence. Whilst this may be true to some extent, it seems doubtful that it can explain the large and continuing drops in homicide and other serious violence.

Security measures influence the context in which crimes may occur by various routes. 'Different security measures work in different ways to reduce the crimes to which they are applied: they increase actual or perceived risk to the offender, and/or they reduce actual or perceived reward for the offender, and/or they increase actual or perceived effort for the offender' (Farrell et al. 2014: 460). Nonetheless, 'the security hypothesis applied to the crime drop can be viewed as simply a specific version of the more general notion that situational crime prevention can be effective' (ibid.).

This makes the theoretical pedigree of the security hypothesis clear. It is rooted in rational choice, routine activities and opportunity theory (Farrell et al. 2014: 481). These perspectives specifically deny that there are any issues about defining crime (the project of this book) and that crime has any deep 'root causes' of the kind analysed by political economy. If, however, it is accepted that crime has complex causes, these theories, despite their empirical support and immediate policy efficacy, are superficial and limited. In a familiar analogy, they concern ways to hold the lid down on social problems, 'liddism' in the term coined by terrorism expert Paul Rogers (Rogers 2010). This perspective turns criminology into liddology: the design of better dustbin lids. It is of course desirable all round to reduce the incidence of criminal acts by effective prevention. But being tough or smart only on crime events, but not on the causes of crime, stores up tensions and troubles. It is perhaps the underlying sense of this that accounts for the public's lack of reassurance, despite the lower rates at which they report victimization.

The next section will seek to apply to the crime drop the framework of the five necessary conditions of crime that were set out earlier. This remains largely a mystery because the grand narratives of neither the Left (political economy) nor the Right (permissiveness, de-civilizing process) that were deployed to explain the crime rise up to the early 1990s seem to fit the decline smoothly. Nonetheless, examining the five conditions will supply some tentative answers.

Labelling Is the explanation of the crime drop that it hasn't actually happened? To what extent might the fall in crime, recorded by both police statistics and victim surveys, nonetheless be a result of shifts in the propensity to label offences, rather than changes in the rate at which they are committed? As always, it is impossible to be sure, but the similar trends in the main measures do suggest that there has been a decline in all western countries, at any rate in the types of crime picked up by those indicators.

At some points, the police statistics and the victim-survey estimates diverged within the last 25 years, and this indicates the perpetual possibility that changes are due to labelling processes. For example, in the early 1990s (Reiner 1996), and in 2013/14 (HMIC 2014) in England and Wales, there is evidence that the rigorous monitoring of performance measures made police record lower proportions of the crimes reported by victims. Similar manipulations have been found in America's NYPD, depressing their recording rate (Eterno and Silverman 2012). Insurance premiums have also been shown to deter victim reporting to the police when crime levels are especially high, again producing artificially reduced police recording rates (Reiner 1996). Conversely, police statistics may create apparent increases in crime that are not borne out by the victimization data if the counting rules change, as they did in England and Wales in 1998 and 2002.

Despite these issues, there is little doubt that the drops throughout the western world in the crimes recorded by conventional measures do map a real change in offending *within the categories that they measure*. However, as seen in previous chapters, this refers only to a particular range of street property offences, committed mainly by and against the poor, and a much smaller number of serious violent offences that take place higher up the social hierarchy.

Many legally defined crimes are scarcely recorded. They are sheltered by legal and social norms of privacy, the corporate form and protection of state secrets. Beyond this, there is a plethora of serious harms and wrongful acts against property and people committed by the powerful, by corporations and states that are immune from criminal sanctions because of a variety of processes keeping them away from criminal law. Although there cannot be precise measurement of the trends, chapters 3 and 4 suggested it was likely that elite crimes were increasing considerably. It is also possible that more crimes are being committed within the same legal categories as those conventionally recorded, but displaced to cyberspace because of better security against street crime (Fitzgerald 2014).

Crime of many very serious kinds has probably increased. Nonetheless, the kinds of offences recorded in criminal statistics have fallen over some twenty years or more. Why?

Motivation The crime drop is puzzling because what have traditionally been seen as the main drivers of crime did not obviously diminish in the 1990s, and certainly not since the 2007/8 economic crash. As shown above, property and serious violent crime are in large part produced by inequality, mediated by the cultural and social psychological processes labelled by Merton as anomie and relative deprivation.

The standard measure of income inequality, the Gini coefficient, increased sharply between 1979 and the early 1990s, the period described above as the era of 'crime explosion' (Belfield et al. 2014: ch. 3).[4] However, it rose with a slower and less even trajectory between the early 1990s and the 'Great Recession', following the 2007/8 financial crash. This fits the earlier period of falling crime.

After the crash, the Gini coefficient fell initially because the incomes of those in employment decreased even faster than benefits, but this will be reversed by current government austerity policies, and measured inequality is heading back to 2008 levels. Absolute poverty actually increased in these years (Belfield et al. 2014: ch. 4). So the initial years of falling crime are linked to some attenuation of the galloping increase of income inequality in the 1980s. However, the recent diminution of Gini coefficient-measured inequality is a reflection of falling living standards for most of the population but with the fastest decline in the middle, rather than the poorest, sections. Certainly, the continuing fall in crime since the crash is difficult to explain by any attenuation of relative deprivation, unless one considers that perhaps expectations may have fallen along with prosperity (Lynch 2013).

As suggested above, when considering the empirical literature on the crime drop, other economic factors show a similar pattern. Overall prosperity, employment and consumer confidence rose from the 1990s to the 2007/8 Great Recession, and inflation declined, playing a part in falling motivations for crime. However, the crime decline continued even after the economic motivational pressures increased following the 2007–8 crisis.

Opportunity The proliferation of attractive, easy-to-steal targets has long been seen as a key factor generating increasing crime, especially by those who deny root-cause theories. During most of the period of the crime fall, however, highly portable and valuable consumer goods became *more* available (laptops, mobile phones, iPods, tablets). There is evidence that, within the overall crime fall, thefts of these sorts of goods increased. For example, the ownership of mobile phones rose in parallel to thefts of them (Curran et al. 2005: 16).

Overall, most of the crime drop occurred at a time of rising consumption levels, when the availability of targets had expanded. Since the Great Recession of 2007/8, the reverse has occurred, so perhaps falling crime since then is partly attributable to declining opportunities. However, it is hard to see this as an important factor in the fall in crime since the early 1990s.

Means The spread of more effective security, the best explanation of the overall crime drop, implies that the standard means used for burglary, thefts of and from cars and other volume property offences have become less effective. This reduced availability of means to commit standard property crimes is the flip side of the security hypothesis and is a strong contender as a proximate explanation of the overall crime drop.

On the other hand, the means for committing other forms of crime have proliferated, notably through the internet (McGuire and Dowling 2013). These offences are scarcely measured, and the ONS is exploring ways of expanding the CSEW to incorporate questions in order to track them (Collins et al. 2014; ONS 2014, 2015). In October 2015, some preliminary estimates were released, showing that the rise in cybercrime may well outweigh the fall in conventionally measured offences and that including them shows that overall crime is rising, not falling (Travis 2015b). However, restricted availability of means to commit those crimes that traditionally form the bulk of the official statistics could be a part of the explanation of the drop in (conventionally measured) crime, an aspect of the security hypothesis. At the same time, means to commit crimes in new ways may have proliferated without registering in the statistics until 2015. This also implies that the broader theories about increasing motivation and declining cultural controls continue to be valid.

Absence of control As discussed earlier, some have argued that a process of re-civilization has occurred, restoring the long march of the civilizing process that had brought down violence and crime more generally since the Middle Ages (Pinker 2011: 145–54; Eisner 2014; Kivivuori 2014). In addition, formal controls began to work better. 'I think two overarching explanations are plausible. The first is that the Leviathan got bigger, smarter, and more effective. The second is that the Civilizing Process, which the counterculture had tried to reverse in the 1960s, was restored to its forward direction' (Pinker 2011: 145).

Formal controls

Did a 'bigger, smarter, and more effective' Leviathan play a part in reducing crime, as Pinker suggests? The above reviews of the evidence suggest that more imprisonment and smarter, more numerous police did play a part in the early stages of crime reduction. However, imprisonment has long been in a phase of diminishing returns, according to most analysts. Police numbers have plateaued or decreased in many jurisdictions since the 2008 recession. In Britain, in particular, numbers have fallen sharply following the election of Conservative-led governments since 2010. Police are expected to do more with less, and so far at any rate dramatic cuts have been accompanied by continued falls in conventionally measured crime. This may well change with the advent of even more draconian reductions in resourcing of police (and indeed criminal justice as a whole). At any rate, it is difficult to attribute recent falls in crime to a larger Leviathan, and the enhanced smartness demanded is becoming superhuman.

Informal controls

The heart of the re-civilization thesis is that 'the Great Crime Decline of the 1990s was part of a change in sensibilities'

(Pinker 2011: 149–50). Whilst the 'permissive' culture of the 1960s relaxed internalized self-controls to a dangerous extent, this led to a counter-revolution of reintroducing stricter normative disciplines that have shaped the post-1980s younger generations. As argued earlier, a major problem with this interpretation is that the only solid evidence of re-civilization is the decline of violence itself.

Eisner does try to find some quantitative evidence of broader cultural change by tracing the frequency of certain words in the Google-books database NGRAM (Eisner 2014: 117–22). For example, his analysis shows that the frequency of the words 'sex', 'drugs' and 'narcissism' (what happened to rock 'n' roll?) increased in the 1970s and 1980s, paralleling the crime rise, but then fell from the late 1990s as crime fell. On the other hand, the frequency of words like 'shame', 'politeness', 'honesty', 'conscientiousness' and 'anger management' increased after about 2000. This, he suggests, indicated a strengthening of the 'moral muscle of self-control' (Eisner 2014: 121).

There are two great problems with this interpretation, even disregarding technical issues of the non-representativeness of the Google database. First, the positive words began to increase in frequency after, not before, the decline in violence set in. Second, the sexual explicitness, focus on violence and drug orientation of popular culture has increased dramatically since the late 1990s, perhaps not in books (though what about the *Fifty Shades of Grey* phenomenon?) but in newer media – videos, pop music, electronic games, the internet.

As indicated earlier, Pinker is well aware of that, but excuses, indeed celebrates, the hyper-explicit sex and violence of Generation X pop culture as 'media-savvy, ironic, postmodern', 'a sign that they live in a society that is so civilized that they don't have to fear being harassed or assaulted' (Pinker 2011: 153–4). On the other hand, Pinker remorselessly focuses on the dark and extreme sides of 1960s counter-culture, street-fighting violent rhetoric from the Rolling Stones, the Black Panthers and the Hell's Angels. There is no hint of what many would see as the dominant aspects of 1960s counter-culture, a search for peace and justice, but which was rapidly co-opted or corrupted by commercial and consumerist forces (Hall et al. 2008; Hall 2012; Hall and Winlow 2015). 'Make love, not war' became 'make love *and* war *and* money', as neo-liberalism defeated Keynesian welfarism, and the Woodstock generation graduated to Wall Street and the West Wing, seeking sex *and* the city.

The key problem with the 're-civilizing process' argument is its neglect of the epochal changes in political economy since the Second World War, looking at cultural change in isolation from it. The post-war reconstruction that was based on a social democratic, welfarist model, deploying Keynesian economic management techniques (accepted in its essentials even by the Conservative and Republican governments of the 1950s up to the early 1970s), witnessed the culmination of a long-term march towards increasing social inclusion and greater equality. This stretched back to the seventeenth-century upheavals in England and the eighteenth-century revolutions in the United States and France. In the English case, it was analysed seminally by Marshall's account of the spread of citizenship (Marshall 1950).

This long-term democratization project went hand in hand with pacification charted by Eisner and other historical studies of declining violence. It is the macro-level base for the 'civilizing process'. Pacification and incorporation into citizenship not only occurred slowly, in fits and starts, and unevenly, but was of course never anything like complete. Even at its apex, before being set into reverse by neo-liberalism, inequality remained large, and violence was in many ways hidden or suppressed (which is why Hall and Winlow persuasively speak of a 'pseudo-pacification' process; cf. Hall 2012; Hall and Winlow 2015: 115–19).

Whilst no doubt much turns on different political and ethical viewpoints, it seems hard to discern in contemporary trends in political economy and culture any clear or consistent move to greater civility. As charted earlier, in western societies we have seen: a massive increase in economic inequality and, now, in poverty; wars of choice by democratically elected governments that have inflicted death and destruction on countless – more precisely, uncounted – innocent victims; rampant crimes of the powerful economic elites; evisceration of economies around the world in the name of financial rectitude that benefits only the wealthy; demonization of people receiving welfare, whether or not they are 'hard-working' families and/or disabled; increasing castigation of immigrants and foreigners; and a reborn rampant nationalism. In this toxic collateral cultural damage flowing from the 'shock doctrine' of neo-liberal 'disaster capitalism' (Klein 2008), the 'civilizing revival' theorists rightly pick out nuggets of ethical progress against the tide of growing egoistic individualism. These include greater justice for black and ethnic minority people, women and gay people. All these victories for fairness and tolerance, however, are clearly rooted in the 1960s, the 'civilized' society boasted of by Home Secretary Roy Jenkins but castigated as 'permissiveness' by the 're-civilization' theorists.

Conclusion: political economy or policing?

The post-1990s crime fall has been a major ingredient in the resurgence of 'can-do' optimism amongst police, criminal justice policy makers and agents around the world. Certainly, nobody can fail to welcome improvements in policing that have saved many lives. But has it refuted the older criminological consensus that policing and prisons were at best short-term palliatives. No one put it better than Raymond Chandler in *The Long Goodbye* (1977 [1953]: 599): 'Crime isn't a disease, it's a symptom. Cops are like a doctor that gives you aspirin for a brain tumour.'

In the face of extensive evidence about the relationship between inequality, economic exclusion and violence, it seems hazardous to conclude that the lid can be held down indefinitely on injustice. The evidence cited earlier clearly suggests that there *are* 'root causes' shaping crime and penal trends. These are related to variations in political economy. They indicate that social democratic political economies are associated with less homicide, violence and serious crime, *and* with less punitive penal policies (Cavadino and Dignan 2006;

Reiner 2007: 95–116, especially Table 4.1, 2012a, 2012b; Lacey 2008; Hall and McLean 2009; Lynch 2013).

This is plausibly due to cultural differences in the moral quality of individualism. Social democracies reflect and encourage reciprocal individualism, in which there is some mutual concern for the welfare of all, as distinct from the competitive individualism of neo-liberalism, which fosters a Darwinian struggle in which only the strongest flourish. The dependence of social harmony on justice is not a post-Enlightenment, modernist grand narrative, outmoded in a post-modernized, globalized era. Psalm 127 tells us that 'if the Lord does not guard the city, the watchman keeps watch in vain', and the Prophet Micah admonished that for this we must 'do justice, love mercy, and walk humbly' (Micah VI: 8). Or, if pagan sources are preferred, *si vis pacem, para iustitiam* ('if you seek peace, pursue justice'). Have we really got a new policing panacea that allows us to disregard these ancient wisdoms?

Crime has complex and multiple causes, so no single-factor accounts (like the conservative control thesis) can withstand close examination. The analysis in terms of five necessary conditions of crime provides a variety of tools for explaining particular turning points. For example, the explosion of crime in the Thatcher years (confirmed by both police statistics and the British Crime Survey) was attributable above all to the pernicious social effects (rapidly rising inequality and social exclusion) of the introduction of neo-liberal economic policies.

The fall in crime since the mid-1990s remains rather more mysterious, as it is difficult to see any attenuation of 'criminality' (the tendency of society to produce criminals). Indeed, the 2015 addition of estimates of cybercrime to the conventional measures suggests that crime beyond the traditionally measured may not be decreasing at all but growing. The Right's *bête noire*, 'permissiveness', continued unabated, as did the economic and social polarization attributable to neo-liberal globalization. The most plausible account of the fall in standard crime is the 'security hypothesis': the huge expansion in the use and efficacy of technical crime prevention techniques, especially car and home security devices. These have held the lid down on a continuing underlying increase in 'criminality'. The UK 2011 riots showed dramatically what happens when the lid is temporarily lifted, as do similar outbreaks elsewhere (Winlow et al. 2015). The key department for tackling crime is the Treasury, not the Home Office or the Ministry of Justice. Smart and fair criminal justice can help, but only as first aid. It is necessary to be not only tough on crime but on its underlying causes, which lie way beyond the ambit of codes, cops, courts and corrections.

Conclusion: Crime: A Capital Concept

'If there's any illness for which people offer many remedies, you may be sure that particular illness is incurable.'
(Anton Chekhov: *The Cherry Orchard*, 1904)

Conflict between human beings and violations of group norms are perennial. They have existed as long as there have been humans and groups. The concept of crime, in its broadest sense of condemnation and censure of some behaviour as seriously wrong and threatening, is arguably also universal in human relationships. In chapters 1 and 2 we saw, however, that a particular modern legal conception of crime, distinguished from other forms of wrongdoing and troublemaking, emerged hand in hand with the development of capitalist nation-states. The essence of this legal conception has three elements: that crime is an offence against the general public interest, embodied in the state (as distinct from harm to specific individuals); that criminal proceedings are aimed at punishing offenders, not securing compensation; and that punishment is justified by the individual responsibility of offenders.

Strong nation-states were a necessary condition of the modern concept of crime. They were essential to the idea that crimes were offences against a general order, not just specific interests. They were also the source of the specific rules detailing what this entailed and overseeing the proceedings that punished violators. They also underwrote the minimum degree of settled existence necessary for a functioning legal system, preventing such a degree of disorder that it becomes impossible to distinguish individual wrongful acts from a generalized war of all against all (whether between or within nation-states).

It was the capitalist form of the nation-state that was essential for the other two elements of the modern conception of crime. The idea that offenders were responsible as individuals for their crimes was a necessary condition for regarding the pains inflicted upon them by legal punishment as morally justified, rather than motivated by revenge or the interests of a despotic authority. And the model of actors (criminal or not) as individually responsible for their deeds was isomorphic with the actual position of people in the capitalist marketplace, whether for labour or goods. All participants in the ideal-typical competitive market were responsible for striking the best bargains they could with their resources, whether these were merely their own bodies or ownership of capital. This was the culture and practice of 'possessive individualism' (Macpherson 1962), underlying the rational choice model of individual action, still presumed today by most economics, and with a flourishing presence in other branches of social science, including criminology. As seen in earlier chapters, this model of the individual actor, rationally choosing whether or not to break the law, was the bedrock of the eighteenth-century classical perspective in criminal law, which remains the core ideology of present-day criminal justice.

A key problem was and is that, whilst the criminal process deems all people equal before the law in that they are presumed capable of exercising individual responsibility, the reality of capitalist social relations is that they are constructed on a basis of fundamental *inequality*, between owners of capital and those who only possess their labour power. In addition, the normal operation of capitalist markets, in the absence of countervailing collective or state action, generates ever-widening inequality.[1]

This creates a pincer movement that traps the lowest levels of the hierarchy of power and privilege into a double lock with regard to crime. What right-wing criminologists like James Q. Wilson pinpoint as the essence of crime – 'predatory street crime' – is most likely to involve the poorest and most excluded sections of society, both as victims and perpetrators. The crimes of the powerless are the most visible and viscerally frightening, as well as easier to measure routinely. But the damage they do (to people's bodies as well as their property) is far outstripped by that inflicted by the crimes of the powerful, although this is largely hidden from plain sight and enmeshed in complex causal chains that complicate responsibility. The public face of crime – in the criminal process, political discourse and the mass media – is thus dominated by the crimes afflicting the poor, who disproportionately pay the price through the pains of victimization and of punishment.

How is this double whammy of social injustice legitimated, in particular to the poorer and excluded sections of society? Certainly, a crucial part is played by the inculcation of ideological perspectives portraying the criminal law as universally beneficial protection against serious and frightening wrongs which are perpetrated by individuals who choose to do harm to others. The criminal process is legitimated by representing it as a fair application of the law to malefactors, operating in accordance with technical procedures that are impartial and effective.

The many fictional television series about the police offer an illustration of this. They can be interpreted as a succession of models of police officers and their work that present them as protecting ordinary people (like the viewer) from dangers they are vulnerable to because of the actions of individuals who have chosen to benefit themselves by victimizing others. The changing details of how the police are legitimated by these programmes accommodates shifting cultural sensibilities about how agents of the state, battling the perils posed by 'villains', can be made plausible and acceptable to a mass audience. In Britain, since the Second World War, this has moved on from portraying the police as impeccably virtuous grown-up boy scouts such as the BBC's PC George Dixon, serving as ideal citizens guarding the community from its own wrongdoers. As news revelations of police malpractice become more common, this has become increasingly implausible.

Police heroes on TV became less virtuous in their personal lives (swearing, drinking, having extra-marital affairs, using violence) whilst still zealously and effectively bringing criminals to justice. During the 1990s, the peccadilloes attributed to police protagonists threatened at times to make them indistinguishable from criminals, but the constant factor remained the idea that they were needed to defeat even more evil threats to ordinary people – I have called this myth 'police fetishism' (Reiner 2010a: 1–2, ch. 6). The most recent formula for presenting the police as effective guardians of the universal public interest embodied in law is the appliance of science. Police procedurals focusing on scientific forensic methods as the panacea for crime solving flourish, quintessentially exemplified by the US television series *CSI* and its many progenies around the world (the different locales for the *CSI* brand itself, but also such popular British programmes as *Silent Witness* or *Waking the Dead*). These construct policing as the pursuit of dangerous offenders, unerringly identifying criminals by utilizing a neutral, objective analysis of evidence.

The constantly changing guard of fictional police heroes is a long way from the reality, which is that the police detect only a tiny minority of the crimes that they record (itself a fraction of those they know about, let alone the unmeasured mass of crimes that actually are committed). It also disguises the vastly disproportionate criminalization of the poor and BAME populations, whilst the crimes of the powerful have virtual immunity from policing.

A precondition of the legitimation of policing and of the criminal process is the legitimation of the criminal law that supposedly underpins them. This was achieved in the course of the nineteenth century by a slow process of reforms of criminal law, procedure and criminal justice agencies. All moved away from direct control by economic and political elites to become the preserve of an array of professionals, who were represented as insulated from the socially powerful. Lawyers, judges and other criminal justice agents were professionalized by more or less extensive education, and were subject to disciplinary bodies independent of outside governmental power. The police, the cutting edge of interaction with the public, continued to be drawn from the mass of the population and relatively poorly educated but were constructed by various organizational strategies as representing the public interest and accountable to the professionalized legal system (Reiner 2010a: ch. 3).

Underpinning this representation of criminal justice as governed by objective, impartial technical processes was a deeper legitimation of substantive criminal law itself (Lacey 2014). This was accomplished primarily by the nineteenth-century progress of parliamentary democracy, transforming a system of aristocratic rule to one in which law making and policy were shaped by the will of the people expressed through the electoral process. The long march of democratic citizenship (Marshall 1950) transformed the image of law (including criminal) from an embodiment of the interest of the ruling class to an expression of popular will.

It is important to note that this process of legitimation is not an injection of false consciousness by the ideological syringes of the mass media and political socialization. The core of its plausibility is twofold. First, the processes of parliamentary democracy do allow the occasional opportunity to change government, crudely to boot the bastards out. True, this has become increasingly a Hobson's choice between neo-liberalism and neo-liberalism lite, but it is a less painful way of changing governing elites than is available under other systems.

The legitimation of criminal law is more directly a result of its dual face. Criminal law simultaneously protects the universal interest of order in general, a precondition of any civilized coexistence, *and* the particular orders of unequal and hierarchical power and privilege. Criminal justice administers both 'parking tickets and class repression' (Marenin 1982). As the criminological realists emphasize, the volume of predatory street crimes, which are the bulk of those processed by criminal justice agencies, do particularly harm the weakest, poorest, most vulnerable people in society. However, as the constructionists stress, the law in action focuses on only a small proportion of wrongful harms (mainly proletarian crimes and offenders), leaving largely untouched the depredations of the powerful.

This contrast leaves the legitimation of law and criminal justice constantly fragile. It is threatened by the disproportionate, often discriminatory, use of police powers, such as stop and search, against visible minorities (Delsol and Shiner 2015) and gives rise to a regular cycle of scandal and reform (indicated in the United Kingdom by the Scarman Report 1981 and the Macpherson Report 1999). Even more fundamentally delegitimating are the occasional uses of criminal law and policing nakedly to buttress the power of economic and political elites against the political actions of the disadvantaged (for example, the 1984–5 miners' strike in the United Kingdom or the worldwide protests against neo-liberal globalization and austerity). These conjunctures evidently tilt criminal law towards the class repression rather than parking-ticket side of the Janus face.

The project of constructing crime, the perennial phenomenon of censure and condemnation of conduct, into its modern criminal law conception involved profound social transformation. It aimed to convert the use of coercive power to buttress economic, social and political elites into an apparently impartial, technocratic, neutral exercise of reason on behalf of the democratically expressed popular will. This was an important element in the development of more integrated, centralized capitalist states which required high degrees of predictability in everyday conduct in labour and goods markets, and disciplined mass urban workforces for industrial production. The new 'demand for order' (Silver 1967) was supplied by the emergence of an apparently independent and professionalized criminal justice system. The legitimation this achieved has always been fragile and is threatened by any hint of connection between the formulation and enforcement of law and socio-economic power.

At its root, the conception of crime as criminal law makes crime a capital concept, intimately bound up with the workings and the vicissitudes of capitalism. It is always subject to critique from different moral positions and because its operation in practice is closely associated with the structures of class and power. Nonetheless, its fragile legitimacy is buttressed by its work against the viscerally alarming depredations of some poor young men against the majority of the deprived, as well as by ideological constructions working upon that.

From its eighteenth-century inception in the early days of capitalist industrialization, criminal law and justice have gone through a long march of growing legitimation, albeit punctuated by periods of threat when the class repression aspect overshadowed the function of general order maintenance. This was partly the result of the strategy of constructing an apparently neutral and technical system. However, the precondition for the success of that legitimation strategy was the long-term incorporation of the mass of society into a common status of democratic citizenship, based on civil, political and ultimately socio-economic rights (Marshall 1950). This was not inevitable but the result of conflict and struggle for the vote, trade union rights, welfare and many other issues. There were periods of profound setback to the project of capitalist pacification: for example, the years immediately before and after the First World War, the 1930s Great Depression and the rise of fascism. Nonetheless, in the three post-Second World War decades, although considerable inequality remained, it was possible to discern the onward progress of a long march towards greater equality, justice and internal peace, underpinned by the Keynesian welfarist consensus. This was reflected in a parallel trajectory towards more consensual criminal justice, embodied in 'penal welfarism' (Garland 1985, 2001) and 'policing by consent' (Reiner 2010a: ch. 3, 2011: Parts I and III).

The neo-liberal onslaught on this project since the end of the 1960s has set everything into reverse, and we seem to be hurtling back to older eras of laissez-faire capitalism, unbridled inequality, unravelling of social security and safety nets, rich people in their gated estates, poor people bedroom-taxed away from even the gates…Destination 1900? 1800? 1700?

At first, the crime and criminal justice consequences of this epochal reversal fitted the backwards trajectory of political economy (Reiner 2007). Recorded crime and actual victimization exploded in the 1980s–early 1990s. Urban and industrial disorder brought levels of violence unseen for more than half a century. Policing and penal policy became ever tougher, more punitive and better resourced under both the Conservatives and New Labour (Newburn 2007; Newburn and Reiner 2007; Lacey 2008; Downes and Morgan 2012). This was well summed up as 'the Free Economy and the Strong State' (Gamble 1994). Commensurate with this, there was evidence of a legitimacy crisis, particularly in policing, although this seems to have been partially reversed since the early 1990s (Reiner 2010a: ch. 3).

And then something mysterious and totally unexpected happened. From the early 1990s, crime began to drop, at first in the United States but then throughout the western world. It confounded the expectations of Right, Left and administrative criminologists alike.

Quickly, however, they came up with theory-saving explanations. The Right and the administrative criminologists saw it as a vindication of faith in tougher and/or smarter, larger criminal justice systems. The Left, and the administrative criminologists too (who also associated economic prosperity with falling crime), could attribute it to benign material conditions in the 1990s and early 2000s. After all, in May 2008 (on the cusp of the Great Recession), Mervyn King, then governor of the Bank of England, had dubbed the previous period the 'NICE' (non-inflationary continuous expansion) decade.

We now know that the apparent prosperity of that period was built on a bubble of debt and exploded soon after King's hubristic naming of the previous decade. Financialization had been the secret weapon of neo-liberal regimes desperate to keep up the living standards of the general population, despite dormant productivity and surging inequality, in which the wealth of the very top layers shot up, up and away into the stratosphere. It all exploded in the credit crunch and subsequent economic crisis, the consequences and uncertain outcome of which we are still living with.

What did not happen was the widely predicted resurgence of rising crime and rampant disorder (despite the massive cuts in policing and criminal justice generally since 2010). True, there has been some growth in political protest against austerity and of rioting (but of the 'consumer' kind, without a political edge; cf. Newburn et al. 2015; Rayman and Smith 2015; Winlow et al. 2015). These do not compare with the outbreaks of the 1980s in frequency, intensity, violence or overt political motivations.

The crime drop is of course apparent only in the types of offences that are recorded by official surveys or police statistics. It is likely that offending has increased in cyberspace (as confirmed by recent Home Office efforts to estimate it), and in other ways that escape the conventional measures. Above all, the economic crisis and the political reaction to it are in themselves the result of, and in turn produce, extremely serious corporate and state elite crimes and harms. There are many signs that we live in an increasingly brutal and heartless age, implied for example by the callous indifference, if not outright contempt, with which many regard the mass drowning of would-be immigrants to Europe or Australia. So there is no warrant for the Panglossian view of some commentators, who attribute the fall in violence in particular to a renewed civilizing process.

Nonetheless, the drop in mainstream recorded criminal activity is undeniable. However, most of this is due to the increase in the quantity and quality of security devices and techniques, preventing the main forms of routine property crime but not tackling criminality, the underlying criminogenic social tendencies. In the absence of any alleviation of the causes of crime, better security techniques probably can only hold the lid down on offending for a time. It is also true that the benefit of the crime fall is unevenly divided along the lines of class, gender and ethnic inequality in both the United States (Parker 2010) and the United Kingdom (Tilley, Tseloni and Farrell 2011). Enhanced security is disproportionately available to the more affluent. And crimes beyond the conventionally measured, and which are targeted by security paraphernalia, are burgeoning.

Does the pause in routine crime offer any opportunity for a resurgence of the movement towards less punitive and more legitimate criminal justice that was engendered by neoliberalism? Survey evidence suggests most people don't believe that crime risks have declined, and 'penal populism' (Pratt 2006) is buoyant, but there are also counter-signs that the crime drop has registered with the public, at least subliminally. The salience of crime as an issue has slipped down opinion polls, and it scarcely figured in the three British general elections since 2005. This could be one of the reasons that the Conservative-dominated governments since 2010 have had the political space to effect considerable reductions in police resourcing and autonomy.

Public attitudes to crime and justice have long been both pessimistic and punitive. Surveys regularly show most people believe crime is perpetually trending upwards, even as the recorded statistics show the opposite. They also believe that penal policy is too lax, despite its evident toughening in recent decades and bursting prisons (after two decades of falling crime). But these perspectives are volatile, and include many contradictions (Ipsos MORI 2010; Paige 2013). Much of this is due to misinformation, primarily drawn from the mass media, which most people cite as their main source of 'knowledge' about crime and justice.

Many studies have shown that, when people are provided with accurate information about sentencing, imprisonment and community penalties, their views move away from the penal populism expressed in polls (Hough and Roberts 2012: 287–9). The contradictory interaction between experience and media representations is evident in the surveys. Most people perceive that crime is not rising in their own areas (of course, for the most unfortunate it may be), but still say it is increasing overall – presumably 'knowledge' from the constant media reporting of sensational cases. When asked about how to cut crime, people favour social strategies such as employment opportunities and youth leisure facilities as the most effective. There is little faith in the crime-reducing potential of imprisonment, so the demand for more of it is presumably purely punitive. But when people are asked what would be the appropriate sentence for specific cases, they come close to current judicial practice. The perception that sentencing is excessively lenient comes from the media highlighting exceptionally heinous crimes or egregious errors by criminal justice authorities.

What emerges from surveys of public concern, as well as the *vox populi* as expressed in phone-in programmes, the blogosphere and other sources, is a scapegoating of vulnerable targets, the common factor being their construction as 'other'. Attitudes expressed towards criminals, but also other folk devils, such as immigrants, welfare and 'overseas aid' recipients, are redolent of a projection of anger about insecurity and relative deprivation onto the even more vulnerable. Anger is also expressed towards more plausible authors of the widespread fear and anxiety engendered by much more precarious economic circumstances, politicians and the economic elite, summed up as 'bankers'. But this ire seems muted by comparison with the venom directed at vulnerable 'others'.

In the United Kingdom, moreover, politicians not in government (Labour, and now the Lib Dems) attract much more contempt and bile than the ruling Tories. In part, this may be because of widespread acceptance of the myth that Labour overspending caused the crisis, rather than the more accurate opposite version: the crisis caused Labour to overspend, seeking to rescue the reckless financial institutions that caused it. The widespread belief that Labour crashed the economy is in large part because of corporate and Conservative dominance of the media.

However, the deeper question is how to explain the receptivity of the mass of the population to the neo-liberal reading of the economic crisis caused by neo-liberalism itself. After all, the economic underpinnings of the neo-liberal austerity strategy, which unnecessarily and counterproductively immiserates most people, have been demolished by a legion of economists, not least the IMF itself.

The mystery of Disraeli's 'angels in marble', the one-third of the working class who have voted Tory for the century and a half since they began to be enfranchised, has been probed by generations of scholars. What is seldom recognized is the possibility of a psychodynamic interpretation (Hall and Winlow 2015), underlying the more rational explanations such as the picking up of crumbs from the table provided by the fruits of imperialism.

This same question was addressed nearly a century ago, in the wake of the Great Depression of the 1930s, by Left-leaning psychoanalysts (several associated with the Frankfurt School) who sought to understand the phenomenon of mass support for hard-line disciplinary solutions, including fascism. Prominent amongst these was Erich Fromm, who specifically tackled the issue of crime and popular punitiveness, deploying a combination of political economy and psychoanalysis (Fromm 2000a [1930], 2000b [1931]; Anderson and Quinney 2000; Cheliotis 2013).

Fromm recognized the reality that conventionally defined crime does indeed harm vulnerable victims. He also accepted that socio-economic pressures lead some deprived people to commit crimes, especially when times are hard, but saw the explanation of why only some resort to harming others in psychodynamic processes separating them from their fellows in the same plight. Whilst ordinary crimes are a problem, the hatred levelled at the offender (rather than the elites that direct the economic system leading to the crimes) is excessive and partly misdirected. The roots of this are sadomasochistic psychic processes whereby the aggressive energy stoked by the suffering of the masses is directed inwards, rather than at the powerful father figures of the dominant elites. This fury is then projected outwards with even greater ferocity against scapegoats lower in the pecking order: convicted criminals but also ethnic and other minorities.

The deep psychodynamic sources of populist punitiveness certainly make tackling it challenging, especially when it is further fuelled by misinformation from a corporate-dominated mass media. Information can only play a limited role, especially when the playing field for public debate is so tilted towards conservative perspectives. The way forward must involve tackling the deeper roots in the overall political economy and culture beyond the criminal justice sphere itself.

What this book has shown is that, paraphrasing Marx on philosophers, 'Criminologists have only *interpreted* the world.' As Marx famously concluded, 'The point, however, is to *change* it.'[2] The problem of the criminal world, as of Marx's world itself, is ultimately a problem of capital, hence this conclusion's title. The origins of dominant modern criminal law lie in the development of capitalism, and its contemporary functioning continues to reflect this. The commission of most of the harmful acts processed by the criminal 'justice' system as crimes (as well as the many that are not recorded) lie in the egoistic and anomic culture generated by capitalism. And the excessively punitive popular hatred of the luckless losers of the criminal justice lottery who are caught (most of whom are factually guilty) results in penal treatments doomed to result in recidivism. This is a self-perpetuating loop that can never succeed in its avowed goal of controlling crime, but functions as one of the scapegoating processes diverting anger and hate away from the economic and political elites, especially in the era of neo-liberalism with its spiralling inequality and insecurity. Yet these elites (especially the 1 per cent labelled by the Occupy movement) are responsible for much greater harms than those committed by the deprived, serious as some of those are. *The* crimes of our times are those of capital.

Notes

Introduction: Crime: Conundrums of a Common-Sense Concept

1 This is distinct from Sumner's sophisticated application of Marxist theory of ideology to crime which he calls 'censure theory' (Amatrudo 2009: 86–8), discussed later in chapter 3.

2 PPI refers to 'Payment Protection Insurance', policies purporting to protect borrowers by carrying on their loan repayments in the event of illness or other circumstances that make it hard for them to continue paying. These policies were widely sold (often covertly) by British banks. These were held by the courts to have been mis-sold in many cases, and banks have been compensating victims for this.

Chapter 1: Legal Conceptions of Crime

1 Chalmers and Leverick 2013 is a rigorous critical analysis of the Coalition government's attempt to restrict the creation of new criminal offences.

2 These types are classified into nine broad categories: violence against the person, sexual offences, robbery, burglary, theft and handling stolen goods, fraud and forgery, criminal damage, drugs and 'other' offences – a massive plethora of statutory prohibitions ranging from concealing an infant death, bigamy, obscene publications and public order to

illegal immigration, VAT, illegal gambling and violations of health and safety at work regulations ('Counting rules for recorded crime', https://www.gov.uk/government/publications/counting-rules-for-recorded-crime).

3 Private prosecution remains technically possible. Most are brought by companies not individuals.

4 An idealized figure of 'the victim' has indeed become increasingly central to the contemporary cultural characterization of crime (Garland 2001; Reiner 2007: ch. 5; Simon 2007: ch. 3).

5 Expressed sharply in the polemical 'logical positivism' of *Language, Truth and Logic* (Ayer 1936).

6 The ambivalent hydra-headedness of Popper's political philosophy is signalled by his membership of the original Mont Pelerin Society, to which neo-liberalism traces its roots (Mirowski and Plehwe 2009).

7 A withering critique of mindless 'voodoo' number crunching in criminology is Young 2011.

8 The reconciliation of the polarities of rigorous empirical and logical analysis, whilst recognizing the irreducible element of unpredictability due to human consciousness and interpretation, and the immanent critique of social conditions growing out of their understanding, is potentially achieved in the ongoing work of critical realism (Sayer 2011).

9 Many textbooks cite the 1931 case in which the great judge Lord Atkin declared: 'The domain of criminal jurisprudence can only be ascertained by examining what acts at any particular period are declared by the State to be crimes, and the only common nature they will be found to possess is that they are prohibited by the State' *(Proprietary Articles Trade Assn.* v. *Alt. Gen. for Canada* [1931] AC at 324).

10 The leading case is *Engel*, in which the Court formulated three criteria for determining whether proceedings are 'criminal'. These are: (i) the domestic classification of the offence; (ii) 'the very nature of the offence'; (iii) the seriousness of the potential punishment. The second criterion, the substance of the offence, has not produced analysis of the principles characterizing behaviour as criminal. Rather, it has involved a set of essentially procedural issues: is there a punitive element to the sanction? Is the offence generally binding or restricted to a specific sub-group? Does the verdict require finding culpability? Are proceedings instituted by a public body?

How are such matters defined in other jurisdictions? In most cases, the third criterion, the severity of potential punishment, has proved decisive (*Engel v. Netherlands* 1979–80, 1 European Human Rights Reports 647).

11 *Clingham v. Royal Borough of Kensington and Chelsea*; *R. v. Crown Court at Manchester ex.p. McCann and others* [2003] 1 A.C. 787.

12 The historian Douglas Hay noted in studying eighteenth-century punishment that 'It was easy to claim equal justice for murderers of all classes, where a universal moral sanction was more likely to be found...The trick was to extend that communal sanction to a criminal law that was nine-tenths concerned with upholding a radical division of property' (Hay 1975: 35). Hay's 'trick' continues today.

13 Key texts include: Taylor 1981; Lea and Young 1984; Kinsey, Lea and Young 1986. More recent contributions to Left realism include Lea 2002, Matthews 2014 and the important work associated with the Teesside Centre for Realist Criminology, established in 2013 (e.g. Hall and Winlow 2012, 2015).

Chapter 2: Moral Conceptions of Crime

1 Jeremy Clarkson was the (often controversial) co-presenter of the BBC television series *Top Gear* from 2002 until 2015.

2 Tort is a civil action for damages as compensation for harmful conduct. An example would be assault, which can lead to prosecution for a crime, and/or civil action for damages.

3 They include: prohibiting marriages where the parties lack the means to support a family; prohibiting voluntary idleness leading to unjustified demands for public support, or failure to support children; fining fathers whose children cannot read; punishing drunkenness in people deemed to have a propensity to violence; punishing sellers of dangerous goods like weapons, poisons or alcohol who fail to comply with licensing and other regulations; and 'offences against decency' (see Harcourt 2014: section 1).

Chapter 4: How Do They Get Away With It? The Non-Criminalization of the Powerful

1 LSE Visiting Professor Roger McCormick has founded a Conduct Costs Project website that seeks to keep track of the

fines and other sanctions levied against financial institutions: http://ccpresearchfoundation.com/index, accessed 3 July 2015.

2 This was definitively established in the landmark 1896 House of Lords decision in *Salomon v. Salomon*, upholding the doctrine of corporate personality set out in the 1862 Companies Act, protecting the shareholders in a company from action to recover debts.

3 Further essential sources for up-to-date information are two websites: Statewatch (which until 2014 published a regular journal) and International State Crime Initiative.

Chapter 5: The Criminal Justice Process and Conceptions of Crime

1 The much-discussed drop in crime since the 1990s has only returned statistics to a level that in the early 1980s was a source of considerable panic about law and order.

2 The over-representation of prisoners from BAME backgrounds is even stronger for young offenders. According to Youth Justice Board data in 2014/15, 40 per cent of prisoners under 18 were black or other ethnic minority (Sloan and Allison 2015).

Chapter 7: Whodunnit and Why? Criminological Conceptions of Crime

1 Just some of the sources documenting links between economic deprivation, injustice and crime: Box 1987; Currie 1985, 1998; Field 1990, 1999; Hale 1998, 1999, 2013; Fielding, Clarke and Witt 2000; Marris 2000; Reiner 2007: ch. 4, 2012a, 2012b; Hall and McLean 2009; Rosenfeld and Messner 2009; Wilkinson and Pickett 2009: ch. 10; Gilligan 2011; Hooghe et al. 2011; Pridemore 2011; Albertson and Fox 2012; Farrall and Jennings 2012; Jennings, Farrall and Bevan 2012; Messner and Rosenfeld 2012; Healy, Mulcahy and O'Donnell 2013; Marktanner and Noiset 2013; Rufrancos et al. 2013; Baumer and Wolff 2014: 277; Buonanno, Drago and Galbiati 2014; Hall and Wilson 2014; Lappi-Seppala and Lehti 2014: 164–77; Levy, Santhakumuran and Whitecross 2014; Rosenfeld 2014; Roeder et al. 2015: 48–54.

2 Full-length volumes on the crime fall include (in addition to many articles): Silverman 1999; Blumstein and Wallman 2000; Karmen 2000; Zimring 2007, 2012; Goldberger and Rosenfeld 2008; van Dijk, Tseloni and Farrell 2012; *Justice Quarterly* 2014; Morgan 2014; Tonry 2014; Roeder et al. 2015.

3 CompStat, Computer Comparison Statistics, is a data-driven model for management introduced in 1994 by NYPD Chief Bratton, and widely credited as the key factor in the city's crime drop (Bratton 1998; Zimring 2012). The Brennan Center for Justice tracked the association between different cities' adoption of similar techniques and their crime falls, concluding 'that CompStat-style programs were responsible for an estimated 5 to 15 percent decrease in crime in cities where it was introduced' (Roeder et al. 2015: 10).

4 The distribution of wealth as well as income has become much more unequal in recent years in Britain and the United States ('How Has Inequality Changed?', The Equality Trust 2015; 'Income Inequality', Institute for Policy Studies 2014).

Conclusion: Crime: A Capital Concept

1 I summarized the processes in Reiner 2007: 3–8. The definitive empirical and theoretical demonstration of the inevitably increasing inequality of wealth under capitalism, in the absence of policies aimed at checking it, is Piketty 2014.

2 This was the eleventh and last of Marx's 'theses on Feuerbach'. It is inscribed on Marx's headstone in Highgate.

References

Aaronson, E. (2014) *From Slave Abuse to Hate Crime: The Criminalization of Racial Violence in American History*. New York: Cambridge University Press.

Aharonson, E. (2010) '"Pro-Minority" Criminalization and the Transformation of Visions of Citizenship in Contemporary Liberal Democracies: A Critique'. *New Criminal Law Review* 13(2): 286–308.

Albertson, K. and Fox, C. (2012) *Crime and Economics*. Abingdon: Routledge.

Alexander, M. (2012) *The New Jim Crow*. New York: New Press.

Allen, J., Livingstone, S. and Reiner, R. (1998) 'True Lies: Changing Images of Crime in British Postwar Cinema'. *European Journal of Communication* 13(1): 53–75.

Amatrudo, A. (2009) *Criminology and Political Theory*. London: Sage.

Amatrudo, A. and Blake, L. (2014) *Human Rights and the Criminal Justice System*. Abingdon: Routledge.

Anderson, K. and Quinney, R. (eds) (2000) *Erich Fromm and Critical Criminology: Beyond the Punitive Society*. Urbana: University of Illinois Press.

Ashworth, A. (2000) 'Is the Criminal Law a Lost Cause?' *Law Quarterly Review* 116(2): 225–56.

Ashworth, A. (2004) 'Social Control and "Anti-Social Behaviour": The Subversion of Human Rights'. *Law Quarterly Review* 120(2): 263–91.

Ashworth, A. and Redmayne, M. (2010) *The Criminal Process*, 4th edn. Oxford: Oxford University Press.

Ashworth, A. and Zedner, L. (2014) *Preventive Justice*. Oxford: Oxford University Press.

Atkinson, R. (ed.) (2014) *Shades of Deviance*. Abingdon: Routledge.

Ayer, A. J. (1936) *Language, Truth and Logic*. London: Gollancz.

Banks, J. and Moxon, D. (2013) 'The Value(s) of Cultural Criminology', in M. Cowburn, M. Duggan, A. Robinson and P. Senior (eds), *Values in Criminology and Criminal Justice*. Bristol: Policy Press.

Banton, M. (1964) *The Policeman in the Community*. London: Tavistock.

Barak, G. (2012) *Theft of a Nation: Wall Street Looting and Federal Regulatory Colluding*. Lanham: Rowman and Littlefield.

Barclay, G. and Tavares, C. (1999) *Digest 4 – Information on the Criminal Justice System in England and Wales*. London: Home Office.

Baritz, L. (1960) *The Servants of Power*. Middletown: Wesleyan University Press.

Baumer, E. and Wolff, K. (2014) 'The Breadth and Causes of Contemporary Cross-National Crime Trends', in M. Tonry (ed.), *Why Crime Rates Fall and Why They Don't*. Chicago: Chicago University Press.

BBC News (2015) 'VW scandal: Company warned over test cheating years ago', 27 September.

Becker, G. (1968) 'Crime and Punishment: An Economic Approach'. *Journal of Political Economy* 76: 175–209.

Becker, H. (1963) *Outsiders*. New York: Free Press.

Becker, H. (1967) 'Whose Side Are We On?' *Social Problems* 14(3): 239–47.

Beckett, K. (1997) *Making Crime Pay*. New York: Oxford University Press.

Belfield, C., Cribb, J., Hood, A. and Joyce, R. (2014) *Living Standards, Poverty and Inequality in the UK: 2014*. London: Institute for Fiscal Studies.

Bell, E. (2011) *Criminal Justice and Neoliberalism*. Basingstoke: Palgrave.

Bell, E. (2015) *Soft Power and Freedom under the Coalition: State-Corporate Power and the Threat to Democracy*. Basingstoke: Palgrave.

Berman, G. (2012) *Prison Population Statistics*. London: House of Commons Library.

Bernstein, R. (1983) *Beyond Objectivism and Relativism*. Philadelphia: University of Pennsylvania Press.

Best, J. (2004) 'Deviance May Be Alive, But Is It Intellectually Lively? A Reaction to Goode'. *Deviant Behaviour* 25(5): 483–92.

Bittner, E. (1974) 'Florence Nightingale in Pursuit of Willie Sutton: A Theory of the Police', in H. Jacob (ed.), *The Potential for Reform of Criminal Justice*. Beverly Hills: Sage.

Blumstein, A. and Rosenfeld, R. (2008) 'Factors Contributing to US Crime Trends', in Goldberger and Rosenfeld (eds), *Understanding Crime Trends*. Washington, DC: National Academies Press.

Blumstein, A. and Wallman, J. (eds) (2000) *The Crime Drop in America*. Cambridge: Cambridge University Press.

Blyth, M. (2015) *Austerity: The History of a Dangerous Idea*. Oxford: Oxford University Press.

Bonger, W. (1969 [1916]) *Criminality and Economic Conditions*. Bloomington: Indiana University Press.

Bourke, J. (1999) *An Intimate History of Killing: Face to Face Killing in Twentieth-Century Warfare*. New York: Basic Books.

Bowling, B. (1999) 'The Rise and Fall of New York Murder'. *British Journal of Criminology* 39(4): 531–54.

Box, S. (1987) *Recession, Crime and Punishment*. London: Macmillan.

Braga, A. and Weisburd, D. (2010) *Policing Problem Places*. New York: Oxford University Press.

Braithwaite, J. (1979) *Inequality, Crime, and Public Policy*. London: Routledge.

Braithwaite, J. and Pettit, P. (1990) *Not Just Deserts: A Republican Theory of Criminal Justice*. Oxford: Oxford University Press.

Brannigan, A. (2013) *Beyond the Banality of Evil: Criminology and Genocide*. Oxford: Oxford University Press.

Bratton, W. (1998) 'Crime is Down: Blame the Police', in N. Dennis (ed.), *Zero Tolerance: Policing a Free Society*, 2nd edn. London: Institute of Economic Affairs.

Brogden, M. and Shearing, C. (1993) *Policing for a New South Africa*. London: Routledge.

Brudner, A. (2009) *Punishment and Freedom*. Oxford: Oxford University Press.

Buonanno, P., Drago, F. and Galbiati, R. (2014) 'Response of Crime to Unemployment: An International Comparison'. *Journal of Contemporary Criminal Justice* 30(1): 29–40.

Burdis, K. and Tombs, S. (2012) 'After the Crisis: New Directions in Theorising Corporate and White-Collar Crime', in S. Hall and S. Winlow (eds), *New Directions in Criminological Theory*. Abingdon: Routledge.

Burney, E. (2009) *Making People Behave: Anti-Social Behaviour, Politics and Policy*, 2nd edn. Cullompton: Willan.

Burrows, J., Tarling, R., Mackie, A., Lewis, R. and Taylor, G. (2000) *Review of Police Forces' Crime Recording Practices*. London: Home Office.

Cambridge English Dictionary, available at http://dictionary.cambridge.org/dictionary/english/censure. Accessed 9 December 2015.

Card, R., Cross, R. and Jones, P. (2014) *Criminal Law*, 21st edn. Oxford: Oxford University Press.

Castelbajac, M. (2014) 'Brooding Over the Dark Figure of Crime: The Home Office and the Cambridge Institute of Criminology in the Run-up to the British Crime Survey'. *British Journal of Criminology* 54(5): 928–45.

Cavadino, M. and Dignan, J. (2006) *Penal Systems: A Comparative Approach*. London: Sage.

Centre for Macroeconomics (2015) *The Importance of Elections for UK Economic Activity*. 28 March, London: CFM. Available at http://cfmsurvey.org/surveys/importance-elections-uk-economic-activity. Accessed 28 November 2015.

Chadee, D. and Ditton, J. (2005) 'Fear of Crime and the Media: Assessing the Lack of Relationship'. *Crime, Media, Culture* 1(3): 322–32.

Chakelian, A. (2015) 'Disabled man killed himself over benefit cut, coroner rules'. *New Statesman*, 21 September.

Chakrabortty, A. (2015) 'David Cameron, a champion of disabled people? Try telling Paula Peters'. *The Guardian*, 8 June.

Chalmers, J. and Leverick, F. (2013) 'Tracking the Creation of Criminal Offences'. *Criminal Law Review* 7: 543–60.

Chambliss, W. and Mankoff, M. (eds) (1976) *Whose Law? What Order?* New York: Wiley.

Chambliss, W., Michalowski, R. and Kramer, R. (eds) (2010) *State Crime in the Global Age*. Abingdon: Routledge.

Chandler, R. (1977 [1953]) *The Long Goodbye*. London: Heinemann/Octopus.

Chatterton, M. (1976) 'Police and Social Control', in J. King (ed.), *Control Without Custody*. Cambridge: Institute of Criminology.

Cheliotis, L. (2013) 'Neoliberal Capitalism and Middle-Class Punitiveness: Bringing Erich Fromm's "Materialistic Psychoanalysis" to Penology'. *Punishment and Society* 15(3): 247–73.

Chevigny, P. (1998) *Edge of the Knife: Police Violence in the Americas*. New York: New Press.

Chibnall, S. (1977) *Law-and-Order News*. London: Tavistock.

Clarke, R. and Mayhew, P. (eds) (1980) *Designing Out Crime*. London: Home Office.

Cockburn, J. S. (1977) *Crime in England 1550–1800*. London: Methuen.

Cohen, L. and Felson, M. (1979) 'Social Change and Crime Rate Trends: A Routine Activity Approach'. *American Sociological Review* 44(4): 588–608.

Cohen, S. (1988 [1979]) 'Guilt, Justice, and Tolerance: Some Old Concepts for a New Criminology', in D. Downes and P. Rock (eds), *Deviant Interpretations*. Oxford: Martin Robertson.

Cohen, S. (1997) 'Crime and Politics: Spot the Difference', in R. Rawlings (ed.), *Law, Society, and Economy*. Oxford: Oxford University Press.

Cohen, S. (2000) *States of Denial*. Cambridge: Polity.

Colbran, M. (2014) *Media Representations of Police and Crime*. Basingstoke: Palgrave.

Collins, D., Kerr, J., Harvey, S., Green, S. and McNaughton Nicholls, C. (2014) *Developing Questions on Fraud and Cyber-crime for the CSEW: Final Report*. London: NatCen Social Research.

Colquhoun, P. (1800) *Treatise on the Commerce and Police of the River Thames*. London: J. Mowman.

Cook, D. (1989) *Rich Law, Poor Law: Different Responses to Tax and Supplementary Benefit Fraud*. Milton Keynes: Open University Press.

Cook, D. (2006) *Criminal and Social Justice*. London: Sage.

Corbett, C. (2003) *Car Crime*. Cullompton: Willan.

Corbett, C. (2010) 'Driving Offences', in F. Brookman, M. Maguire, H. Pierrepoint and T. Bennett (eds), *Handbook of Crime*. Cullompton: Willan.

Cornish, D. and Clarke, R. (eds) (1986) *The Reasoning Criminal*. New York: Springer-Verlag.

Cottee, S. (2013) 'Judging Offenders: The Moral Implications of Criminological Theories', in M. Cowburn, M. Duggan, A. Robinson and P. Senior (eds), *Values in Criminology and Criminal Justice*. Bristol: Policy Press.

Cotterrell, R. (2015) 'The Concept of Crime and Transnational Networks of Community', in V. Mitsilegas, P. Alldridge and L. Cheliotis (eds), *Globalisation, Criminal Law and Criminal Justice*. Oxford: Hart.

Cowburn, M., Duggan, M., Robinson, A. and Senior, P. (eds) (2013) *Values in Criminology and Criminal Justice*. Bristol: Policy Press.

Cowling, M. (2008) *Marxism and Criminological Theory*. Basingstoke: Palgrave.

Crawford, A. and Evans, K. (2012) 'Crime Prevention and Community Safety', in M. Maguire, R. Morgan and R. Reiner (eds), *The Oxford Handbook of Criminology*, 5th edn. Oxford: Oxford University Press.

Crawford, A., Jones, T., Woodhouse, T. and Young, J. (1990) *The Second Islington Crime Survey*. London: Middlesex Polytechnic Centre for Criminology.

Croall, H. (2001) *Understanding White Collar Crime*. Milton Keynes: Open University Press.

CSEW (2014) *Crime in England and Wales, Year Ending March 2014*. London: Office for National Statistics. Available at http://www.ons.gov.uk/ons/dcp171778_371127.pdf. Accessed 2 December 2015.

Curran, K., Dale, M., Edmunds, M., Hough, M., Millie, A. and Wagstaff, M. (2005) *Street Crime in London*. London: Government Office for London.

Currie, E. (1985) *Confronting Crime*. New York: Pantheon.

Currie, E. (1998) *Crime and Punishment in America*. New York: Holt.

Dahrendorf, R. (1985) *Law and Order*. London: Sweet and Maxwell.

Davies, N. (1999) 'Watching the detectives: How the police cheat in the fight against crime'. *The Guardian*, 18 March.

Davies, N. (2003a) 'Fiddling the figures'. *The Guardian*, 11 July.

Davies, N. (2003b) 'Exposing the myth of the falling crime rate'. *The Guardian*, 10 July.

Davies, N. (2008) *Flat Earth News*. London: Chatto and Windus.

Davies, P., Francis, P. and Jupp, V. (eds) (1999) *Invisible Crimes: Their Victims and Their Regulation*. Basingstoke: Palgrave.

Davies, P., Francis, P. and Jupp, V. (eds) (2014) *Invisible Crimes and Social Harms*. Basingstoke: Palgrave.

Dawe, A. (1970) 'The Two Sociologies'. *British Journal of Sociology* 21(2): 207–18.

Dean, M. (2012) *Democracy under Attack: How the Media Distort Policy and Politics*. Bristol: Policy Press.

Dellwing, M., Kotarbe, J. and Pino, N. (eds) (2014) *The Death and Resurrection of Deviance: Current Ideas and Research*. New York: Palgrave.

Delsol, R. and Shiner, M. (eds) (2015) *Stop and Search: The Anatomy of a Police Power*. Basingstoke: Palgrave.

Devlin, P. (1965 [1959]) *The Enforcement of Morals*. Oxford: Oxford University Press.

Dick, P., Silvestri, M. and Westmarland, L. (2014) 'Women Police: Potential and Possibilities for Police Reform', in J. Brown (ed.), *The Future of Policing*. Abingdon: Routledge.

Dominick, J. (1978) 'Crime and Law Enforcement in the Mass Media', in C. Winick (ed.), *Deviance and Mass Media*. Beverly Hills: Sage.

Dorling, D. (2004) 'Prime Suspect: Murder in Britain', in P. Hillyard, C. Pantazis, S. Tombs and D. Gordon (eds), *Beyond Criminology: Taking Harm Seriously*. London: Pluto.

Dorling, D. (2015) *Injustice: Why Social Inequality Still Persists*. Bristol: Policy Press.

Downes, D. (1966) *The Delinquent Solution*. London: Routledge.

Downes, D. and Morgan, R. (2012) 'Overtaking on the Left? The Politics of Law and Order in the "Big Society"', in M. Maguire, R. Morgan and R. Reiner (eds), *The Oxford Handbook of Criminology*, 5th edn. Oxford: Oxford University Press.

Downes, D. and Rock, P. (2012) *Understanding Deviance*, 5th edn. Oxford: Oxford University Press.

Duff, R. A., Farmer, L., Marshall, S., Renzo, M. and Tadros, V. (eds) (2014) *Criminalization: The Political Morality of the Criminal Law*. Oxford: Oxford University Press.

Duffy, B., Wake, R., Burrows, T. and Bremner, P. (2008) *Closing the Gaps: Crime 7 Public Perceptions*. London: Ipsos MORI Social Research Institute.

Durkheim, E. (1951 [1897]) *Suicide*. London: Routledge.

Durkheim, E. (1964 [1895]) *The Rules of Sociological Method*. Glencoe: Free Press.

Durkheim, E. (1973 [1893]) *The Division of Labor in Society*. Glencoe: Free Press.

Dworkin, G. (1999) 'Devlin was Right: Law and the Enforcement of Morality'. *William and Mary Law Review* 40(3): 927–46.

Dworkin, R. (2002) *Sovereign Virtue: The Theory and Practice of Equality*. Cambridge: Harvard University Press.

Dworkin, R. (2013) *Justice for Hedgehogs*. Cambridge: Harvard University Press.

Eck, J. and Maguire, E. (2000) 'Have Changes in Policing Reduced Violent Crime?', in A. Blumstein and J. Wallman (eds), *The Crime Drop in America*. Cambridge: Cambridge University Press.

Eisner, M. (2001) 'Modernisation, Self-Control and Lethal Violence: The Long-Term Dynamics of European Homicide Rates in Theoretical Perspective'. *British Journal of Criminology* 41: 618–38.

Eisner, M. (2014) 'From Swords to Words: Does Macro-Level Change in Self-Control Predict Long-Term Variation in Levels of Homicide?', in M. Tonry (ed.), *Why Crime Rates Fall and Why They Don't*. Chicago: Chicago University Press.

Elias, N. (1969) *The Civilizing Process*, Vol. I: *The History of Manners*. Oxford: Basil Blackwell.

Elias, N. (1982) *The Civilizing Process*, Vol. II: *State Formation and Civilization*. Oxford: Basil Blackwell.

Emmerson, B. and Ashworth, A. (2012) *Human Rights and Criminal Justice*, 3rd edn. London: Sweet and Maxwell.

Engels, F. (2009 [1844]) *The Condition of the Working Class in England*. London: Penguin.

Equality Trust (2015) 'How has inequality changed?' Available at https://www.equalitytrust.org.uk/how-has-inequality-changed. Accessed 3 December 2015.

Eterno, J. and Silverman, E. (2012) *The Crime Numbers Game*. Boca Raton: CRC Press.

Farmer, L. (1996) 'The Obsession with Definition'. *Social and Legal Studies* 5(1): 57–73.

Farrall, S., Jackson, J. and Gray, E. (2009) *Social Order and the Fear of Crime in Contemporary Times*. Oxford: Oxford University Press.

Farrall, S. and Jennings, W. (2012) 'Policy Feedback and the Criminal Justice Agenda: An Analysis of the Economy, Crime Rates, Politics and Public Opinion in Post-War Britain'. *Contemporary British History* 26(4): 467–88.

Farrall, S. and Lee, M. (eds) (2008) *Fear of Crime: Critical Voices in an Age of Anxiety*. Abingdon: Routledge.

Farrell, G., Tilley, N. and Tseloni, A. (2014) 'Why the Crime Drop?' in M. Tonry (ed.), *Why Crime Rates Fall and Why They Don't*. Chicago: Chicago University Press.

Farrington, D. (2001) *What Has Been Learned from Self-Reports about Criminal Careers and the Causes of Offending?* London: Home Office.

Farrington, D. (2007) 'Childhood Risk Factors and Risk-Focused Prevention', in M. Maguire, R. Morgan and R. Reiner (eds), *The Oxford Handbook of Criminology*, 4th edn. Oxford: Oxford University Press.

Feinberg, J. (1984–1990) *The Moral Limits of the Criminal Law*, 4 vols. New York: Oxford University Press.

Felson, M. and Clarke, R. (1998) *Opportunity Makes the Thief*. London: Home Office.

Felson, M. and Eckert, M. (2015) *Crime and Everyday Life*, 5th edn. Los Angeles: Sage.

Field, S. (1990) *Trends in Crime and Their Interpretation: A Study of Recorded Crime in Post-War England and Wales*. London: Home Office.

Field, S. (1999) *Trends in Crime Revisited*. London: Home Office.

Fielding, N., Clarke, A. and Witt, R. (eds) (2000) *The Economic Dimensions of Crime*. Basingstoke: Palgrave.

Fitzgerald, M. (2014) 'The curious case of the fall in crime'. London: Centre for Crime and Justice Studies. Available at http://www.crimeandjustice.org.uk/resources/curious-case-fall-crime. Accessed 3 December 2015.

Fitzgerald, M., Hough, M., Joseph, I. and Qureshi, T. (2002) *Policing for London*. Cullompton: Willan.

Flatley, J. and Bradley, J. (2013) *Analysis of Variation in Crime Trends*. London: ONS.

France, A. (2002 [1894]) *The Red Lily*. Boston: IndyPublish.

Fromm, E. (2000a [1930]) 'The State as Educator: On the Psychology of Criminal Justice', in K. Anderson and R. Quinney (eds), *Erich Fromm and Critical Criminology: Beyond the Punitive Society*. Urbana: University of Illinois Press.

Fromm, E. (2000b [1931]) 'On the Psychology of the Criminal and the Punitive Society', in K. Anderson and R. Quinney (eds), *Erich Fromm and Critical Criminology: Beyond the Punitive Society*. Urbana: University of Illinois Press.

Fuller, L. (1958) 'Positivism and Fidelity to Law – A Reply to Professor Hart'. *Harvard Law Review* 71(4): 630–72.

Gabor, T. (1994) *Everybody Does It! Crime by the Public*. Toronto: University of Toronto Press.

Gallie, W. B. (1957) 'Essentially Contested Concepts'. *Proceedings of the Aristotelian Society* 56(1): 167–98.

Gamble, A. (1994) *The Free Economy and the Strong State*. Basingstoke: Macmillan.

Garland, D. (1985) *Punishment and Welfare*. Aldershot: Gower.

Garland, D. (2001) *The Culture of Control*. Oxford: Oxford University Press.

Garrett, B. (2015) *Too Big to Jail: How Prosecutors Compromise with Corporations*. Cambridge: Harvard University Press.

Gatrell, V., Lenman, B. and Parker, G. (eds) (1980) *Crime and the Law*. London: Europa.

Gerbner, G. (1995) 'Television Violence: The Power and the Peril', in G. Dines and J. Humez (eds), *Gender, Race, and Class in Media: A Critical Text-Reader*. Newbury Park: Sage.

Gibson, O. and Neate, R. (2015) 'Fifa in crisis as officials who presided over "World Cup of fraud" are arrested'. *The Guardian*, 27 May.

Giddens, A. (1977) *Studies in Social and Political Theory*. London: Hutchinson.

Giddens, A. (1979) *Central Problems in Social Theory: Action, Structure and Contradiction in Social Analysis*. Basingstoke: Macmillan.

Gilens, M. (2012) *Affluence and Influence: Economic Inequality and Political Power in America*. Princeton: Princeton University Press.

Gilligan, J. (2011) *Why Some Politicians Are More Dangerous than Others*. Cambridge: Polity.

Gobert, J. and Punch, M. (2003) *Rethinking Corporate Crime*. London: Butterworths.

Godfrey, B. and Lawrence, P. (2014) *Crime and Justice since 1750*, 2nd edn. Abingdon: Routledge.
Goldberger, A. and Rosenfeld, R. (eds) (2008) *Understanding Crime Trends*. Washington, DC: National Academies Press.
Goldstein, R. (2006) 'Hugh Thompson, 62, who saved civilians at My Lai, dies'. *New York Times*, 7 January.
Gottfredson, M. and Hirschi, T. (1990) *A General Theory of Crime*. Stanford: Stanford University Press.
Graif, C. and Sampson, R. (2009) 'Spatial Heterogeneity in the Effects of Immigration and Diversity on Neighborhood Homicide Rates'. *Homicide Studies* 13(3): 242–60.
Green, P. and Ward, T. (2004) *State Crime*. London: Pluto.
Green, P. and Ward, T. (2012) 'State Crime: A Dialectical View', in M. Maguire, R. Morgan and R. Reiner (eds), *The Oxford Handbook of Criminology*, 5th edn. Oxford: Oxford University Press.
Greer, C. (2003) *Sex Crime and the Media*. Cullompton: Willan.
Greer, C. and McLaughlin, E. (2010) 'We Predict a Riot? Public Order Policing, New Media Environments and the Rise of the Citizen Journalist'. *British Journal of Criminology* 50(6): 1041–59.
Greer, C. and McLaughlin, E. (2011a) '"This is not Justice": Ian Tomlinson, Institutional Failure and the Press Politics of Outrage'. *British Journal of Criminology* 52(2): 274–93.
Greer, C. and McLaughlin, E. (2011b) 'Trial by Media: Phone-Hacking, Riots, Looting, Gangs and Police Chiefs', in T. Newburn and J. Peay (eds), *Policing: Politics, Culture and Control*. Oxford: Hart.
Greer, C. and Reiner, R. (2012) 'Mediated Mayhem: Media, Crime, Criminal Justice', in M. Maguire, R. Morgan and R. Reiner (eds), *The Oxford Handbook of Criminology*, 5th edn. Oxford: Oxford University Press.
Guzman, Z. (2015) 'Target, Amazon pull Confederate goods from websites'. *CNBC*, 23 June.
Hale, C. (1998) 'Crime and the Business Cycle in Post-War Britain Revisited'. *British Journal of Criminology* 38: 681–98.
Hale, C. (1999) 'The Labour Market and Post-War Crime Trends in England and Wales', in P. Carlen and R. Morgan (eds), *Crime Unlimited?*. Basingstoke: Palgrave Macmillan.
Hale, C. (2013) 'Economic Marginalization and Social Exclusion', in C. Hale, K. Hayward, A. Wahidin and E. Wincup (eds), *Criminology*, 3rd edn. Oxford: Oxford University Press.
Hales, J., Nevill, C., Pudney, S. and Tipping, S. (2009) *Longitudinal Analysis of the Offending, Crime and Justice Survey 2003–06*. London: Home Office.

Hall, J. (1952 [1935]) *Theft, Law and Society*, 2nd edn. Indianapolis: Bobbs-Merrill.
Hall, S. (2012) *Theorizing Crime and Deviance*. London: Sage.
Hall, S. and McLean, C. (2009) 'A Tale of Two Capitalisms: Preliminary Spatial and Historical Comparisons of Homicide Rates in Western Europe and the USA'. *Theoretical Criminology* 13(3): 313–39.
Hall, S. and Wilson, D. (2014) 'New Foundations: Pseudo-pacification and Special Liberty as Potential Cornerstones of a Multi-Level Theory of Homicide and Serial Murder'. *European Journal of Criminology* 11(5): 635–55.
Hall, S. and Winlow, S. (eds) (2012) *New Directions in Criminological Theory*. Abingdon: Routledge.
Hall, S. and Winlow, S. (2015) *Revitalizing Criminological Theory*. Abingdon: Routledge.
Hall, S., Winlow, S. and Ancrum, C. (2008) *Criminal Identities and Consumer Culture*. Cullompton: Willan.
Hall, Stuart, Critcher, C., Jefferson, T., Clarke, J. and Roberts, B. (1978) *Policing the Crisis*. London: Macmillan.
Harcourt, B. (1999) 'The Collapse of the Harm Principle'. *Journal of Criminal Law and Criminology* 90(1): 109–94.
Harcourt, B. (2014) 'Beccaria's "On Crimes and Punishments": A Mirror on the History of the Foundations of Modern Criminal Law', in M. Dubber (ed.), *Foundational Texts in Modern Criminal Law*. Oxford: Oxford University Press.
Harrington, M. (1962) *The Other America*. New York: Simon and Schuster.
Hart, H. (1958) 'Positivism and the Separation of Law and Morals'. *Harvard Law Review* 71(4): 593–629.
Hart, H. (1961) *The Concept of Law*. Oxford: Oxford University Press.
Hart, H. (1968) *Law, Liberty and Morality*. Oxford: Oxford University Press.
Hart, H. (1983) *Essays in Jurisprudence and Philosophy*. Oxford: Oxford University Press.
Hay, D. (1975) 'Property, Authority and the Criminal Law', in D. Hay, P. Linebaugh and E. P. Thompson (eds), *Albion's Fatal Tree*. London: Allen Lane.
Hay, D. and Snyder, F. (eds) (1989) *Policing and Prosecution in Britain, 1750–1850*. Oxford: Oxford University Press.
Hayward, K. and Young, J. (2012) 'Cultural Criminology', in M. Maguire, R. Morgan and R. Reiner (eds), *The Oxford Handbook of Criminology*, 5th edn. Oxford: Oxford University Press.

Healy, D., Mulcahy, A. and O'Donnell, I. (2013) 'Crime, Punishment and Inequality in Ireland'. *GINI Discussion Paper* 93. Amsterdam: Institute for Advanced Labour Studies.

Heidensohn, F. and Silvestri, M. (2012) 'Gender and Crime' in M. Maguire, R. Morgan and R. Reiner (eds), *The Oxford Handbook of Criminology*, 5th edn. Oxford: Oxford University Press.

Hennigan, K. M., Delrosario, M. L., Heath, L., Cook, J. D. and Calder, B. J. (1982) 'Impact of the Introduction of Television Crime in the United States: Empirical Findings and Theoretical Implications'. *Journal of Personality and Social Psychology* 42(3): 461–77.

Henry, S. (2009) *Social Deviance*. Cambridge: Polity.

Henry, S. and Lanier, M. (eds) (2001) *What is Crime?* Lanham: Rowman and Littlefield.

Hillyard, P., Pantazis, C., Tombs, S. and Gordon, D. (eds) (2004) *Beyond Criminology: Taking Harm Seriously*. London: Pluto.

Hinton, M. (2005) *The State on the Streets: Police and Politics in Argentina and Brazil*. Boulder: Lynne Rienner.

Hirschi, T. (1969) *Causes of Delinquency*. Berkeley: University of California Press.

HMIC (2014) *Crime Recording: A Matter of Fact*. London: Her Majesty's Inspectorate of Constabulary.

Hobsbawm, E. (1972) 'Social Criminality: Distinctions between Socio-political and Other Forms of Crime'. *Bulletin of the Society for the Study of Labour History* 25: 5–6.

Home Office (2015) Counting Rules for Recorded Crime, available at https://www.gov.uk/government/uploads/system/uploads/attachment_data/file/452294/count-general-august-2015.pdf. Accessed 2 December 2015.

Hooghe, M., Vanhoutte, B., Hardyns, W. and Bircan, T. (2011) 'Unemployment, Inequality, Poverty and Crime: Spatial Distribution Patterns of Criminal Acts in Belgium, 2001–2006'. *British Journal of Criminology* 51(1): 1–20.

Hope, T. (2013) 'The Effect of "Third Party" Pressure on Police Crime Recording Practice', Evidence to Public Administration Select Committee. Available at http://data.parliament.uk/writtenevidence/WrittenEvidence.svc/EvidenceHtml/3315. Accessed 3 December 2015.

Hopkins, K. (2012) *The Pre-Custody Employment, Training and Education Status of Newly Sentenced Prisoners*. London: Ministry of Justice.

Horder, J. (2014) 'Bureaucratic "Criminal" Law: Too Much of a Bad Thing?' *LSE Law Society and Economy Working Paper Series* 01-2014.

Horsley, M (2014) 'The "Death of Deviance" and the Stagnation of Twentieth Century Criminology', in M. Dellwing, J. Kotarba and N. Pino (eds), *The Death and Resurrection of Deviance: Current Ideas and Research*. New York: Palgrave.

Hough, M and Mayhew, P. (1983) *The British Crime Survey*. London: Home Office.

Hough, M. and Roberts, J. (2012) 'Public Opinion, Crime, and Criminal Justice', in M. Maguire, R. Morgan and R. Reiner (eds), *The Oxford Handbook of Criminology*, 5th edn. Oxford: Oxford University Press.

Huffington Post (2013) 'Affluenza defense: rich Texas teen gets probation for killing 4 pedestrians while driving drunk'. 12 December.

Huggins, M. (1998) *Political Policing: The United States and Latin America*. Durham: Duke University Press.

Huggins, M. (2002) *Violence Workers: Police Torturers and Murderers Reconstruct Brazilian Atrocities*. Berkeley: University of California Press.

Hulsman, L. (1986) 'Critical Criminology and the Concept of Crime'. *Contemporary Crises* 10(1): 63–80.

Human Rights Watch (2008) *Courting History: The Landmark International Criminal Court's First Years*. New York: Human Rights Watch.

Husak, D. (2004) 'Crimes outside the Core'. *Tulsa Law Review* 39(4): 755–80.

Husak, D. (2008) *Overcriminalization: The Limits of the Criminal Law*. New York: Oxford University Press.

Hutton, W. (2015) 'Criminal bankers have brazenly milked the system. Let's change it'. *The Guardian*, May 24.

Institute for Policy Studies (2014) 'Income Inequality'. Washington, DC. Available at http://inequality.org/income-inequality. Accessed 3 December 2015.

Ipsos MORI (2010) *Where are the Public on Crime and Punishment?* London: Ipsos MORI.

Jeffery, C. R. (1957) 'The Development of Crime in Early English Society'. *Journal of Criminal Law, Criminology and Police Science* 47: 647–66.

Jennings, W., Farrall, S. and Bevan, S. (2012) 'The Economy, Crime and Time: An Analysis of Recorded Property Crime in England and Wales 1961–2006'. *International Journal of Law, Crime and Justice* 40(3): 192–210.

Jewkes, Y. (2004) *Media and Crime*. London: Sage.

Jewkes, Y. (ed.) (2006) *Crime Online: Committing, Policing and Regulating Cybercrime*. Cullompton: Willan.

Jewkes, Y. and Yar, M. (eds) (2009) *Handbook of Internet Crime*. Cullompton: Willan.

Jones, O. (2014) *The Establishment: And How They Get Away with It*. London: Allen Lane.

Jones, T., MacLean, B. and Young, J. (1986) *The Islington Crime Survey*. Aldershot: Gower.

Jupp, V., Davies, P. and Francis, P. (1999) 'Features of Invisibility', in P. Davies, P. Francis and V. Jupp (eds), *Invisible Crimes*. Basingstoke: Palgrave.

Justice Quarterly (2014) Special Issue on the New York Crime Drop, 31 January.

Kant, I. (1993 [1785]) *Ethical Philosophy: The Complete Texts of 'Grounding for the Metaphysics of Morals' and 'Metaphysical Principles of Virtue'*, 3rd edn. Cambridge: Hackett.

Karmen, A. (2000) *New York Murder Mystery*. New York: New York University Press.

Karstedt, S. and Farrall, S. (2004) 'The Moral Maze of the Middle Class', in H.-J. Albrecht, T. Serassis and H. Kania (eds), *Images of Crime II*. Freiburg: Max Planck Institute.

Karstedt, S. and Farrall, S. (2006) 'The Moral Economy of Everyday Crime: Markets, Consumers and Citizens'. *British Journal of Criminology* 46(6): 1011–36.

Karstedt, S. and Farrall, S. (2007) *Law-Abiding Majority? The Everyday Crimes of the Middle Classes*. London: Centre for Crime and Justice Studies.

Keay, D. (1987) Interview for *Woman's Own*. Available at http://www.margaretthatcher.org/document/106689.

Kennedy, M. (1970) 'Beyond Incrimination'. *Catalyst* 5: 1–37.

Kinsey, R., Lea, J. and Young, Y. (1986) *Losing the Fight against Crime*. Oxford: Basil Blackwell.

Kivivuori, J. (2014) 'Understanding Trends in Personal Violence: Does Cultural Sensitivity Matter?', in M. Tonry (ed.), *Why Crime Rates Fall and Why They Don't*. Chicago: Chicago University Press.

Klein, N. (2008) *The Shock Doctrine*. London: Penguin.

Krugman, P. (2015) 'The austerity delusion'. *The Guardian*, April 29.

Lacey, N. (1995) 'Contingency and Criminalisation', in I. Loveland (ed.), *Frontiers of Criminality*. London: Sweet and Maxwell.

Lacey, N. (2001) 'In Search of the Responsible Subject: History, Philosophy and Criminal Law Theory'. *Modern Law Review* 64(2): 350–71.

Lacey, N. (2008) 'Philosophy, Political Morality and History: Explaining the Enduring Resonance of the Hart–Fuller Debate'. *New York University Law Review* 83: 1059–87.

Lacey, N. (2014) 'What Constitutes Criminal Law?', in R. A. Duff, L. Farmer, S. Marshall, M. Renzo and V. Tadros (eds), *Criminalization: The Political Morality of the Criminal Law*. Oxford: Oxford University Press.

Lacey, N. and Zedner, L. (2012) 'Legal Constructions of Crime', in M. Maguire, R. Morgan and R. Reiner (eds), *The Oxford Handbook of Criminology*, 5th edn. Oxford: Oxford University Press.

Lacey, N., Wells, C. and Quick, O. (2003) *Reconstructing Criminal Law: Text and Materials*, 3rd edn. London: Lexis Nexis UK.

Lappi-Seppala, T. and Lehti, M. (2014) 'Cross-Comparative Perspectives on Global Homicide Trends', in M. Tonry (ed.), *Why Crime Rates Fall and Why They Don't*. Chicago: Chicago University Press.

Law Commission (2010) *Criminal Liability in Regulatory Contexts*. London: Law Commission.

Lea, J. (1999) 'Social Crime Revisited'. *Theoretical Criminology* 3(3): 307–25.

Lea, J. (2002) *Crime and Modernity*. London: Sage.

Lea, J. and Young, J. (1984) *What is to Be Done about Law and Order?* London: Penguin.

Lee, S. (1987) *Law and Morals*. Oxford: Oxford University Press.

Levi, M. (1987) *Regulating Fraud*. Abingdon: Routledge.

Levi, M. (2006) 'The Media Construction of Financial and White-Collar Crimes'. *British Journal of Criminology* 46(6): 1037–57.

Levitt, S. (2004) 'Understanding Why Crime Fell in the 1990s: Four Factors That Explain the Decline and Six That Do Not'. *Journal of Economic Perspectives* 18(1): 163–90.

Levy, L., Santhakumuran, D. and Whitecross, R. (2014) *What Works to Reduce Crime? A Summary of the Evidence*. Edinburgh: Scottish Government.

Linebaugh, P. (1976) 'Karl Marx, the Theft of Wood, and Working-Class Composition: A Contribution to the Current Debate'. *Crime and Social Justice* 6: 5–16.

Linebaugh, P. (2006) *The London Hanged: Crime and Civil Society in the Eighteenth Century*. London: Verso.

Linebaugh, P. (2014) *Stop, Thief! The Commons, Enclosures, and Resistance*. Oakland: PM Press.

Livingstone, S. (1996) 'On the Continuing Problem of Media Effects', in J. Curran and M. Gurevitch (eds), *Mass Media and Society*, 2nd edn. London: Edward Arnold, pp. 305–24.

Loader, I. and Walker, N. (2007) *Civilizing Security*. Cambridge: Cambridge University Press.

Lukes, S. (2003) *Liberals and Cannibals: The Implications of Diversity*. London: Verso.

Lukes, S. (2008) *Moral Relativism*. London: Profile.

Lynch, M. (2013) 'Reexamining Political Economy and Crime: Exploring the Crime Expansion and Drop'. *Journal of Crime and Justice* 36(2): 250–64.

Lyng, S. (1990) 'Edgework: A Social Psychological Analysis of Voluntary Risk Taking'. *American Journal of Sociology* 95(4): 851–86.

Machin, D. and Mayr, A. (2013) 'Personalising Crime and Crime-Fighting in Factual Television: An Analysis of Social Actors and Transitivity in Language and Images'. *Critical Discourse Studies* 10(4): 356–72.

Macpherson, C. B. (1962) *The Political Theory of Possessive Individualism*. Oxford: Oxford University Press.

Maguire, M. (2007) 'Crime Data and Statistics', in M. Maguire, R. Morgan and R. Reiner (eds), *The Oxford Handbook of Criminology*, 4th edn. Oxford: Oxford University Press.

Malinowski, B. (1926) *Crime and Custom in Savage Society*. London: Routledge.

Marenin, O. (1982) 'Parking Tickets and Class Repression: The Concept of Policing in Critical Theories of Criminal Justice'. *Contemporary Crises* 6(3): 241–66.

Marks, M. (2005) *Transforming the Robocops: Changing Police in South Africa*. Durban: University of Kwazulu-Natal Press.

Marktanner, M. and Noiset, L. (2013) 'Social Versus Conservative Democracies and Homicide Rates'. *International Journal of Social Economics* 40(4): 292–310.

Marlow, A. (2014) 'Thinking about the Fall in Crime'. *Safer Communities* 13(2): 56–62.

Marris, R. (2000) *Survey of the Research Literature on the Economic and Criminological Factors Influencing Crime Trends*. London: Volterra Consulting.

Marshall, T. H. (1950) *Citizenship and Social Class*. Cambridge: Cambridge University Press.

Marx, K. (1852) *The Eighteenth Brumaire of Louis Bonaparte*. Available at www.marxists.org/archive/marx/works/1852/18th-brumaire/.

Marx, K. (1976 [1867]) *Capital*, Vol. 1. London: Penguin.

Marx, K. and Engels, F. (1998 [1848]) *The Communist Manifesto*. London: Verso.

Matravers, M. (2000) *Justice and Punishment: The Rationale of Coercion*. Oxford: Oxford University Press.

Matravers, M. (2011) 'Political Theory and the Criminal Law', in R. A. Duff and S. Green (eds), *Philosophical Foundations of the Criminal Law*. Oxford: Oxford University Press.

Matthews, R. (2014) *Realist Criminology*. Basingstoke: Palgrave.

Matza, D. and Sykes, G. (1961) 'Juvenile Delinquency and Subterranean Values'. *American Sociological Review* 26(5): 712–19.

Mawby, R. (2010) 'Chibnall Revisited: Crime Reporters, the Police and "Law-and-Order News"'. *British Journal of Criminology* 50(6): 1060–76.

Mayhew, P. (2014) *Crime Data Integrity*. London: HMIC. Available at http://www.justiceinspectorates.gov.uk/hmic/wp-content/uploads/crime-data-integrity-literature-review.pdf. Accessed 2 December 2015.

McAra, L. and McVie, S. (2012) 'Critical Debates in Developmental and Life-Course Criminology', in M. Maguire, R. Morgan and R. Reiner (eds), *The Oxford Handbook of Criminology*, 5th edn. Oxford: Oxford University Press.

McCabe, S. and Sutcliffe, F. (1978) *Defining Crime*. Oxford: Blackwell.

McCarthy, Mary (1972) *Medina*. New York: Harcourt Brace Jovanovich.

McCormack, S. (2015) 'Cops bought Dylann Roof Burger King hours after Charleston shooting'. *Huffington Post*, June 23.

McGuire, M. and Dowling, S. (2013) *Cybercrime: A Review of the Evidence*. London: Home Office.

Melissaris, E. (2012a) 'Toward a Political Theory of Criminal Law: A Critical Rawlsian Account'. *New Criminal Law Review* 15(1): 122–55.

Melissaris, E. (2012b) 'Property Offences as Crimes of Injustice'. *Criminal Law and Philosophy* 6(2): 149–66.

Mendoza, K.-A. (2015) *Austerity*. Oxford: New Internationalist.

Merton, R. (1938) 'Social Structure and Anomie'. *American Sociological Review* 3: 672–82 (revised in R. Merton [1957] *Social Theory and Social Structure*. London: Free Press).

Messner, S. and Rosenfeld, R. (2012) *Crime and the American Dream*, 5th edn. Belmont: Wadsworth.

Mill, J. S. (1998 [1859]) *On Liberty*. Oxford: Oxford University Press.

Mills, C. W. (1959) *The Sociological Imagination*. New York: Oxford University Press.

Ministry of Justice (2013) *Statistics on Race and the Criminal Justice System*. London: Ministry of Justice.

Mirowski, P. (2014) *Never Let a Serious Crisis Go to Waste: How Neoliberalism Survived the Financial Meltdown*. London: Verso.

Mirowski, P. and Plehwe, D. (eds) (2009) *The Road from Mont Pelerin: The Making of the Neoliberal Thought Collective*. Cambridge: Harvard University Press.

Moore, M. (1997) *Placing Blame: A General Theory of the Criminal Law*. Oxford: Clarendon Press.

Morgan, N. (2014) *The Heroin Epidemic of the 1980s and 1990s and Its Effect on Crime Trends: Then and Now*. London: Home Office.

Morris, N. (2006) 'Blair's "frenzied law-making"'. *The Independent*, August 16.

Morrison, W. (2006) *Criminology, Civilisation and the New World Order*. Abingdon: Routledge.

Moxon, D. (2011) 'Marxism and the Definition of Crime'. *In-Spire Journal of Law, Politics and Societies* 5(2): 102–20.

Moxon, D. (2013) 'Marxist Criminology: Whose Side, Which Values?', in M. Cowburn, M. Duggan, A. Robinson and P. Senior (eds), *Values in Criminology and Criminal Justice*. Bristol: Policy Press.

Moxon, D. (2014) 'Willem Bonger' in J. M. Miller (ed.), *The Encyclopedia of Theoretical Criminology*. Malden: Wiley-Blackwell.

Naughton, M. (2012) *Rethinking Miscarriages of Justice*. Basingstoke: Palgrave.

Nelken, D. (2012) 'White-Collar and Corporate Crime', in M. Maguire, R. Morgan and R. Reiner (eds), *The Oxford Handbook of Criminology*, 5th edn. Oxford: Oxford University Press.

Newburn, T. (1991) *Permission and Regulation*. London: Routledge.

Newburn, T. (2007) '"Tough on Crime": Penal Policy in England and Wales', in M. Tonry and A. Doob (eds), *Crime and Justice 36*. Chicago: University of Chicago Press.

Newburn, T. and Reiner, R. (2007) 'Crime and Penal Policy', in A. Seldon (ed.), *Blair's Britain*. Cambridge: Cambridge University Press.

Newburn, T. and Rock, P. (2005) *Living in Fear: Violence and Victimisation in the Lives of Single Homeless People*. London: Shelter.

Newburn, T., Cooper, K., Deacon, R. and Diski, R. (2015) 'Shopping for Free? Looting, Consumerism and the 2011 Riots'. *British Journal of Criminology* 55: 987–1004.

Nobles, R. and Schiff, D. (2000) *Understanding Miscarriages of Justice*. Oxford: Oxford University Press.

Norrie, A. (2014) *Crime, Reason and History*, 3rd edn. Cambridge: Cambridge University Press.

O'Hara, M. (2015) *Austerity Bites*. Bristol: Policy Press.

ONS (2014) *Assessment of Compliance with the Code of Practice for Official Statistics: Statistics on Crime in England and Wales*. London: Office for National Statistics.

ONS (2015a) *Crime in England and Wales, Year Ending September 2014*. http://www.ons.gov.uk/ons/dcp171778_392380.pdf.

ONS (2015b) *Extending the Crime Survey for England and Wales (CSEW) to Include Fraud and Cybercrime*. London: Office for National Statistics.

Osiel, M. (1997) *Mass Atrocity, Collective Memory and the Law*. Piscataway: Transaction.

Osiel, M. (2008) *Obeying Orders: Atrocity, Military Discipline and the Law of War*. Piscataway: Transaction.

Oxford Dictionaries, available at http://www.oxforddictionaries.com/definition/english. Accessed 9 December 2015.

Paige, J. (2013) 'British public wrong about nearly everything, survey shows'. *The Independent*, July 9.

Palmer, J. (1977) 'Evils Merely Prohibited'. *British Journal of Law and Society* 3(1): 1–16.

Parker, K. (2010) *Unequal Crime Decline*. New York: New York University Press.

PASC (2014) *Caught Red-Handed: Why We Can't Count on Police Recorded Crime Statistics*. London: Public Administration Select Committee.

Pashukanis, E. B. (1978 [1924]) *Law and Marxism: A General Theory*. London: Pluto.

Pearson, G. (1983) *Hooligan*. London: Macmillan.

Pemberton, S. (2004) 'A Theory of Moral Indifference: Understanding the Production of Harm by Capitalist Society', in P. Hillyard, C. Pantazis, S. Tombs and D. Gordon (eds), *Beyond Criminology: Taking Harm Seriously*. London: Pluto.

Pemberton, S. (2015) *Harmful Societies*. Bristol: Policy Press.

Phillips, C. and Bowling, B. (2012) 'Ethnicities, Racism, Crime, and Criminal Justice', in M. Maguire, R. Morgan and R. Reiner (eds), *The Oxford Handbook of Criminology*, 5th edn. Oxford: Oxford University Press.

Piketty, T. (2014) *Capital in the Twenty-First Century*. Cambridge: Harvard University Press.

Pinker, S. (2011) *The Better Angels of Our Nature: Why Violence Has Declined*. London: Allen Lane.

Popper, K. (1945) *The Open Society*. Abingdon: Routledge.

Popper, K. (1959 [1935]) *The Logic of Scientific Discovery*. London: Hutchinson.

Pratt, J. (2006) *Penal Populism*. Abingdon: Routledge.

Pridemore, W. A. (2011) 'Poverty Matters: A Reassessment of the Inequality–Homicide Relationship in Cross-National Studies'. *British Journal of Criminology* 51(5): 739–72.

Priestley, J. B. (2001 [1947]) *An Inspector Calls*. London: Penguin.

Pring, J. (2015) 'One in five benefit-related deaths involved sanctions, admits DWP'. *Disability News Service*, 15 May.

Punch, M. (1996) *Dirty Business: Exploring Corporate Misconduct*. London: Sage.

Punch, M. (2007) *Zero Tolerance Policing*. Bristol: Policy Press.

Punch, M. (2009) *Police Corruption*. Cullompton: Willan.

Punch, M. (2010) *Shoot to Kill: Police, Firearms and Fatal Force*. Bristol: Policy Press.

Punch, M. (2012) *State Violence, Collusion and the Troubles: Counter Insurgency, Government Deviance and Northern Ireland*. London: Pluto.

RAC (2014) *Report on Motoring*. Walsall: Royal Automobile Club.

Radzinowicz, L. (1948) *A History of English Criminal Law and its Administration from 1750*: Vol. I. London: Stevens.

Radzinowicz, L. (1956) *A History of English Criminal Law and its Administration from 1750*: Vol. III. London: Stevens.

Rakoff, J. (2014) 'The financial crisis: why have no high-level executives been prosecuted?' *New York Review of Books*, January 9. http://www.nybooks.com/articles/archives/2014/jan/09/financial-crisis-why-no-executive-prosecutions. Accessed 28 November 2015.

Rakoff, J. (2015) 'Mass incarceration: the silence of the judges'. *New York Review of Books*, 21 May.

Ramsay, P. (2012) *The Insecurity State*. Oxford: Oxford University Press.

Rawls, J. (1971) *A Theory of Justice*. Cambridge: Harvard University Press.

Rawls, J. (1993) *Political Liberalism*. New York: Columbia University Press.

Rayman, T. and Smith, O. (2015) 'What's Deviance Got to Do with it? Black Friday Sales, Violence and Hyper-Conformity'. *British Journal of Criminology*. Available at http://bjc.oxfordjournals.org/content/early/2015/06/02/bjc.azv051.abstract. Accessed 3 December 2015.

Redmayne, M. (2015) *Character in the Criminal Trial*. Oxford: Oxford University Press.

Reiman, J. and Leighton, P. (2012) *The Rich Get Richer and the Poor Get Prison*, 10th edn. New York: Routledge.

Reiner, R. (1996) 'The Case of the Missing Crimes', in R. Levitas and W. Guy (eds), *Interpreting Official Statistics*. London: Routledge.

Reiner, R. (2007) *Law and Order: An Honest Citizen's Guide to Crime and Control*. Cambridge: Polity.

Reiner, R. (2010a) *The Politics of the Police*, 4th edn. Oxford: Oxford University Press.

Reiner, R. (2010b) 'Citizenship, Crime, Criminalization: Marshalling a Social Democratic Perspective'. *New Criminal Law Review* 13(2): 241–61.

Reiner, R. (2011) *Policing, Popular Culture and Political Economy.* Farnham: Ashgate.

Reiner, R. (2012a) 'Casino Capital's Crimes: Political Economy, Crime, and Criminal Justice', in M. Maguire, R. Morgan and R. Reiner (eds), *The Oxford Handbook of Criminology*, 5th edn. Oxford: Oxford University Press.

Reiner, R. (2012b) 'Political Economy and Criminology: The Return of the Repressed', in S. Hall and S. Winlow (eds), *New Directions in Criminological Theory.* Abingdon: Routledge.

Reiner, R., Livingstone, S. and Allen, J. (2000) 'No More Happy Endings? The Media and Popular Concern about Crime since the Second World War', in T. Hope and R. Sparks (eds), *Crime, Risk and Insecurity.* London: Routledge.

Reiner, R., Livingstone, S. and Allen, J. (2001) 'Casino Culture: The Media and Crime in a Winner–Loser Society', in K. Stenson and R. Sullivan (eds), *Crime and Risk Society.* Cullompton: Willan.

Reiner, R., Livingstone, S. and Allen, J. (2003) 'From Law and Order to Lynch Mobs: Crime News since the Second World War', in P. Mason (ed.), *Criminal Visions.* Cullompton: Willan.

Roberts, P. (1996) 'From Deviance to Censure: A "New" Criminology for the Nineties'. *Modern Law Review* 59(1): 125–44.

Roberts, P. (2014) 'Criminal Law Theory and the Limits of Liberalism', in P. Simester, A. Du Bois-Pedain and U. Neumann (eds), *Liberal Criminal Theory.* Oxford: Hart.

Roberts, S. (1979) *Order and Dispute.* London: Penguin.

Robinson, C. and Scaglion, R. (1987) 'The Origin and Evolution of the Police Function in Society: Notes Toward a Theory'. *Law & Society Review* 21(1): 109–54.

Robinson, C., Scaglion, R. and Olivero, J. M. (1994) *Police in Contradiction: The Evolution of the Police Function in Society.* Westport: Greenwood.

Rock, P. (2004) *Constructing Victims' Rights.* Oxford: Oxford University Press.

Roeder, O., Eisen, L.-B. and Bowling, J. (2015) *What Caused the Crime Decline?* New York: Brennan Center for Justice, NYU Law School.

Rogers, P. (2010) *Losing Control: Global Security in the 21st Century*, 3rd edn. London: Pluto.

Rosenfeld, R. (2014) 'Crime and Inflation in Cross-National Perspective', in M. Tonry (ed.), *Why Crime Rates Fall and Why They Don't.* Chicago: Chicago University Press.

Rosenfeld, R. and Messner, S. (2009) 'The Crime Drop in Comparative Perspective: The Impact of the Economy and Imprisonment on American and European Burglary Rates'. *British Journal of Sociology* 60(3): 445–71.

Rosoff, S., Pontell, H. and Tillman, R. (2014) *Profit without Honor: White Collar Crime and the Looting of America*, 6th edn. Upper Saddle River: Prentice Hall.

Rowbotham, J., Stevenson, K. and Pegg, S. (2013) *Crime News in Modern Britain: Press Reporting and Responsibility, 1820–2010*. Basingstoke: Palgrave.

Rufrancos, H., Power, M., Pickett, K. and Wilkinson, R. (2013) 'Income Inequality and Crime: A Review and Explanation of the Time-Series Evidence'. *Sociology and Criminology* 1(1). Available at https://www.equalitytrust.org.uk/sites/default/files/Income%20Inequality%20and%20Crime%20-%20A%20Review%20and%20Explanation%20of%20the%20Time%20series%20evidence_0.pdf. Accessed 3 December 2015.

Ruggiero, V. (2013) *The Crimes of the Economy: A Criminological Analysis of Economic Thought*. Abingdon: Routledge.

Ruggiero, V. (2015) *Power and Crime*. Abingdon: Routledge.

Rundle, K. (2013) *Forms Liberate: Reclaiming the Jurisprudence of Lon L. Fuller*. Oxford: Hart.

Rushe, D. (2015) 'Wall Street wolves still on the prowl as survey reveals taste for unethical tactics'. *The Guardian*, 19 May.

Sands, P. (2006) *Lawless World*. London: Penguin.

Sands, P. (2009) *Torture Team: Uncovering War Crimes in the Land of the Free*. London: Penguin.

Sayer, A. (2011) *Why Things Matter to People: Social Science, Values and Ethical Life*. Cambridge: Cambridge University Press.

Schechter, D. (2010) *The Crime of Our Time: Why Wall Street is Not Too Big to Jail*. New York: Disinformation Company.

Schlesinger, P. and Tumber, H. (1994) *Reporting Crime*. Oxford: Oxford University Press.

Schramm, W., Lyle, J. and Parker, E. (1961) *Television in the Lives of Our Children*. Stanford: Stanford University Press.

Schur, E. (1965) *Crimes without Victims*. Englewood Cliffs: Prentice Hall.

Schwartz, R. and Miller, J. (1964) 'Legal Evolution and Societal Complexity'. *American Journal of Sociology* 70(2): 159–69.

Schwendinger, H. and Schwendinger, J. (1975) 'Guardians of Order or Defenders of Human Rights?', in I. Taylor, P. Walton and J. Young (eds), *Critical Criminology*. London: Routledge.

Scraton, P. (2007) *Power, Conflict and Criminalisation*. Abingdon: Routledge.

Sen, A. (2015) 'The economic consequences of austerity'. *New Statesman*, 4 June.

SEU (2002) *Reducing Re-Offending by Ex-Prisoners*. London: Social Exclusion Unit.

Seymour, R. (2014) *Against Austerity*. London: Pluto.

Shafik, M. (2014) 'Making Markets Fair and Effective'. Speech at LSE, 27 October. Available at http://www.bankofengland.co.uk/publications/Pages/speeches/2014/771.aspx. Accessed 28 November 2015.

Sharpe, J. A. (1984) *Crime in Early Modern England, 1550–1750*. London: Longman.

Sharpe, J. (2001) 'Crime, Order, and Historical Change', in J. Muncie and E. McLaughlin (eds), *The Problem of Crime*. London: Sage.

Shepherd, J. (1990) 'Violent Crime in Bristol: An Accident and Emergency Department Perspective'. *British Journal of Criminology* 30(2): 289–305.

Silver, A. (1967) 'The Demand for Order in Civil Society', in D. Bordua (ed.), *The Police*. New York: Wiley.

Silverman, E. (1999) *NYPD Battles Crime: Innovative Strategies in Policing*. Boston: Northeastern University Press.

Silverman, J. (2011) *Crime, Policy and the Media: The Shaping of Criminal Justice, 1989–2010*. Abingdon: Routledge.

Simester, A. P. and Sullivan, G. R. (2013) *Criminal Law*, 5th edn. Oxford: Hart.

Simester, A. P. and von Hirsch, A. (2011) *Crimes, Harms, and Wrongs: On the Principles of Criminalisation*. Oxford: Hart.

Simon, J. (2007) *Governing Through Crime*. Oxford: Oxford University Press.

Sivarajasingam, V., Wells, J. P., Moore, S., Page, N., Morgan, P., Matthews, K. and Shepherd, J. P. (2012) *Violence in England and Wales: An Accident and Emergency Perspective*. Cardiff: Violence and Society Research Group, Cardiff University.

Skidelsky, R. (2014) 'The Osborne Audit: what have we learned?' *New Statesman*, 17 March.

Skidelsky, R. (2015) 'George Osborne's cunning plan: how the chancellor's austerity narrative has harmed recovery'. *New Statesman*, 29 April.

Slapper, G. (1999) *Blood in the Bank*. Aldershot: Ashgate.

Slapper, G. and Tombs, S. (1999) *Corporate Crime*. London: Longman.

Sloan, A. and Allison, E. (2015) 'Sharp rise in the proportion of young black and ethnic minority prisoners'. *The Guardian*, 24 June.

Smith, A. (1982 [1782–4]) *The Wealth of Nations*. London: Penguin.

Smith, D. (2007) 'Crime and the Life Course', in M. Maguire, R. Morgan and R. Reiner (eds), *The Oxford Handbook of Criminology*, 4th edn. Oxford: Oxford University Press.

Social Trends (1993). London: HMSO.

Sparks, R. (1992) *Television and the Drama of Crime*. Milton Keynes: Open University Press.

Sparks, R., Genn, H. and Dodd, D. (1977) *Surveying Victims*. Chichester: Wiley.

Sparrow, A. (2011) 'David Cameron announces recall of parliament over riots'. *The Guardian*, 9 August.

Squires, P. (ed.) (2008) *ASBO Nation: The Criminalisation of Nuisance*. Bristol: Policy Press.

Standing, G. (2011) *The Precariat: The New Dangerous Class*. London: Bloomsbury.

Stephen, J. F. (1967 [1873]) *Liberty, Equality, Fraternity*. Cambridge: Cambridge University Press.

Stephen, J. F. (1883) *A History of the Criminal Law of England*. London: Macmillan.

Stern, S. (2014) 'Blackstone's Criminal Law: Common-Law Harmonization and Legislative Reform', in M. Dubber (ed.), *Foundational Texts in Modern Criminal Law*. Oxford: Oxford University Press.

Stiglitz, J. (2015) *The Great Divide*. New York: Norton.

Stowell, J. I., Messner, S. F., McGeevor, K. F. and Raffalovich, L. E. (2009) 'Immigration and the Recent Violent Crime Drop in the United States'. *Criminology* 47(3): 889–928.

Streeck, W. (2014) *Buying Time: The Delayed Crisis of Democratic Capitalism*. London: Verso.

Stuckler, D. and Basu, S. (2013) *The Body Economic: Why Austerity Kills*. New York: Basic Books.

Stuntz, W. (2001) 'The Pathological Politics of Criminal Law'. *Michigan Law Review* 100(3): 505–608.

Sumner, C. (1979) *Reading Ideologies*. London: Academic Press.

Sumner, C. (ed.) (1990) *Censure, Politics and Criminal Justice*. Milton Keynes: Open University Press.

Sumner, C. (1994) *The Sociology of Deviance: An Obituary*. Buckingham: Open University Press.

Sumner, C. (2012) 'Censure, Culture and Political Economy: Beyond the Death of Deviance Debate', in S. Hall and S. Winlow (eds), *New Directions in Criminological Theory*. Abingdon: Routledge.

Surette, R. (2014) *Media, Crime, and Criminal Justice*, 5th edn. Belmont: Wadsworth.

Sutherland, E. (1949) *White Collar Crime*. New York: Holt, Rinehart and Winston.

Sutherland, E. (1983) *White Collar Crime: The Uncut Version*. New Haven: Yale University Press.

Sykes, G. and Matza, D. (1957) 'Techniques of Neutralisation'. *American Sociological Review* 33: 46–62.

Tappan, P. (2001 [1947]) 'Who is the Criminal?', in S. Henry and M. Lanier (eds) (2001), *What is Crime?* Lanham: Rowman and Littlefield.

Taylor, A. (2007) 'A taxing problem'. *The Guardian*, 10 January.

Taylor, H. (1998a) 'The Politics of the Rising Crime Statistics of England and Wales, 1914–1960'. *Crime, History and Societies* 2(1): 5–28.

Taylor, H. (1998b) 'Rising Crime: The Political Economy of Criminal Statistics since the 1850s'. *Economic History Review* LI: 569–90.

Taylor, H. (1999) 'Forging the Job: A Crisis of "Modernisation" or Redundancy for the Police in England and Wales 1900–39'. *British Journal of Criminology* 39: 113–35.

Taylor, I. (1981) *Law and Order: Arguments for Socialism*. London: Macmillan.

Taylor, I. (1997) 'The Political Economy of Crime', in M. Maguire, R. Morgan and R. Reiner (eds.), *The Oxford Handbook of Criminology*, 2nd edn. Oxford: Oxford University Press.

Taylor, I. (1999) *Crime in Context*. Cambridge: Polity.

Taylor, I., Walton, P. and Young, J. (1973) *The New Criminology*. London: Routledge.

Taylor, L. (1972) 'The Significance and Interpretation of Replies to Motivational Questions: The Case of Sex Offenders'. *Sociology* 6(1): 23–40.

Thompson, E. P. (1971) 'The Moral Economy of the English Crowd in the Eighteenth Century'. *Past & Present* 50(1): 76–136.

Thompson, E. P. (1975) *Whigs and Hunters*. London: Penguin.

Thompson, E. P. (2009) *Customs in Common*. London: Merlin.

Tilley, N. (ed.) (2005) *Handbook of Crime Prevention and Community Safety*. Cullompton: Willan.

Tilley, N., Tseloni, A. and Farrell, G. (2011) 'Income Disparities of burglary risk and security availability during the crime drop'. *British Journal of Criminology* 51(2): 296–313.

Tombs, S. and Whyte, D. (eds) (2003) *Unmasking the Crimes of the Powerful: Scrutinizing States and Corporations*. New York: Peter Lang.

Tombs, S. and Whyte, D. (2007) *Safety Crimes*. Cullompton: Willan.

Tombs, S. and Whyte, D. (2015) *The Corporate Criminal*. Abingdon: Routledge.

Tonry, M. (ed.) (2014) *Why Crime Rates Fall and Why They Don't*. Chicago: Chicago University Press.

Travis, A. (2015a) 'Crime rate in England and Wales soars as cybercrime is included for first time'. *The Guardian*, 15 October.

Travis, A. (2015b) 'Crime rate to rise by 40% after inclusion of cyber-offences'. *The Guardian*, 15 October.

Treanor, J. and Rushe, D. (2015) 'Banks hit by record fine for rigging forex markets'. *The Guardian*, 20 May.

Turner, L. (2014) 'PCCs, Neo-liberal Hegemony and Democratic Policing'. *Safer Communities* 13(1): 13–21.

Ugwudike, P. (2015) *An Introduction to Critical Criminology*. Bristol: Policy Press.

UK Government (2014) 'Criminal Justice System: Aims and Objectives'. Available at http://webarchive.nationalarchives.gov.uk/20101019153126/http:/www.cjsonline.gov.uk/aims_and_objectives. Accessed 7 December 2015.

UKSA (2013) *UK Statistics Authority Assessment of Crime Statistics*. London: UKSA.

Van Dijk, J. (2006) 'What Goes Up, Comes Down: Explaining the Falling Crime Rates'. *Crime in Europe – Newsletter of the European Society of Criminology* 5(3): 3, 17–18.

Van Dijk, J., Tseloni, A. and Farrell, G. (eds) (2012) *The International Crime Drop*. Basingstoke: Palgrave.

Van Krieken, R. (2002) 'The Paradox of the "Two Sociologies": Hobbes, Latour and the Constitution of Modern Social Theory'. *Journal of Sociology* 38(3): 255–73.

Vold, G., Bernard, T., Snipes, J. B. and Gerould, A. L. (2010) *Theoretical Criminology*, 6th edn. New York: Oxford University Press.

Waldron, J. (2002) 'Is the Rule of Law an Essentially Contested Concept (in Florida)?' *Law and Philosophy* 21(2): 137–64.

Wall, D. (2007) *Cybercrime*. Cambridge: Polity.

Wallerstein, J. S. and Wyle, C. J. (1947) 'Our Law-Abiding Law-Breakers'. *Probation* 25: 107–12.

Walmsley, R., Howard, L. and White, S. (1992) *The National Prison Survey 1991*. London: HMSO.

Walters, R. (2003) *Deviant Knowledge*. Cullompton: Willan.

Walters, R. (2009) 'The State, Knowledge Production and Criminology', in R. Coleman, J. Sim, S. Tombs and D. Whyte (eds), *State, Power, Crime*. London: Sage.

Walzer, M. (2006) *Just and Unjust Wars*. New York: Basic Books.

Weber, M. (1949) *The Methodology of the Social Sciences*. Glencoe: Free Press.

Weber, M. (1964 [1947]) *The Theory of Social and Economic Organization*. Glencoe: Free Press.

Weber, M. (2004 [1917–19]) *The Vocation Lectures*. Indianapolis: Hackett.

Wells, C. (2001) *Corporations and Criminal Responsibility*. Oxford: Oxford University Press.

Wells, H. (2011) 'Risk and Expertise in the Speed Limit Enforcement Debate: Challenges, Adaptations and Responses'. *Criminology and Criminal Justice* 11(3): 225–41.

Western, B., Travis, J. and Redburn, S. (2015) *The Growth of Incarceration in the United States*. Washington, DC: National Research Council.

Whyte, D. (2007) 'The Crimes of Neo-Liberal Rule in Occupied Iraq'. *British Journal of Criminology* 47(2): 177–95.

Whyte, D. (ed.) (2009) *Crimes of the Powerful*. Maidenhead: Open University Press.

Whyte, D. (2010) 'The Neo-Liberal State of Exception in Occupied Iraq', in W. Chambliss, R. Michalowski and R. Kramer (eds), *State Crime in the Global Age*. Abingdon: Routledge.

Whyte, D. (2012) 'Between Crime and Doxa: Researching the Worlds of State-Corporate Elites'. *State Crime Journal* 1(1): 188–9.

Whyte, D. (ed.) (2015) *How Corrupt is Britain?* London: Pluto.

Wilkinson, R. (2005) *The Impact of Inequality*. New York: New Press.

Wilkinson, R. and Pickett, K. (2009) *The Spirit Level: Why More Equal Societies Almost Always Do Better*. London: Penguin.

Williams, G. (1955) 'The Definition of Crime'. *Current Legal Problems* 8: 107.

Wilson, J. Q. (2013 [1975]) *Thinking about Crime*, rev. edn. New York: Basic Books.

Wilson, J. Q. and Herrnstein, R. (1985) *Crime and Human Nature*. New York: Simon and Schuster.

Winlow, S. and Atkinson, R. (eds) (2012) *New Directions in Crime and Deviancy*. Abingdon: Routledge.

Winlow, S. and Hall, S. (2013) *Rethinking Social Exclusion*. London: Sage.

Winlow, S., Hall, S., Treadwell, J. and Briggs, D. (eds) (2015) *Riots and Political Protest*. Abingdon: Routledge.

Wintour, P. (2014) 'Benefit sanctions regime for unemployed to be investigated by MPs'. *The Guardian*, 23 October.

Wittgenstein, L. (2001 [1921]) *Tractatus Logico-Philosophicus*. Abingdon: Routledge.

Wolfenden, J. (1957) *Report of the Committee on Homosexual Offences and Prostitution*. London: Her Majesty's Stationery Office.

Wren-Lewis, S. (2013) 'Aggregate Fiscal Policy under the Labour Government, 1997–2010'. *Oxford Review of Economic Policy* 29(1): 25–46.

Wren-Lewis, S. (2015) 'The economic consequences of George Osborne: covering up the austerity mistake'. *New Statesman*, 22 April.

Wrightson, K. (1980) 'Two Concepts of Order: Justices, Constables and Jurymen in Seventeenth-Century England', in J. Brewer and J. Styles (eds), *An Ungovernable People: The English and Their Law in the Seventeenth and Eighteenth Centuries*. London: Hutchinson.

Yar, M. (2013) *Cybercrime and Society*, 2nd edn. London: Sage.

Young, J. (1975) 'Working Class Criminology', in I. Taylor, P. Walton and J. Young (eds), *Critical Criminology*. London: Routledge.

Young, J. (1986) 'The Failure of Criminology: The Need for a Radical Realism', in R. Matthews and J. Young (eds), *Confronting Crime*. London: Sage.

Young, J. (1999) *The Exclusive Society*. London: Sage.

Young, J. (2003) 'Merton with Energy, Katz with Structure: The Sociology of Vindictiveness and the Criminology of Transgression'. *Theoretical Criminology* 7: 389–414.

Young, J. (2007) *The Vertigo of Late Modernity*. London: Sage.

Young, J. (2011) *The Criminological Imagination*. Cambridge: Polity.

Young, M. (1991) *An Inside Job*. Oxford: Oxford University Press.

Zedner, L. (2011) 'Putting Crime Back on the Criminological Agenda', in M. Bosworth and C. Hoyle (eds), *What is Criminology?* Oxford: Oxford University Press.

Zimring, F. (2007) *The Great American Crime Decline*. New York: Oxford University Press.

Zimring, F. (2012) *The City that Became Safe: New York's Lessons for Urban Crime and Its Control*. New York: Oxford University Press.

Index

Note: page numbers in italics refer to figures or tables